KU-215-770

SHOOT TO KILL

SHOOT TO KILL

by

SCOTT GRAHAM

BLAKE

Published by Blake Publishing Ltd,
3 Bramber Court, 2 Bramber Road, London W14 9PB, England

First published in paperback in Great Britain in 2002

ISBN 1 857825 05 5

All rights reserved. No part of this publication may be
reproduced, stored in a retrieval system, or in any form or by
any means, without the prior permission in writing of the
publisher, nor be otherwise circulated in any form of binding or
cover other than that in which it is published and without a
similar condition including this condition being imposed on the
subsequent purchaser.

British Library Cataloguing-in-Publication Data:
A catalogue record for this book is available from
the British Library.

Typeset by Jon Davies

Printed and bound in Great Britain by
Bookmarque

3 5 7 9 10 8 6 4 2

Text copyright Graham/Davies 2002

Pictures reproduced by kind permission of
PA and Pacemaker Press

Contents

Author's Note

After completing the first draft of this book, it was submitted to the Ministry of Defence for their observations. At no time did I wish to put at risk the lives of any of my colleagues who have been involved, or are involved, in the security forces in Northern Ireland.

As a result, various names, places and operational details have been amended at the request of the MOD.

Scott Graham, 2002

Author's Note

Glossary

Ard fheis	Policy-making conference
Armalite	Rifle
ASU	Active Service Unit
BAOR	British Army of the Rhine
Bashas	An army hostel
Bergen	Military Pack
Black and Tans	Members of an English volunteer police force, who were recruited to put down the Irish uprising of the 1920s
B-specials	The former volunteer Ulster police force which was disbanded in the 1970s
Det	On detachment from a British regiment, usually the SAS, to carry out dangerous undercover surveillance operations
E4A	Plain clothes wing of the RUC
Gimpy	General purpose machine-gun
Gimpy links	Machine-gun rounds
GPMG	General purpose machine-gun
HMSU	Headquarters Mobile Support Unit
INLA	Irish National Liberation Army
LUP	Lying-up point
NICRA	Northern Ireland Civil Rights Association
OP	Observation point
Pigs	Armoured personnel carriers
Provos	The provisional wing of the IRA
PTI	Physical training instructor
Q Vehicle	An undercover army vehicle
R&R	Rest and recuperation
RUC	Royal Ulster Constabulary
RV	Rendezvous
SOP	Standing observation post
SP	Special projects
TCG	Tasking Co-ordination Group
UCBT	Under-car booby trap
UDR	Ulster Defence Regiment
VCP	Vehicle check point

1

THE WIND SWEPT THE rain in strong gusts that day in the late spring of 1974. Shoppers and office workers hurried by with their heads down, some shielding their faces with their hands, for the wind would have blown umbrellas inside out. I noticed the young men and women clutching at their raincoats as the wind tore at them and a smile crossed my face at seeing one young woman's skirt lifted high above her knee, causing shrieks and laughter from her friends. But their laughter was quickly swept away by the noise of the wind.

I walked on steadily down Arthur Street, not caring about the rain beating in my face, not caring that I was becoming steadily soaked, nor that my curly, short hair was now drenched and straight. It was probably the months of training in appalling weather, or the fact that appearances never worried me, that made me indifferent to such matters. I was on my way to the King Arthur, a well-known pub in Belfast city centre, where I hoped to spend an hour or so revelling in the sight of pretty girls enjoying a lunch time drink.

I approached the pub, pushed open the door, took off my black leather jacket and shook it to get rid of all the rain and took the stairs two at a time to the large lounge bar on the first floor. At first, I was rather disappointed as I looked around the room, for the place was usually quite full of office girls having a quiet Friday drink with friends. In the past, I had stopped by for a pint and would sit and watch the office girls chatting excitedly, sometimes exchanging glances and wondering how many of them were fancy free and looking forward to a night on the town later that day.

As I walked into the room, a few of the girls looked up, as though checking me out. I knew I looked rather like a drowned rat so I went to the gents and tried to make myself more presentable. As usual, I went and stood at the bar and looked around the room, checking the girls sitting at the small tables dotted about. Most of the young people had drinks in front of them, some with shorts but the majority drinking lager and, along the bar, young men were drinking pints of beer and Guinness.

'Yes, Sir, what can I get for you?' asked a young, pimply-faced youth who looked little more than 18.

I had always appreciated the barmen of Belfast. They are efficient, polite and quick to serve a new customer. They seem to take a pride in their speed of service and their line of chat. Nearly every time I bought a drink in a Belfast pub there would be gentle banter from the barman so that one felt relaxed and welcome.

'I'm not sure what I fancy,' I replied. 'Give me a pint of lager while I think what I would really like.'

'Coming up, Sir,' the barman replied, 'and when you've made up your mind, I'll get you what you want,' and he smiled as he pulled me a pint.

Automatically, I looked at my watch and winced. I had forgotten to change my army issue watch before setting out from camp, so I pulled down the sleeve of my jacket to cover it, hoping people wouldn't notice that the watch I was wearing that night screamed 'Army', a heavy macho-type worn by most British squaddies. Whenever I left camp, I would invariably change my watch to a different, more delicate one, though it looked a bit cissy on the muscles of my forearms.

I handed over a £1 note and looked at the change he gave me, all in the new coins Britain had introduced with decimalisation. I was against it from the start. I just wasn't convinced that the change from good old-fashioned pounds, shillings and pence to the new-fangled denominations was a good idea. I would still think in the old currency, calculating everything in the notes and coinage I remembered and would then convert them to the new decimals. Whenever I bought a pint or went shopping, I would always think to myself how expensive everything had become since the change over — especially on a soldier's pay.

I turned round, leaned against the bar, took a long pull on my pint and surveyed the scene. I liked going out on my own. My mates at camp always wanted me to join them, to go out as a group, get pissed and have a laugh. I never liked that. I was a loner and enjoyed my own company, making my own fun, meeting people who lived a different life from the Army. And I felt psychologically stronger being on my own, making my own decisions, living my life the way I wanted, rather than following the dictates of fashion.

The lounge was a large room and the long windows to the right of the bar looked down on to the street which was usually bustling. But not this night. It seemed the wind and the rain had chased everyone home or into their nearest pub, where they could enjoy a quiet drink and wait for the rain to subside.

Most of the young women seemed to be in groups, talking to each other in animated discussions, while the other young women sat in quiet, almost intimate conversations with their young fellas. There were only a few old people in the room, regulars I presumed. I expected that this was a young people's pub, because the older men and women didn't like having to climb the long flight of stairs for a drink. And there was another point — the prices in the King Arthur lounge were a little higher than bar prices in most other Belfast pubs.

I had only taken a few sips when I saw her, sitting chatting to a girlfriend near the window in a corner of the room. Occasionally, she would look out of the window as though waiting for someone to arrive before returning to chat with her friend. I noticed that both girls were drinking halves of lager and I smiled ruefully, knowing that buying them a drink or two wouldn't cost me the earth. On the seat between them were their raincoats.

I watched them for a few minutes but, my attention was particularly drawn to the dark-haired girl wearing a plain white blouse and jeans but very little make-up, if any at all. And I couldn't see any jewellery either, no rings or bracelets, not even earrings. She seemed young, perhaps around 20 or 21. She was sitting with her legs crossed with long dark hair, parted in the centre, which reached below her shoulders. She had lovely dark eyes and a pale, typically Irish complexion, as though her skin had been soothed by soft rains and not too much harsh sunlight. Her girlfriend, a little older and dressed in a dark-blue skirt and office-type white blouse was also attractive but, though naturally attracted to both of them, I continued to look around the room, convinced that such good-looking girls must be waiting for boyfriends to arrive.

By the time I had finished my first pint and ordered another, however, the two girls were still chatting together and I had managed to catch the eye of the dark-haired girl on two or three occasions. Once, as I lifted the glass to my mouth, I happened to look over and catch her attention. I quickly raised the glass as though drinking a toast to her, wishing her good health, and I think a smile crossed her lips before she looked away and resumed her conversation.

Perhaps some 15 minutes later, the other girl left the table, presumably to go to the toilet, and I decided to act. I picked up my pint and walked over. Deliberately, I didn't walk too quickly because I didn't want to alarm her or seem too eager. At a tick under 6ft tall and weighing 15 stone, I knew that some girls became wary whenever I approached them.

'Take your time' I told myself, 'don't rush her ... play it cool. You've never seen or met her before and the odds are that she will probably be waiting for her boyfriend to appear at any moment.'

She looked up as I approached and I realised in that instant that she was, indeed, a very good-looking girl. She had the most beautiful dark hair and eyes, and her skin was more delicate the closer I came to her. I sensed one problem. She seemed young, too young for me, certainly no more than 18. I couldn't yet judge how tall she would be and I wondered, in that brief instant before I spoke to her, whether her legs were as long and as lovely as the rest of her body.

'Could I get you a drink?' I asked, trying to sound as casual as possible.

She smiled back as though welcoming me and I leant towards her because I knew I would have difficulty understanding her Irish brogue. I had always had difficulty understanding the broader Irish tongue, though I had served in the Province on previous tours of duty. I found some of the Irish phraseology difficult to understand, and occasionally

I had trouble deciphering the accent. The last thing I wanted that evening was to appear so bloody English that the girl wouldn't even consider talking to me. Some of the Northern Irish girls were fine talking to army types but others, particularly Republicans or Catholics, would run a mile if they thought for one moment they were being approached by a British soldier.

But this night I was in luck.

'If you're buying,' she replied in a beautiful, fresh Irish voice. 'I'll have a half of lager,' and she picked up her nearly empty glass and shook it slightly, intimating that she had virtually finished the drink she was holding.

'And your friend?' I asked, smiling back at her.

'She'll have the same, if that's all right with you?'

'That's fine by me,' I replied and turned on my heel making my way through the tables to the bar a few yards distant. As I ordered the drinks, I decided to take another look at her, to see if she was interested or not, or whether she was just accepting a drink because someone had offered to buy her one. I turned sharply and caught her looking at me. My glance had not taken her unawares, however, for she smiled quite openly as though enjoying the intimacy. In that instant, I noticed her near-perfect set of teeth and her genuine smile which seemed innocently childlike.

I hoped the young barman would live up to the usual tradition and serve me quickly so that I could return and have a few words with my new-found friend before the other girl returned to the table. All that concerned me then was the fear that the girl was too young. Instinctively I liked her and hoped she was at least 18. I was 24 and I never usually went out with girls under 21 because they always seemed too young and inexperienced. And there was a further point. I had always looked older than my true age and most strangers believed me to be about thirty!

I walked back quickly and put down the two lagers.

'By the way, I'm Scott. What's your name?'

'My name's Mairead, Mairead Farrell,' she said and I wasn't sure whether I had heard correctly or not and cursed myself for not having an ear for the Irish brogue. I felt a bit of a fool but I had to find out her name.

'Mary?' I queried. 'I didn't quite catch what you said.'

'Listen to me; my name's Mairead,' and she spoke slowly and phonetically so that I could understand. 'It's the Irish for Mary, that's all,' she said, 'but if that's too difficult, you can just call me Mary.'

'What would you prefer?' I asked, hoping that was the diplomatic reply.

'Well, I am Irish and Mairead is my name so, if it's all right with you's, I'd prefer to be called Mairead.'

'Quite right,' I replied. 'I'll never call you Mary again. Mairead it is.'

I picked up my pint and raised my glass. 'To Mairead,' and she smiled.

'To Scott,' she said and sipped her lager.

'Is Scott your real name or do they call you that

because you's come from Scotland?' she asked.

'No,' I replied, 'I've never been there in my life. I'm from Worcestershire, in the south Midlands, but I travel around all the time.'

'What you's do?' asked Mairead. 'Don't tell me you's in the Army.'

'Good God, no,' I declared emphatically. 'I'm a welder ... I work in the shipyards,' and I nodded to what I hoped was the direction of the docks.

Whenever I met anyone in Northern Ireland, I always told them I was a welder in the shipyards. I knew that to admit to being a member of the British Army was asking either to be filled in by a bunch of republican sympathisers, or worse, far worse, if they happened to be members of the Provos. Republican girls would often be equally offensive, usually spitting on the ground in disgust and walking away, as though being a member of the British Army was the lowest form of life.

I had chosen welding as my job because I knew I could easily be taken for a welder. Mates would often tell me that I looked like one with my strong, rough hands and my weather-beaten face as though I was used to working all day in all weathers. Not that I looked suntanned, more that I worked outside in all weathers and all conditions most days of my life.

And there was another reason why I would always tell people, especially girls, that I worked as a welder. In that way, whenever the Army posted me back to England, or overseas, I could simply say that I had another welding job in Germany, the Netherlands or working on the oil rigs of the North Sea. And I knew a little about welding, at least enough to hold my own in a conversation with a man who might really be an expert. I made it my duty to know the rates of pay and the type of jobs and conditions welders were expected to endure. I also had a few made-up names ready in case such conversations should arise.

'And what do you do for a living?' I asked Mairead.

'I work in an insurance office in Belfast,' she said.

'What do you do there?' I asked, trying to sound interested, making small talk.

'Same as everyone else,' she said, 'answering the phone, talking to people, trying to answer their queries.'

'Is the pay good?'

'What you's think?' she answered, not wanting to be dragged into a conversation about her work.

'At least in welding you get well paid with all the overtime on offer,' I said.

Before the conversation could go any further, Mairead's friend walked up to the table, a smile on her face.

'You two didn't take long getting to know each other,' she said, speaking in a Northern Irish accent, 'and me gone only a couple of minutes. Are you going to introduce me, or not?' she said, looking at Mairead.

'This is Scott,' Mairead replied. 'He's bought you a drink.'

'Well, he's not all bad,' the girl replied. 'Are you in the Army?'

'No he's not,' Mairead butted in, 'he's a welder at the shipyards.'

'I'm Leslie,' said the girl holding out her hand for me to shake. 'Pleased to meet you. Thanks for the drink. What's your name?'

'Scott ... Scott Graham,' I replied, my first chance to get a word in edgeways since Leslie had returned to the table.

Trying to behave like a gentleman, I lent over and pulled up a chair for Leslie, a girl somewhat older than Mairead with lighter, brown hair and freckles on her nose. She looked smart and purposeful and I began to think that I had indeed struck lucky that night, for here I was chatting to two good-looking girls, both of whom I fancied, sitting in a comfy Irish pub drinking a few pints of lager and with no competition from hairy-arsed mates trying to butt in or ruin my chances. I began to relax but knew that could be a mistake at this stage. If I wanted to get to know them better, I needed to make more of an impression.

'And what do you do for a living?' I asked Leslie.

'She works with me,' Mairead said quickly, and I noticed a knowing look flash between the two girls.

'Yes,' replied Leslie. 'We work together in an insurance office. Not far from here. We often pop in for a drink in the evening, especially when it's blinding with rain, like tonight.'

I began to smell trouble, realising that something didn't quite add up. Though I had only met the girls for a matter of a few minutes, I instinctively felt that one, or both of them, was lying. But I didn't know why they were lying to me. My gut instinct advised me to leave there and then, but I also felt strangely drawn to Mairead and knew that I wanted to see her again, to get to know her better. So I decided to stay and try to discover what was going on, not only because I felt attracted to Mairead, but also because I wondered whether there was a deeper significance to the reason for their lies. I also realised that my assumptions might be totally wrong and they might be two girls having a quiet drink on their own, checking out the talent, a night out without boyfriends.

Together, the three of us talked of Belfast, of films and pop music, and they touched on the Troubles — the frequent house-to-house searches; the police guarding the entrance to every major city centre shop, checking women's handbags; the road-blocks; and the constant presence of armed RUC officers and the Army patrolling the streets of Belfast day and night. I could tell from the way they spoke that neither young woman was happy with the presence of troops on the streets. Indeed, both girls seemed quite passionate in their attitude towards the British troops, wanting them to get out of Northern Ireland. I listened to what they said and asked a few questions, but I gave no hint as to whether I agreed or disagreed with them. In any case, I wasn't in the frame of mind to discuss politics; I was much more interested in winning the attention of Mairead.

As we talked, I kept looking at Mairead and I noticed that whenever we looked at each other, she would examine my eyes, my face and my mouth and then hold my gaze for a few seconds before looking away. Her quiet, almost childlike manner and her large, open eyes seemed to suggest that she had seen and experienced a great deal, but she gave little away. Mairead's obvious passion about the British involvement in Northern Ireland didn't quite fit with her willingness to sit and chat to an Englishman in a bar in Belfast. It made me a little suspicious, and aware of the possibility that she was far more assured and in control than I gave her credit for. I was excited and intrigued, and determined to explore things further.

I was aware of something else, as well. The way she looked at me, without saying anything or giving any hint of wanting to know me better, convinced me that there was a strong sexual attraction between the two of us. When she left the table to go to the toilet, I suddenly realised I was mentally undressing her. I also realised, for the first time, that Mairead was only about 5ft 2in tall, and in good trim, with an athletic, though not a full figure, a neat, tight backside and good legs. As she walked away from the table, I couldn't keep my eyes from her and I realised in that instant that I was being watched by Leslie. She said nothing, but her eyes revealed that she knew exactly what I was thinking at that moment and I felt myself blush, caught in the act of watching Mairead walking away from me, and imagining her naked.

When Mairead returned, Leslie made an excuse and left the two of us to talk alone.

'Where do you live?' I asked as soon as Leslie was out of earshot.

'Stewartstown Road,' she said and watched for my reaction. She wasn't sure that, as a stranger, I would know from her reply whether she was a Catholic or a Protestant; and she had no idea whether that was important or of no consequence whatsoever. She watched my face for any tell-tale sign and waited for a comment.

I realised that the area where she lived was in West Belfast and I wasn't sure whether Stewartstown Road was a mixed area or a Catholic one, but I knew it wasn't Protestant.

'Damn,' I thought to myself, 'I wonder whether she's a Catholic? If she is, that will make things far more difficult; if she's a Prod, we're home and dry, but if she's a Mick that could spell trouble.' I had never been out with a Catholic girl in Ireland, for the unit had always been advised to keep away from republican areas for fear of being targeted by the Provos.

'I don't know that area very well,' I lied. 'Is that some way from the Falls?'

I just wanted to hear her reply, to test her, because I knew the Falls area was the heart of the Catholic community, republican territory, where the Provisional IRA recruited most of their members, as well as those young men who made up the bulk of the active service units. It was an area all but out of bounds to off-duty British troops. Indeed, when on duty, they would only patrol the Falls in armoured Land Rovers, and when on foot, a heavily-armed, four-man 'brick' patrol would take great care, never entering the area without automatic weapons at the ready and wearing flak-jackets.

'The other side of the Falls,' she said, as though trying to convince me.

'Do you have any trouble there?' I enquired, trying to sound unconcerned.

'Not really,' Mairead lied again, a smile of reassurance on her face. 'We have the odd spot of bother, but nothing serious. It's not as bad as the Falls, though some Protestant families are beginning to move away.'

'Do you like living there?' I ventured, hoping to draw her further.

'It's home,' she said. 'It's where I grew up, where I went to school, where my friends all live. I wouldn't live anywhere else.'

'So, I could come and see you there?' I asked, though the words had hardly left my mouth when I realised I was pushing my luck too quickly.

'I wouldn't do that,' warned Mairead, looking serious for the first time since our conversation began an hour or so earlier.

'Why's that?' I asked, looking concerned.

'Well, you's got an English accent,' she said, obviously trying not to look me in the eye, 'and some people might think you were Army. And they don't like the Army around where I live. Well, certainly not since Bloody Sunday.'

'But that was in 'Derry, wasn't it?' I asked, though I knew the answer. I knew only too well that in January 1972, troops from the Parachute Regiment — my regiment — had opened fire indiscriminately on hundreds of nationalists, mostly teenagers, who were hooting and jeering the Paras, and throwing stones and bottles at the troops. Suddenly, and without warning, the Paras had opened fire, chasing and firing on the panic-stricken marchers as they ran for cover. When the firing ended, 13 Catholics lay dead and 29 were wounded.

'It makes no difference,' Mairead said with an emphasis in her voice I had not previously detected, 'it's still the British Army.' And I felt a tinge of anger, of recrimination, in her voice.

It was time to change the subject. Instinctively, I felt once again that I should walk away from this meeting, forget all about Mairead whatever-her-name-was and pretend the evening and the conversation had never taken place. But when I looked at her again, I knew it would be difficult to do that. I realised there was already a strong sexual attraction and I believed the young girl sitting in front of me felt that same urgency, the same attraction. On only a few occasions in my young life had I enjoyed the same immediate chemistry between me and a girl, an attraction which I knew in my bones was reciprocated. We had met in a bar, two total strangers, and although we were on opposite sides of the fence, perhaps natural enemies, there was already a bond between us.

As all these stupid thoughts raced through my head, I knew there and then that I wanted to take Mairead to bed, but I wasn't confident that she felt that strongly towards me. I began to fear that I was simply imagining her interest because I wanted her to feel sexually attracted to me and yet I believed signs of interest were there. Then I began to doubt myself. There seemed to be a wide gulf in our ages, which time could never bridge and yet I convinced myself that, with every week, every month that passed, Mairead would mature so that the gap in our ages wouldn't matter a damn. I had to know how she felt, though I knew I was stupid to rush her.

'Could we meet again?' I asked.

'I don't see's why not,' she replied with little enthusiasm in her voice. 'Do you want to see me or are you just being polite?'

'Don't you realise I want to see you again?' I asked, wondering whether she was being genuine or simply looking for a way out of an awkward predicament.

'Course I do; can't you tell?' she asked. 'I'm all nerves inside; I'm up to a hundred.'

'No you're not,' I said, my heart thumping at the thought that all my doubts had been simply a lack of self-confidence. I smiled at her, glad that the awkwardness of the last few minutes had disappeared.

'I am that,' Mairead protested. 'Honestly.'

I had to hold her, to kiss her.

'Give me a kiss then?' I urged jokingly, little thinking that Mairead would dream of giving a stranger a kiss in the middle of a Belfast pub.

'All right, you'll see,' she said and got up from her chair and gave me a peck on the cheek before promptly sitting down.

Her action surprised me, but I then knew that she did indeed feel some attraction for me, however slight. I was convinced that Mairead would never have given me a kiss if she hadn't wanted to see me again.

'Can I see you again, then?' I asked, pressing the point.

'Aye,' she replied, once again looking away, embarrassed by her own answer.

'Next week, then,' I said, 'in this pub, around 7.30 next Wednesday night. Can you manage that?'

'Course I can,' she said. 'Don't you think my Mam would let me out?'

'Good,' I replied, 'that's a date then. Great.'

'In case anything goes wrong,' I said, 'could I have your home phone number? Sometimes I'm moved at very short notice and I wouldn't want to stand you up.'

'So you're a gentleman,' she said with a laugh and happily gave me her number.

I got to my feet and smiled down at her and wondered whether I should return the compliment and give Mairead a kiss on the cheek. But I thought better of it and told myself to play it cool. Instead, I decided to shake her hand, warmly, so that I wouldn't appear too forward, too eager. Leslie came over from where she had been chatting to other girls and I shook her by the hand, too.

'Be seeing you, then,' I said, looking straight at Mairead.

'Aye,' she replied with a smile and turned towards Leslie who had immediately sat down. As I walked through the doorway, on the way downstairs I looked back once and waved to the two girls who had been anticipating my action, and they waved back. Once through the door, I looked through the glass window and saw them talking earnestly to each other. In the fresh, cool air outside, I felt once again the wind and the rain on my face and it felt good. I was late for the RV and needed to push on.

But I didn't forget where I was and checked a couple of times to see that no one was following me. Invigorated and happy with my afternoon's work, I thought of my next date with Mairead and wondered what she was thinking. I met the other lads who had spent the day on the town and listened in silence to their exploits as we drove back to camp in one of the civvy vans the army provided for us during such expeditions into town.

2

I LEARNED LATER THAT Mairead had enjoyed a happy childhood, the second youngest and the only girl in a close-knit family of six children. She lived throughout her childhood above a hardware shop run by her father in the Falls, the hardest, most republican area of Belfast. Then the family moved to a house in a relatively middle-class Catholic area off Stewartstown Road in the city.

Because of the very fact that she was the only girl with five brothers, Mairead would spend time playing with other Catholic girls of her own age in and around the neighbourhood. Being always small for her age, and with five brothers to contend with, Mairead needed to be both strong-willed and streetwise.

And yet, being small for her age, the bright-eyed

Mairead was protected by her brothers and she never suffered any trouble from other boys or girls in the neighbourhood or at the local Catholic primary school she attended. But, like her own mother, Mairead was a bright child and easily coped with the harder work at Rathmore Catholic Grammar School where she proved a highly popular, though serious, young girl.

But the political events which dominated West Belfast during her formative years would play a dominant role throughout her life. She was only nine years old when the Northern Ireland Civil Rights movement was formed, an organisation which demanded the most basic of human rights, such as one person, one vote; the re-mapping of gerrymandered election boundaries; the enactment of anti-discrimination laws; the establishment of government machinery to handle citizens' complaints; a points system based on need for the allocation of council houses; the repeal of the Special Powers Act; and the disbanding of the hated B-Specials.

During the following few years, however, NICRA's activities — holding marches, singing the famous song of the oppressed 'We Shall Overcome' and staging sit-ins at crucial times — began to interest her as the Ulster Unionists took exception to the demands of the Catholic minority for social justice and a more equal society. And before her teens Mairead would witness the brutality of the RUC, led and manned by Protestants, baton charging and clubbing peaceful marchers and demonstrators.

The young Mairead also noted that unprovoked, vicious attacks on peaceful demonstrators were bringing thousands more demonstrators on to the streets. In 'Derry, in October 1968, 15,000 Catholics — the largest single protest ever mounted in Northern Ireland — marched in protest against the brutality of the RUC and the B-Specials. Outnumbered by 50 to 1, the RUC beat a retreat and went back to their police barracks.

Even at that age, however, Mairead felt the tension rising within her family and among her friends as the Protestant backlash gathered force and she learned of the violence that was being unleashed on the Catholic marchers, who by now formed the great majority of the Civil Rights movement.

From her grandfather on her mother's side, Mairead learned of earlier exploits of the Republican movement which she would ask him to repeat ad nauseam. Her grandfather had been interned by the notorious Black and Tans at Ballinamore, County Leitrim, for refusing to drive the Tans on a train during the Second World War. His job as a train driver gave him a great opportunity to watch the coming and goings of the Tans around County Leitrim and he would tell her of the details he passed on to the Republicans.

In 1969, at the age of 11, Mairead witnessed at first hand the harsh violence that would become a part of her life. Loyalist vigilante groups had formed themselves into a number of 'defence' organisations and were constantly invading Catholic areas, particularly the Falls Road. By the summer of 1969,

Catholics in the Falls were seriously concerned, frightened for their children and their homes, as the loyalists scattered leaflets threatening a full-scale invasion of the surrounded community.

Some nationalists in Belfast appealed to the IRA headquarters in Dublin to send some guns north so the Catholics could defend themselves in case of a serious invasion by loyalist vigilante groups. The IRA leadership in Dublin did not want to know. In any case, they had no arms to send.

On the night of 14 August 1969, loyalist gangs went on the offensive, storming the Falls where Mairead and her family and friends lived, setting fire to Catholic homes in the maze of streets that connected the two ghettos to one another. The attack went on throughout the following day. Within 36 hours, more than 200 Catholic homes had been burned to the ground or badly gutted. Some of Mairead's schoolfriends had their homes, and all their furniture, clothes and belongings destroyed.

As the flames lit up the night sky, the RUC joined in the fray, driving up and down the Falls Road in their shielded Land Rovers with Browning heavy machine-guns mounted on the top and firing at anything that moved. The police, however, did not take to the streets to defend the Catholic minority, which was under attack, but supported the invading loyalists. For hours, they fired sporadic bursts from heavy calibre machine-guns, spitting out ten rounds a second with a range up to 2.5 miles, mainly at Catholic men, women and children fleeing from their burning homes. These heavy weapons were completely inappropriate for use in a densely populated urban area and they took a heavy toll. In all, ten people were killed and about 100 were wounded during the 36-hour attack. All were Catholics.

The Catholic community was extremely fearful for its safety because of more murderous attacks by the loyalist gangs or the heavily-armed RUC. Fortifications made from gutted homes and cars were thrown up in streets leading to the Protestant Shankill area; young Catholic men, armed only with wooden staves, guarded the area; and Catholics living in streets adjacent to Protestant neighbourhoods fled their homes and took refuge in more secure areas in the heart of the Falls. Hundreds of families, representing thousands of people, were taken into over-crowded Catholic homes and offered shelter. Soup kitchens were opened in the streets to feed the homeless, many of whom had lost everything in the fires that engulfed and destroyed their homes.

All these horrifying events, witnessed by the young Mairead, had a profound effect on her and many of her young, impressionable friends.

Mairead and her friends, like many Catholics in West Belfast and 'Derry, welcomed the arrival of British troops in the Province and saw them as saviours, waving and cheering enthusiastically as the troops moved in to protect the besieged Catholic population. Within two weeks, 6,000 British troops had been sent to Ulster to keep the peace. But the honeymoon between the Catholics and the British troops would not last long.

Even at this stage, the Irish Republican Army, was conspicuous by its absence. Older Catholic families could remember the IRA organising the defence of the Catholic community during the 1920-22 pogroms, and again following the sectarian clashes of 1935, but in August 1969 the IRA was nowhere to be seen. Allegedly, ten IRA men, in middle age, turned out armed with First World War pistols, but no one recalls seeing them.

During the next three years, the ordinary Catholics of West Belfast and 'Derry, men and women who were only concerned with protecting their families and their homes, formed barricades and safe areas within Catholic ghettos, in an effort to keep out both loyalist gangs and the RUC. But the British authorities in London decreed that the barricades should be removed and the highways kept open. The people tasked with carrying out those orders were the British troops.

As a result, friction developed daily between the Army and the Catholic minority and the hope which had been there in 1969 ebbed away, replaced by distrust, animosity and, finally, confrontation. Whenever the British forces tried to dismantle the road-blocks and barricades the Catholic youths would retaliate with stones, bricks and bottles. Soon, Molotov cocktails were thrown and the mood between the troops and the young Catholic men turned from friendly antagonism to anger and open hostility. The rivalry quickly became a trial of strength.

When Mairead's parents moved from living

above the shop to a house in Andersonstown, however, Mr Farrell decided to keep the hardware shop open and each day he would have to make the trek back and forth between the barricades and the Army lines. Each time he would be stopped and searched, his car turned inside out as the troops examined it with a fine toothcomb, not only checking the engine compartment and the boot but also the interior. On many occasions, Mairead would accompany her father and she resented the road-blocks and the searches as much as he did.

And yet, with the support of her parents and the help of her teachers, Mairead continued to study hard at her grammar school and each night would buckle down and complete the demanding homework she was required to do. But Mairead and her friends, nearly all girls, were rapidly becoming 'politicised'. They began seeing not only the loyalists and the RUC as the enemy, but also the British troops.

At the age of 13, Mairead had been woken before dawn one day in August 1971 to the sound of dustbins being banged, the traditional alarm in republican areas warning of an attack. And the word the women screamed that night was 'Internment ... internment'. Under orders from London, British troops stormed their way into Catholic homes and dragged out young men, some wearing only their pants, and virtually threw them into the back of vehicles. The din went on for hours and by that night, 342 Catholic men had been arrested without any charges, though fewer than 100 were actually members of the IRA. Within 24 hours, the Army had to release 116 of the men and the rest were then officially interned.

That particular exercise shocked many Catholics, especially the young who realised that Britain no longer believed in justice and fair play when the Government was prepared to imprison innocent people simply because they were Catholics. But worse would follow.

Mairead was 14 and studying for her 'O'-levels when Bloody Sunday finally tore apart for ever the rocky relationship between British troops and the Catholics of Northern Ireland. The shooting dead of 13 innocent Catholics on a sunny, crisp Sunday afternoon in January 1972 by members of the Parachute Regiment under-standably affected the intelligent Mairead to a great extent. At a stroke, it changed her beliefs and her life.

She would never forgive the British Army for opening fire on 15,000 innocent people who were demonstrating peacefully in the Bogside that day. She watched the television pictures over and over again and read the newspapers that reported on the aftermath. She knew that several hundred Catholic teenagers had assembled their barricades in the Bogside as they had done many times that winter, taunting the soldiers and throwing stones and petrol bombs. Some stones and bottles were thrown that day as the teenagers booed and jeered the troops in an almost ritualistic face-off.

The teenagers began to retreat as the troops fired tear-gas in the crowd and they could see a hated water-cannon approaching. It was January and though the sun was shining it was still a cold day. None of them wanted a dousing with ice-cold water.

Then suddenly, and without warning, the Paras opened fire and the panicked marchers and onlookers ran for cover. The teenagers threw themselves down onto the streets, cowered in doorways and took shelter behind cars and in alleyways. Still the shooting continued and television pictures would show later that the firing was methodical, aimed and deliberate. Some men waved white handkerchiefs in a desperate effort to persuade the Paras to stop shooting, but the troops took no notice. When the onslaught finished, 13 Catholics, mostly teenagers, had been killed and 29 wounded. One of them would die several weeks later.

What angered the Catholics of Northern Ireland, however, was that the official version of events made it seem as though there had been a major gun-battle in the Bogside that day. Several of the dead were said to have been armed or hurling petrol or nail bombs at the troops. Four of the thirteen killed were reported by the RUC as being on their wanted list.

No one believed the Army's claims, including all the journalists who had witnessed the events in the Bogside. Each of the army and police allegations would later be withdrawn, although a commission established by the British Government would state in April 1972 that the troops had done nothing wrong. Almost two years later, however, in December 1974, the British Government finally acknowledged some degree of army error and the Ministry of Defence then announced that it would pay a total of £41,500 in compensation to the families of those killed in 'Derry as a gesture of 'conciliation and goodwill'.

At the conclusion of his inquest into the shootings, however, the 'Derry city coroner made this statement:

'It strikes me that the Army ran amok that day and they shot without thinking of what they were doing. They were shooting innocent people. These people may have been taking part in a parade that was banned, but I don't think that justifies the firing of live rounds indiscriminately. I say it without reservation ... it was sheer unadulterated murder.'

That single event struck a chord in Mairead Farrell, one that she would never forget and never forgive. From that time onwards, Mairead would never believe the British Army or Government officials or Government Ministers whenever they issued statements about any event or controversy. She was a young girl who had been brought up in the Catholic tradition of always telling the truth, and she had believed that Authority would always state the facts honestly and correctly. At a stroke, the attempted cover-up by government officials of 14 murders had ended for ever her faith in the British tradition of justice and fair play. And it set her on a path which would always make her challenge and confront any statements or claims made by the British Army, the British Government and, of course, the hated RUC.

At school, Mairead formed cliques among her friends who had also been affected by the tragic events of Bloody Sunday, and they would discuss ways in which they could get their own back on the troops and the police, whom they now saw as the enemy of the Catholic population.

Mairead and her friends had also learnt by heart the short statement made by Sinn Fein leaders after Bloody Sunday:

'The only way you can avenge these deaths is by being organised, trained and disciplined until you can chase that cursed Army away. I would personally prefer to see all the British Army going back dead. But the people will not succeed with stones and bottles. They should come into one organisation which will organise and train them. You should not shout "Up the IRA!" You should join the IRA!'

Unbeknown to her parents, Mairead formed strong friendships with two or three other girls and they would spend their evenings and Saturdays around the republican clubs, bars and cafés, trying to learn as much as they could about the cause, the Provos and the IRA. Much of their information would come from teenage boys who probably knew little more than they did, but they were learning fast.

At home, Mairead would start conversations about the Troubles, desperate for the support of her parents and her brothers. But Mairead's parents never wanted to be involved with the Troubles and preferred to keep out of such political arguments and activities. Mairead would urge her family to take action and become involved with the republican cause.

But Mairead would not be deterred by her family's lack of enthusiasm. She felt she was made of sterner stuff, following in her grandfather's footsteps, and she determined to continue the family tradition started decades before. She would boast to her friends of her grandfather's exploits, and the fact that he had been interned. But her parents hoped that Mairead's hard-line approach to the Troubles would soon pass, and her mother encouraged Mairead to study hard, pass all her examinations and go on to university. She believed her daughter was the brightest of the family and it was her duty to obtain a university education and get a good job.

Mairead did work hard at school, partly to please her mother, and she passed in Modern Languages and English. Her mother encouraged Mairead to return to school and take 'A'-levels in Modern Languages, thereby virtually guaranteeing her a university place at Queen's in Belfast, but Mairead preferred to start work, earn some money and throw herself into supporting the burgeoning Sinn Fein movement. She explained to her mother that when she had earned enough money and kicked the British out of Ireland, she would go to university, but that could wait until later.

Mairead joined *Oglaigh Na hEireann* as a volunteer in 1974 while still at school, along with other schoolfriends. She wanted to help in any way possible. She was keen, bright and committed to the cause and the organisation welcomed her with open arms.

Mairead's teenage enthusiasms and passions became centred on the struggle of the oppressed Catholic population against the obscene dominance of its British rulers, and she and her friends would discuss the events which surrounded them with the benefit of knowledge and experience. The effect of British rule could be witnessed from the windows of their homes, and they could not fail to be personally and emotionally involved. Political events such as internment, the H-Blocks, the removal of political status from IRA prisoners, all these were topics which the young nationalists devoured, and they expected their families and friends to devour them with as much relish.

Although Mairead's enthusiasm was met only with half-hearted encouragement by her family, she determined to continue her personal struggle against the British at a more intense level, and worked alongside other committed teenagers for the nationalist cause. As volunteers within *Oglaigh Na hEirreann*, it was accepted that the young recruits could soon become active service members, and so welcome the chance to take on more significant and dangerous tasks.

Another factor which also attracted the young Mairead, and girls like her, was the sexual equality which existed within the organisation. Unlike other walks of life in Belfast at the time, men and women were expected and encouraged to accept responsibility and to carry out tasks equally, something which became a very attractive proposition for those women who wished to offer their energy and enthusiasm in every bit as practical a way as their male companions.

Mairead, did not tell her mother that in reality she was spending much of her time leading three totally separate lives. Ostensibly, Mairead lived a quiet life at home, being a dutiful and helpful daughter to her hard-pressed mother, helping with the vast amounts of cooking, washing-up and ironing.

She also spent her evenings with the teenage Catholic boys, some of whom, like her, were now IRA members. Like them, she was happy to run errands or they made themselves useful as look-outs or became involved in petty crime, stealing, shop-lifting and selling the goods door-to-door on the Catholic housing estates where money was always short and jobs hard to come by.

Mairead was eager to run errands for the IRA, deliver messages or carry out various duties because she then felt that she was actively helping the republican cause which she had vowed to assist in any way possible. Indeed, the more time she spent discussing the republican cause and the ways of achieving a united Ireland, the happier she was. By the time she was 16 Mairead had concluded, as a Catholic and a nationalist, that the only political state worth having was a 32-county, socialist republic. And the only means of achieving that was through armed struggle. Yet she would keep all these interests from her parents and her brothers.

And then there was the third part of her life — the young, well-built British welder she had met in a Belfast bar one day and to whom she became greatly attracted. That relationship, however, caused Mairead problems because she found it difficult, on occasions almost impossible, to reconcile her growing hatred towards the British authorities and her feelings for the carefree young welder who was rapidly winning her heart. She was 17 and attracted to a strange and exciting man — she believed that she was falling in love.

3

3

Two weeks passed before I saw Mairead again. A few days after our first meeting, I phoned and spoke to her at her family home. Fortunately, she answered the call, because I had no wish to speak to her parents.

'Mairead, is that you?' I asked. 'It's Scott here. We met a few days ago in the King Arthur.'

'Yes, I know,' she replied, sounding somewhat agitated. 'Do you think I've no brain in my head? But why are you ringing me here? I thought we had arranged a date for next week.'

'We did,' I explained, 'but something's come up. I can't see you as we planned. Could you make it the following week, same place, same time?'

'Aye,' she said.

'So what have you been doing?' I asked, wanting

to continue the conversation, to see whether she was still as keen as I hoped.

'Working,' she replied and added nothing.

'Can't you talk just now?' I asked, giving her an excuse to cut short the conversation.

'No,' she replied. 'I'll see you's as planned ... goodbye.'

And with that, the phone went dead.

Two weeks later, she was waiting for me, sitting at the same table as at our first meeting, in the corner of the lounge at the King Arthur. I had checked out the area around the pub to see if there were any suspicious people hanging around, for I didn't want to become a victim in some carefully laid trap. There was certainly nothing suspicious, so I ran up the stairs and, within seconds, I spotted her. Before walking over, I checked out the bar, but there seemed to be no groups of young men taking any notice of my arrival. As Mairead sat smiling at me, I couldn't help thinking how lovely she looked. She seemed excited and immediately got up and gave me a kiss on the cheek as I sat down. I liked that immediate feeling of intimacy.

'What can I get you?' I asked.

'A lager, thanks,' and she smiled.

We sat talking for two hours and, the more we drank and the more we talked, the closer we became. She would take a sip of her lager and then look at me, eyeball to eyeball, and say nothing. At first, it seemed somewhat disconcerting, but I could tell from the manner of her movements and her smiles and laughter that she, too, was enjoying my company. In no way did I want to ruin my chances, so I played the evening as coolly as I could without appearing disinterested.

Suddenly, she leaned forward, put one hand around my chin and kissed me full on the mouth. I wanted to hold her tight, wrap my arms around her and hug her, but thought we would then become the centre of attention and I knew she wouldn't want that. Instead, I held her hand in mine and then rubbed my hand slowly along her thigh. She didn't flinch and I took my hand away, picked up my pint and made a toast, 'To us.'

'To us,' she repeated and I was confident that we would soon become lovers.

'Will you's walk me to the bus station?' she said as the evening closed and the clock approached 10pm. 'It's a nice night for walking, not like the first time we met.'

'Love to,' I said. 'Shall we go?'

We picked up our jackets and walked down the stairs. I tried to check if there was anyone hanging around but it proved difficult because I didn't want Mairead to see that I was being cautious. I felt that would suggest to her that I was, in fact, Army, and not some Brit welder on the town. Being a Para in Belfast means you must keep your wits about you at all times, and as we walked along the road towards the central bus station, I kept checking that we weren't being followed. I was eight or nine inches taller than Mairead and I put my arm around her shoulders and she held me around the waist, occasionally squeezing me to see if I was ticklish.

'You's got some muscles on you's,' she said, somewhat surprised. 'I didn't realise I was going out with a muscle man.'

I laughed off the remark and told her that my job kept me fit.

'I like a man with muscles,' she said quietly and she looked up and kissed me.

As we approached the bus station, however, I noticed Mairead seemed to become anxious, looking behind her and checking the people ahead of us.

'What's the matter?' I asked.

'Nothing,' she replied. 'You's just thinking things that aren't true.'

I agreed with her but I knew something was worrying her.

Two hundred yards from the bus station she stopped and turned towards me, reaching up and giving me a kiss on the mouth, a rather quick, stabbing kiss with little or no emotion.

'I must be going,' she said and began to walk away.

'Where are you going?' I asked. 'We're not there yet ... wait a minute.'

'It's better this way,' she said. 'I'll explain next time we meet.'

And without a pause for breath she went on, 'You do want to see me again, don't you's?'

'Yes,' I replied, 'but when? What's the hurry?'

'Phone me, please phone, tomorrow evening about seven-thirty. OK?' And she was gone, almost running to the station and never looking back.

The thought suddenly crossed my mind that, despite my caution, I had walked into a trap. The Army were constantly reminding us to be careful about being compromised by Catholic girls, pretending to make advances, luring young soldiers into alleyways and derelict houses and then slipping away while half-a-dozen or more young Provo thugs beat the hell out of the poor soldier, caught alone and unawares, unable to protect himself. I would never forget the three Scottish soldiers who had been lured into a 'honey trap' by three Catholic girls, and had ultimately been shot dead by an IRA gang.

I stood with my back to the wall and looked around but there was no one nearby and I was in full view of 20 or more people, some respectable middle-aged couples making their way to the bus station. I felt certain there was no trap. I turned and walked away to the RV, where my mate had agreed to pick me up at 10.30pm. As I regained my confidence, I told myself not to be so bloody foolish. Mairead was simply a young girl and she seemed to like me. Though she had seemed to act in an odd way, I convinced myself I was worrying for no reason. She would explain everything at our next meeting.

We arranged to meet the following week and I told her that I would pick her up from her home in Stewartstown Road. That suggestion met with an instant objection.

'No, no, you can't do that,' she said, obviously trying to think of a valid reason for not letting me

SCOTT GRAHAM

near her home. 'I don't exactly live on the Stewartstown Road, and it would be difficult for you to find.'

'I've got a car,' I said, 'there will be no problem.'

'There will be,' she said in hushed tones, as though not wanting her parents to hear her conversation. 'You don't understand; I'll explain everything to you's when I see you.'

'Can I pick you up from work then?' I asked.

'No, no, you can't do that,' Mairead protested and I began to feel suspicious once again.

Finally, we arranged to meet outside a pub a couple of miles from her home. She was waiting, standing quietly as arranged outside, dressed once more in jeans and a sweater, her hair shining and immaculate, the smile on her face almost angelic.

'Drive,' she said, before she had hardly shut the car door.

'What's the panic?' I asked her. 'You look as if you've seen a ghost.'

'No,' she said, calming down as we drove away. 'Can we go out of Belfast and find a nice pub away from people?'

'Yes,' I agreed, 'I know a place a few miles out where we can chat and have a drink in peace.'

As we drove out of Belfast that evening, she ran her hand along my thigh and gave me pecks on the cheek and I asked whether she would give me a 'proper kiss' later.

'I might,' she said, 'I haven't started with you's yet, you know,' and she laughed as I put my arm around her and pulled her close to me. Already, I felt protective towards her. Perhaps it was the simple fact that she was such a petite girl who seemed to need protection; maybe it was her warm, natural smile that appealed.

We drove north-west out of Belfast and when the traffic had all but disappeared we found a country pub with a large car park which was almost devoid of cars. I guessed that the bar would be all but empty, a perfect place to chat and have a quiet drink in private.

I bought Mairead a half of lager and ordered a pint of Guinness for myself.

'I didn't know you drank Guinness,' she said as I sat down.

'You do now,' I replied. 'When I'm in the mood, a few pints of Guinness go down like nectar.'

'And you's an Englishman,' she said. 'You sound more Irish.'

But there was also a serious side to the conversation that night.

Mairead began by saying that she wasn't sure whether we should continue to see each other and I asked her why.

'Well, you know where I live and you must know that I am a Catholic girl from a Catholic family. But there's more than that. My father was an ardent Republican, though he wants nothing to do with the IRA. He doesn't believe in violence and nor do I.'

She paused as though thinking what to say next, and I urged her to continue.

'Well, you're English and I could never tell my friends or my family that I was going out with an Englishman. It's nothing against you personally, you understand. But none of my friends like or trust the English. We all know that the English are against the Irish people — not the Northern Irish Protestants, of course, just the Catholics — and the English are against anyone who believes that one day there should be a united Ireland. We know that the Army is here to protect the Prods and make sure that Ireland will never be united.'

She paused.

'Well?' I said questioningly.

'Well,' Mairead went on, not looking at me, 'I think the same. You and me are on opposite sides. You're British and I'm Irish. The way we see it, the British came to conquer Ireland 300 years ago and they treated the Irish terrible. We were taught in school that the English were responsible for the potato famine when thousands of Irish people died of starvation. The English are still here, still telling us what to do, still in command of us and they've brought the Army over here again and once again they're killing innocent Irish people. You's must understand that I want an Ireland free of the English and their Army. I know you's not Army but you're still a foreigner here, at least to us Catholics you are. All my friends, everyone I know, wants the English to leave us alone and get out of our country.'

For a couple of seconds I looked into my pint, thinking hard. This was strong stuff and I hardly knew her.

'Don't you want to go out with me?' I asked, trying to change her mood and make her think of our relationship rather than talking and discussing politics. The last thing I wanted was to meet some beautiful, desirable young woman and to have to spend every evening discussing the politics of Northern Ireland. I had very different ideas as to how our relationship should proceed and it didn't include the Irish question.

'Yes, of course I do,' she protested. 'You's know I do; you're my kind of man.'

'Thanks,' I said, trying to lighten the tone of the conversation, 'I like you, too.'

Mairead turned and threw herself at me, burying her head in my chest and I could feel her body shaking as if she was crying with frustration, anger and an inability to rationalise what was going on between her emotions and her political heart. I tried to lift her head to see which of many conflicting emotions were dominant but she wouldn't let me, wanting to keep her tears and her indecision to herself, not wanting me to witness the feelings that in that instant she had been unable to control.

For a few minutes she stayed there, composing herself, and she took a tissue from her handbag and wiped away her tears. Then, rather surprisingly, she gave her nose a good, hard blow. I liked that.

'Would you like a vodka?' I asked, thinking that a stiff drink might help her.

'Thanks, I would,' she said. 'How did you know I like vodka?'

''Cos you're that type of girl,' I said, and laughed.

She finally lifted her head and smiled at me, yet she seemed limp and lifeless as though the trauma of everything raging through her mind had exhausted her. I left her to compose herself while I went to the bar, bought her a vodka and waited patiently while the barman pulled me another pint of Guinness. I looked round and she gave me a weak smile and I felt like a complete shit.

I had enlisted in the Parachute Regiment at the age of 18 and had adored the life. I had already served three tours of duty in Northern Ireland and I knew in my heart that many of the Paras, my mates, were indeed anti-Catholic, anti-Republican and, understandably, anti-IRA. Many was the time that Paras would make derogatory remarks about 'Fenian bastards', and I had realised some time earlier that many Paras believed the quicker the Irish Catholic rebellion in the North could be put down, the sooner they could quit Northern Ireland and get on with real soldiering.

Now I wasn't sure what to do about Mairead. I felt guilty for having lied through my teeth about my job, and yet I felt that she needed protecting. I also felt a kindness towards her that was unusual for me in the relations I had experienced with other girls. As I walked back to the table, I decided to see what happened, for there was no denying I was strongly attracted to her.

'I've been thinking,' I told her. 'I understand there's a problem, but if you want to continue seeing me then that's fine by me. I'm sure we could make arrangements so that we could meet away from the area where you work and live so then no one who knew you would ever know you were going out with an Englishman.'

'Do you think that would really be possible?' she asked, sounding not too convinced by my argument.

'I don't see why not,' I said. 'Look at us here. No one knows who we are or where we're from and you don't feel awkward, do you?'

'No, not at all,' Mairead replied, a half-smile crossing her face. 'I've never felt happier with anyone else in my life ... honest.' And she leant forward and kissed me full on the mouth.

That remark and that kiss determined my decision. Gone was any idea of leaving her and forgetting all about her. I decided there and then that we should see how we could enjoy time together, not drinking in Belfast pubs where she might be recognised, but getting away from the city and spending time together in the country.

After two more drinks, we left and walked to the car and, as soon as we closed the doors behind us, we began to kiss. It seemed to me that she was so hungry for affection and love, almost devouring me in her passion, pushing herself against my chest as she kissed me with vehemence and openness.

'Let's go somewhere quieter,' I suggested.

'Good idea,' she said, and we drove away in search of seclusion.

Within five minutes we had found the perfect

place, a lane with hedges on either side. A few hundred yards down the road, I saw a farm gate leading on to a field and the welcome cover of a huge tree. I pulled in and stopped. We couldn't see a car, a house, even a farm building. Fifteen minutes later, after the most passionate, lustful kissing, fondling and cuddling, and with Mairead half-naked, we decided it was time to return to Belfast. I knew Mairead didn't want to stay out late and I knew that I had to be back in barracks. I dropped Mairead a few hundred yards short of her road and we agreed to meet the following week. As I drove back to camp, I felt exhilarated and happy. We hadn't had sex, and yet I felt I had spent a great evening with a girl of whom I was growing mighty fond. I couldn't wait until our next date.

When I left Mairead that night, I had no idea that it would be some weeks before we would meet again. I was posted back to the mainland on a course. As soon as I knew of my posting back to England I phoned and told her that I had been asked to undertake a rush job working on an oil rig that was being constructed in Scotland, that the pay was wonderful and that I would try to keep in touch. I listened for any doubt in her voice but there appeared to be none; it seemed that she believed my welding story. That was a relief.

I kept my word as much as I could and phoned once a week for a chat. But it was obvious that back home Mairead was a worried young woman, fearful perhaps that her parents or one of her many brothers might find out that she was dating an

Englishman, something which she was determined to keep as quiet as possible. As a result, our phone chats were indeed short and to the point but, I managed to convince myself, we were still in touch.

Two months later, I was back in Northern Ireland, stationed at Palace Barracks in Holywood, a district seven miles east of Belfast City Centre. At first, I didn't tell Mairead I had returned to the Province because I wanted first to check the lie of the land. I had been living in bashas in Belfast and did not know the area round Holywood, except that there seemed to be no trouble in that district. It was home to many lawyers, judges and senior civil servants who lived in large, imposing detached houses in areas that were never targeted by republican or loyalist gangs of young men looking for trouble. Holywood seemed a quiet, middle-class area, somehow untouched by the mayhem that was then going on in many towns across the Province.

I also wanted to check out where I might be patrolling, fearful that one day I might be with a squad of Paras in the Falls area of Belfast, the Catholic ghetto, and find myself face to face with Mairead. I would spend time in my Paras uniform and flak-jacket, looking into the mirror to see whether I was still recognisable to someone who knew me well but who always saw me in civvies, usually jeans, a shirt and a black leather jacket. I knew that if ever Mairead discovered that I was, in fact, a British soldier, our relationship would be at an end. And I didn't want that.

I called Mairead and arranged to meet her at the War Memorial, originally a Second World War memorial, a couple of hundred yards from Holywood railway station. I borrowed a car from a mate and arrived early, parking the car in a side-street near our rendezvous. I had driven around the immediate area twice, checking that no one was around. The place seemed nearly deserted. Then I waited in the car where I could see her approaching but in such a position so that neither she nor anyone else would be aware that I was waiting.

I saw the train arrive and waited a few minutes for her to walk out, through the underpass beneath the dual carriageway to the War Memorial. She was wearing a shirt and short skirt and carrying a jacket. I noticed the wind pulling at her shirt and could see the outline of her breasts. I felt my mouth go dry and wondered what it would be like to hold her again, and when we would actually make love.

I jumped out of the car and walked over to the corner of the street. No one was around and I gave a short, low whistle to attract her attention. She looked up, a little startled, saw me and smiled and began half-walking, half-running towards me. We met in the shadow of a house on the corner of the street and kissed as though we had been lovers for years, desperate to see each other again. As I pressed her body close to mine, I could feel her heart pounding and that made me feel great.

When we broke, Mairead said, 'How you's been, I've missed you. I think you've been weight training; you've got such gorgeous muscles.'

'That's what comes from working in the open air, swinging up and down oil rigs all day,' and we both laughed.

'Where we going?' she asked excitedly.

'Anywhere,' I said, 'but first let's go and have a drink in the country ... I could do with a pint.'

As we walked to the car she held my arm and gave me kisses on my biceps, at the same time as making sexy noises as though she wanted my arms to envelop her. We never reached a pub that night. As we drove along, we kept stroking each other's thighs and I knew I had to make love to her. I found a lane and drove along until I found a spot where other lovers must have parked, an opening with shrubs and trees where the car could not be seen from the road. We kissed momentarily and then I suggested we should move into the back seat. We jumped out of the car and into the back. Within minutes, Mairead was all but naked and she sat astride me as I lay back on the car seat.

'You must be careful,' she warned. 'Promise me you'll be careful.'

'I promise,' I said, and I meant it.

'That's all right, then,' she said, and she began to kiss me all over my face, neck, chest and abdomen. She ran her nails down my chest, deliberately leaving marks. I could hardly control myself and gently began to make love to her. Within minutes, it was all over but that was only the start. For the following two hours, we made love in that car, the windows completely steamed up, our bodies entwined in every possible position. I realised that Mairead probably had very little sexual experience but her passion was breathtaking.

'I think you deserve a drink,' I said to her and she laughed.

'You's the one that needs a drink,' she said.

When we had dressed and tidied ourselves and Mairead had managed to comb her hair into some sort of order, we headed off to find a pub. We found the Cultra Arms, a lovely pub with a large car park behind the exclusive Culloden Hotel. I needed a drink and quickly downed two pints of lager and ate some sandwiches while Mairead quietly sipped a half of lager.

As I finished the second pint she whispered in my ear, 'Does sex always make you that thirsty?'

'It does with you,' I joked. 'I didn't think you would ever want to stop.'

'Get on with you's,' she said, embarrassed by my remark. 'You know I'm a good Catholic girl at heart. We're just having a wee bit of fun.'

'A wee bit of fun,' I quipped. 'What are you like when you get serious, then?'

'Don't you's start,' she said. 'You's making me blush all over.'

'All over? Can I see that, then?' and I pretended to start undoing the buttons of her blouse.

'Jesus, Holy Mary and Joseph,' she exclaimed. 'What do you think you's doing in a public house,' and she slapped my hand. Then she held the hand and kissed it. 'That was wonderful,' she said, looking up into my eyes, 'that's what every girl dreams of in a man.'

Now it was my turn to blush. No one had ever said anything like that to me before and I knew she was being sincere. It made me feel very close to her. I put my arm round her shoulders and kissed her gently on the cheek.

'Thanks,' she said.

We drove back to Holywood station and I dropped her off with the promise that we would meet the following week. I watched as she walked into the station, a warmth in my heart, and I drove off because I knew she would not want me hanging around waiting to see her get on the train. No matter what we had going between us, I realised that, deep down, Mairead was a serious young woman who, for some reason, did not want to be compromised by being seen with me, an Englishman working in Northern Ireland.

Although the sex had now become a vital part of our developing relationship, I was still aware of the curiosity and danger which lay at the heart of our interest in each other. Mairead's political and social background was a world away from mine, and I could only guess at the extent of her involvement in the nationalist struggle. In turn, my secret life as a soldier could never be revealed to her. We were both living our own lies, and we seemed drawn to one another in a way that was both compelling and intensely exciting.

I reasoned that Mairead's political fervour stemmed from the fact that Irish traditions ran deep and that the Catholics, as a people, felt bitterly aggrieved by the way they had been treated through the centuries by successive English rulers. And now it was happening all over again to the new generation. This time, the rule of law was being imposed by a tough, no-nonsense, professional British Army that was being used by their political masters in London to crack the whip and subdue the Catholic minority population, and I knew and understood why the Brits were treated with such contempt.

It was only a matter of days later that I happened to bump into a friend, a mate by the name of Derek, whom I had met while playing football in the Province during my first tour of duty. He was about my age and worked as a Detective Constable with the RUC. We liked the occasional beer together, especially after a match, and we would swap stories and discuss girlfriends. Over a beer, he told me that he had recently rented a cottage in the country outside Holywood and suggested I came over to see his new place. He had been living with his parents in Belfast and usually stayed in the cottage at weekends when not on duty. Without saying a word about Mairead, I thought how wonderful it would be if I could persuade him to let me use the cottage now and again, though I was worried that he was a member of the RUC.

The following weekend, I went to visit the single-storey stone cottage, a small, two-bedroom place in the middle of a field. It must have been at least 100 years old and was in a pretty dilapidated condition. But there was a rudimentary bathroom, the bath and hand-basin both stained from years of dripping taps, and what passed for a kitchen with an ancient electric cooker, a large stone sink and hot water from a wall-heater. There was no sign that the place had ever been decorated and covering the windows were old sheets hanging from bits of wire. The living room was small, too, but there was a fireplace where it seemed wood had been burned for decades, for the whole room smelt of smoke and the walls seemed stained with generations of wood fires. None of that bothered me. Far more importantly, there were two bedrooms and both had double beds squeezed into them somehow with hardly enough room to walk along either side. In each bedroom were old wooden wardrobes, the doors so warped with damp that they wouldn't shut.

'Perfect,' I muttered to myself as I walked around the place.

It wasn't perfect by any stretch of the imagination, but it would be a wonderful hideaway for me and Mairead, a place where we could hole up and stay for the occasional night or even weekend, weather permitting. I looked up at the roof and wondered whether, in fact, it was rain-proof, envisaging lying in bed and hearing the rain above, waiting for the drips to start penetrating the ceiling and dropping on to the bed beneath. But I banished that thought from my mind and decided to concentrate on the positive, for it seemed I might have found somewhere for Mairead and me to continue our wonderful affair.

'I know what you're thinking,' Derek said with a laugh as I walked round the cottage. 'If I'm not around and you want to borrow it, be my guest. But remember, it isn't exactly a Hilton hotel. I don't think you could bring any fancy women here for a night of lust. They would take one look and walk away.'

I looked at him. 'Are you being serious? Could I really borrow it occasionally?'

'It's a deal,' Derek said. 'I'll show you the wood shed and where I keep the key so that you can let yourself in whenever you want it. If you can give me a call first to let me know, it might make life easier.'

'Of course I'll do that,' I said, 'but I've just met a wee girl who might like to spend the odd night in a country cottage away from Belfast.'

'Good luck,' he said, 'but watch the water heater in the bathroom. It's a bit dodgy. The first time I lit it the bloody thing nearly exploded. I had someone take a look at it and it seems OK now. But you won't get much of a bath out of it.'

'Does the cooker work?' I enquired.

'Aye, I've had a fry-up on it but I'm not sure the oven works. I've never tried it but it looks pretty clapped out. It's really a place to escape to in the summer but the rent is next to nothing.'

'Is there a fridge anywhere?'

'No,' replied Derek.

'I'll tell you what I'll do. If I start to use the place I'll go and buy a small, second hand fridge. Is that a deal?'

'Done,' he said. 'Just let me know when you'll be wanting it.'

A couple of days later, I phoned Mairead and told her that I had a surprise for her.

'What is it?' she asked.

'No,' I said, 'I won't tell you. It's something I've got to show you first, to see if you like it or not.'

She persisted but I refused, and days later I was driving her from Holywood Station to the cottage a few miles away. I turned off the main road and slowly weaved along country lanes for about three miles until I came to the cottage, hardly visible 200 yards or so from the road in the evening sunlight.

'What do you think of it?' I asked.

'Think of what?'

'The cottage.'

'That tumble-down place?' she asked, surprised.

'Do you want to take a look?'

'Is it yours, or something?' she asked. 'Have you rented it?'

'Ssshh, I'll tell you everything later. Do you want to take a look?'

Now Mairead was genuinely excited and we left the car at the five-barred iron gate and clambered over. At the top of the gate, she jumped into my arms and I held her and whirled her round while she shouted for me to put her down.

As we made our way in the gathering dusk along the track, Mairead said, 'It looks a wee bit spooky.'

'It's fine,' I said, reassuringly. 'I came here to

take a look a few days ago. It's a bit of a wreck inside, but it is a cottage in the country, it's got running water and a double bed.'

At that, she punched me on my upper arm in mock anger. 'You's,' is all she said and I put my arm around her and we walked together to the front door.

I found the key in the barn nearby where Derek had said he would keep it, but it wouldn't turn the lock. I knew there was only one door and felt sure it should work.

'Do you want me to have a go?' Mairead asked, looking up at me. 'Sometimes a woman's touch works wonders.'

'Go on, good luck, 'cos I can't open the damn thing.'

Neither could Mairead. After one more try, I decided to put my shoulder to the door, only gently, and with a loud crash of splintering wood, the door flew open.

'Shit,' I said. 'Now look what I've done.'

'You's don't know your own strength,' she said, laughing at me.

The door had all but come off its hinges and I was holding it in one hand, trying to stop the entire door falling to the ground in pieces. I inspected the damage and realised that at least one hinge, if not two, would be necessary to fix the door. I also thought the door would need an entirely new lock. It was after 9.00pm and I knew there would be no shops open at that hour.

'I'll fix it before we go,' I said shaking my head

in disbelief. 'Come in and have a look round.'

'It's a bit damp,' she said, 'as though no one's lived here for years.'

I watched her face as she walked from room to room, scrutinising everything, trying to guess if she liked the idea of the cottage or whether it really was too grotty to contemplate staying there for a night, let alone a weekend.

'What do you think?' I asked.

'Not much,' she said, 'but let me ask you one question.'

'What's that?'

'Would we be here on our own?'

I had no idea whether Derek would ever want to stay while we were there, but I presumed he would not. 'Of course,' I said reassuringly, 'just the two of us.'

'Well, I suppose I could do something with it,' she said, turning towards me, 'but you would have to help.'

'Anything you say,' I said, warming to her enthusiasm.

'We could buy sheets for the bed and a duvet ... we could paint the bedroom and the living room.'

'And the kitchen and bathroom?' Mairead added, giving me an old-fashioned look.

'And the kitchen and bathroom,' I repeated.

'Great,' she said, 'that's settled ... we'll have it ... where do you's want me to sign?' and she hugged me.

'Really, it'll be great,' she said, 'I'm sure it will. But you will help?'

'Of course,' I said.

I went outside to the old barn, which was half full of fresh hay and searched around for a hammer and some nails so that I could secure the front door until I found the time to fix some new hinges and a lock. The nails weren't in good shape and the hammer seemed 50 years old or more, but they did the trick.

'Come and see the barn,' I said when I had finished patching up the door. It was obvious the barn was still in frequent use and I wondered where the hay had come from, because I couldn't see any fields nearby that had been recently harvested.

As we walked into the barn, I picked up Mairead and ran with her in my arms towards the bales of hay about 20 yards away. Mairead screamed at me, 'What are you doing? Put me down, put me down.'

And I did. I threw her into some soft hay from a few feet away. Then I dived on top of her as she screamed and tried to fight me off, laughing and hitting me and shouting at me. I pinned her down, holding her arms wide, and leant forward, giving her a gentle kiss on the mouth.

'You,' she said quietly as we began to kiss, '... you terrible man.'

Within minutes, Mairead was naked and we were making love. Her hair was covered in hay. Indeed, her body was half buried in the stuff as we rolled over, taking it in turns to be on top. When we had finished, Mairead asked me to lie still, and soon we started again. She just didn't want me to stop and we didn't for a while. When, finally, we lay still, she said, 'Jesus, that was fantastic,' and we lay close together, hugging each other as the dusk turned to night and to darkness.

As we drove back to the station and I dropped Mairead off, I wondered how long the affair could last. I knew I was living a lie. I also knew that I could never tell her the truth.

4

THROUGHOUT THE AUTUMN AND much of the winter of 1974/75, Mairead and I would spend at least one evening a week together at the cottage. We worked hard on the tumble-down place, making it respectable and comfortable and trying to make it homely. We washed down walls and splashed on paint; we bought cheap rugs for the floors and a large second-hand sofa for the living room which took up most of the available space. We loved to lie on the sofa together in the evenings, covered by the duvet from the bed, while the wood fire filled the room with warmth, and often smoke. Occasionally, very occasionally, Mairead would be able to stay the odd night.

They were wonderful times. I found that I was drinking less and enjoying life more. And Mairead seemed to mature so quickly. Whenever she stayed the night, she wanted to enjoy being with a man, asking to cook the morning fry-ups on the old stove, brewing the tea and only occasionally permitting me to do the washing-up!

She would never talk about her work or about the people she worked with. 'That's boring,' she would say whenever I raised the topic.

And I, in turn, adopted a similar attitude. Sometimes, I would talk about a certain mate or think up some story concerning my job as a welder but, by and large, we never mentioned work, preferring to talk about each other and the fun we had together. Because we never saw each other more than once a week much of our time together would be spent having a drink and a snack together in a country pub and then racing back to the cottage to make love for an hour or two, before it was time for her to return home.

In the summer, we would spend our evenings together in the hay barn or on the edge of a nearby lake, sitting on the grass, watching the birds and the clouds and enjoying the solitude. Our chats and our games would usually dissolve into love-making, about which Mairead became more passionate and confident. It was as if we had escaped into each other's arms for a moment, managing to push away the reality of Belfast and the parts we played in it, in favour of a romantic ideal which seemed almost too good to be true. I had been accused of not having a romantic nature, and maybe that had been the case, but Mairead brought it out of me.

As sex became more passionate, and Mairead grew more forceful, we began to carry permanent reminders of our time together. I would shower back at the army base on my own because of the scars her finger nails made on my chest and back, and she would tell me how careful she had to be at home because of the love-bites on her breasts and inner thighs.

In the winter months, we would play card games together in front of the fire with a bottle of wine for company and nearly every game would end up with Mairead dressed only in stockings and a suspender belt.

'If I lose the next game,' she would joke, 'you know what you must do, don't you?' And within seconds of being dealt the cards, she would forfeit the game and leap on me.

But life wasn't always fun for Mairead, who sometimes revealed a very serious side to her nature for someone so young.

If incidents occurred in which Catholics were given a rough time by the British Army, the RUC or the Ulster Loyalists, she would want to talk about it. Sometimes, she would be truly outraged by the treatment meted out to her relatives, friends and neighbours, in fact anyone who lived in West Belfast or attended a Catholic church.

During those years in the 1970s when responsible politicians hinted that Ulster was on the brink of civil war, the brunt of the verbal and physical attacks were aimed at the Catholic minority of Northern Ireland, mainly in Belfast and

'Derry. The Republicans would hijack cars and lorries and set them ablaze to form barricades against the troops and the police who were determined to maintain command of the streets. Of course, the Republicans hit back and hundreds of people were killed and wounded in those terrifying years on both sides of the divide. And the security forces would take the brunt of the attacks as they tried to keep the peace. I would witness at first hand many attacks against the security forces, especially the RUC and, in particular, against my mates, soldiers of the hated Parachute Regiment. I knew from my talks with Mairead that the Regiment would never be forgiven for Bloody Sunday and every opportunity would be taken by IRA volunteers, Republicans or even young kids to attack the Regiment with stones, bottles, Molotov cocktails and, increasingly, bombs and bullets.

Sometimes, when we were talking she would raise the subject, telling me of incidents she had witnessed. One evening, Mairead told me, 'Last night, I was walking home when I saw a detachment of Paras stop and question some kids because they were throwing stones. I watched as the troops manhandled the kids, swearing at them and pushing them around, ordering them to disperse, threatening them with a rifle butt across their heads. The older kids, teenagers, would give them cheek and the soldiers would threaten them with rubber bullets if they didn't "fuck off".

'I saw two soldiers grab hold of a young kid who could have only been ten or twelve and give him five or six hard cuffs round the head. He answered back and they put him against a wall and punched him in the stomach. Then one put his knee in his groin and the kid went down. I ran over and told them to leave him alone and they told me to run off home. But they did let the lad go.'

On another occasion, Mairead told me that one of her neighbours' homes had been wrecked by the Army the night before. She said, 'Without asking any questions, two 'pigs' arrived outside a woman's house, as well as two RUC Land Rovers. Some soldiers went to the front door while police ran round to the back. The soldiers smashed down the front door and went in shouting at everyone, yelling at them to stand against the wall while others were told to lie face down on the floor. They were in there for an hour, ripping out every cupboard in the house, tearing up carpets and floorboards, ripping down ceilings. Apparently, they had been tipped off that weapons and ammo were hidden there, but they found nothing, absolutely nothing.

'Then, as the woman was screaming at them for wrecking her home, the soldiers just walked out, clambered into the pigs and drove away. The distraught woman was told to make a claim at the town hall.'

That night, Mairead would not be placated. As she related the story, her voice became more strident and emotional. 'That poor woman knew that if she did claim compensation from the authorities there would be form-filling, delays, reports, investigations, objections and months, if not years, of haggling before she received a penny. Now that's not fair; in fact, it's despicable behaviour, and yet no one does anything whatsoever about it. And why? I'll tell you why, Scott. Because she's a Catholic living in a republican area. That's why.'

On that occasion Mairead was genuinely distressed. 'The fuckers,' she said, 'they wrecked this poor woman's home. She had an old woman living with her and three kids. She pleaded with the soldiers to stop searching, protesting her innocence, insisting they were making a mistake. They took not the slightest notice; they didn't care a fuck. Now perhaps you can start to understand why the Catholics hate the Army. They set out to oppress and humiliate us and they do. Now do you understand?'

I knew Mairead was right and I told her so. 'I totally agree,' I said, 'but not all soldiers behave like that. There are good and bad in every walk of life, Mairead. Don't you agree?'

'I suppose so,' she said, 'but things like that make me angry and frustrated. It shouldn't happen.'

On another night, when I collected Mairead from Marino, the railway station not many miles from our cottage, I could see that she was really unhappy. In fact she was fuming, hardly able to contain herself. As she climbed into the car, I could tell she was desperate to tell me something. She barely managed to kiss me before she she looked down between her feet and let out a growl of frustration.

'What's up ... what's the matter?' I asked.

'Please will you's take me for a drink, Scott?'

'Yes, of course,' I replied and drove off. She barely spoke a word as we drove along and I kept looking at her, watching as she repeatedly thumped her knees in frustration. I decided it would be better to give her a drink first before asking any questions. We pulled up at a pub and went in.

'Could I have a vodka?' she asked, without a trace of a smile on her lips. I had never seen her in this mood before, a sort of controlled anger.

'Yes, of course,' I said.

I ordered the drink and a pint of Guinness for myself. I was still waiting for my pint when she put her empty glass down on the bar.

'Now could I have a pint of lager?'

'A pint of lager?' I asked in surprise. 'I've never seen you drink a pint of lager before.'

'You will tonight,' she said and I glanced at the barman who gave me a knowing look, apparently understanding that I was with someone who wanted to drown her sorrows, and quickly. Within a few minutes she had drunk that, too.

'That's better,' she said as she put the glass down and wiped her mouth with the back of her hand. 'Now I feel better.'

'What the hell's going on ?' I asked quietly.

'They took away a load of men last night; fathers and brothers of friends of mine around where I live,' she explained. 'There were scuffles and fights and the RUC, backed by the Army, split open some of their heads, smashed their faces and broke up some homes during what they said were "arrests". They took them away for questioning.'

'What for?'

'For fuck all,' she said quietly and with anger. 'I saw them, Scott. I was inside when I heard the dustbins, the signal that our people are under attack from the RUC, the Army or the Loyalists. I ran outside and down the street towards the Falls. There were police blocks keeping people away. We grabbed some rocks and stones and began throwing them, trying to help those they were arresting. They took no notice of us. I watched as about eight or nine men, mostly young men, but also two or three older ones, were arrested, frog-marched towards the pigs and the vans waiting to take them away. Their heads were split open with blood running down their faces. They had to drag two young fellas because they had taken such a beating. It was awful.'

'Why were they being arrested?' I asked again, knowing full well that there had to be some good reason to raid people's homes and drag them away in the middle of the night, although I had witnessed such actions before.

'They told the women they were wanted for questioning. But, Scott,' she said almost in tears, 'they treated them worse than animals.'

I knew that to be true from witnessing some arrests in which the RUC and, I must confess, some Parachute Regiment troops, had been involved, often resorting to heavy-handed tactics as though deliberately trying to goad the Catholics into action so they could find an excuse for putting the boot in, showing them who was in command and, at the same time, wanting to humiliate the young Catholic men in front of their women and children.

I had no wish to argue with Mairead on this occasion but I knew that there were two sides to the story. I knew that many teenagers would do their utmost to rile the troops, calling them names, throwing stones and bottles, trying to provoke them into retaliating. And the teenagers didn't care a damn if any of the troops were injured in scuffles; indeed, any injury to any soldier was construed as a minor victory, a time for rejoicing. Cheers would always erupt if any soldier went down after being hit by a missile.

For a while, Mairead said nothing and it appeared that her anger was subsiding. I felt genuinely sorry for her and the Catholics who had been treated in such a manner, but I also knew that she was probably unaware of all the facts. Someone was planting bombs, shooting at soldiers, torching homes and inciting riots and the RUC, backed by the Army, had to intervene otherwise there would be the real possibility of civil war. But I kept those thoughts to myself, prepared to argue the matter with her on another occasion when I hoped she would be more rational.

'What do you think?' Mairead asked, challenging me.

'I think it's disgraceful,' I replied. 'Arresting people should be the responsibility of the police with nothing whatsoever to do with the Army. The

Army is meant to be acting as the referee between the two communities, not taking sides.'

'But they shouldn't beat up people like that for no reason, should they?' she asked.

'No, they should not,' I replied.

I bought Mairead another half of lager and a fresh pint of Guinness for myself. As we drank slowly, and munched our way through a couple of packs of peanuts, Mairead looked as though she wanted to continue talking about what had distressed her.

'Go on,' I said, 'I'm sure there's something else on your mind ... tell me.'

'I've been thinking,' she said. 'I have become so outraged at what I've seen and with events like Bloody Sunday that I want to become involved, to do something to help the cause. So many people stand around condemning the RUC and the Army but they do nothing about it. I want to be of some use, some help, because I think it's just so terribly, terribly unfair. But I don't know what to do or what I could do to help. I've been thinking about it for some time, especially when I see what I saw last night. And there have been other things I have seen. Once, I was so appalled at the Army beating hell out of a young Catholic kid that I was sick, there and then. It was awful, awful. And afterwards I cried that night, not just for the boy, but because I felt so helpless, so useless.'

'What would you do?' I asked.

'I don't know. I suppose I could join the IRA if they would have me. I do so want to help, Scott, to do something, but I don't know what I could do.'

I had never heard Mairead talk like that before. I knew she was unhappy, even bitter, at the treatment meted out to the Catholics, but she seemed to ignore the fact totally that the IRA had killed and maimed people, and happily bombed indiscriminately. But that night was not the time nor the place to suggest an alternative viewpoint. She would have believed I was taking an anti-Catholic view and I had no wish to add to her distress.

We went for a quiet walk together, just a few hundred yards along the country road from the pub and I put my arm round her and comforted her. Tonight wasn't the night for going back to the cottage, and she seemed to appreciate that. We returned and drove back to Marino so that she could catch the train to Belfast where she would then get a bus back home. She was tired and depressed and, I guessed, somewhat confused.

Before she left me, she kissed me on the cheek and said, 'Thanks ... thanks for understanding. Sorry I've been ...'

'I understand,' I said, butting in. 'I understand, you know that.'

'Call me,' she said, 'tomorrow at seven-thirty. I'll be feeling better by then.'

During March and April of 1975, however, I was posted back to Aldershot to the Parachute Regiment headquarters where I undertook arms training for Junior NCOs. I told Mairead that I had to fly to West Germany, working in the shipyards on a two-month assignment. A job had come up which meant long hours and overtime, and lots of money. The firm also provided free accommodation and food. I told her that I didn't want to leave but that it would be stupid not to take such a golden opportunity. She seemed to understand but I don't think she liked the idea.

'If you must, you must,' is all she said, making it obvious that she would have preferred me to stay. It was on occasions like that, when I was telling her bare-faced lies, that I felt like a total shit. I don't think at that time she had any idea that I was, in fact, a soldier, and she certainly hadn't guessed that I was a Para. But I kept telling myself that for much of the time she seemed to be enjoying herself and the relationship and that there was no real reason to break it off. There had been no mention of a commitment to each other or marriage or any of that nonsense. And I knew she was young and had probably never had a serious boyfriend before me. I told myself that she would enjoy many other relationships in her life when we split. She was great looking, obviously intelligent and wonderfully passionate; in fact, she had everything a bloke could want in a girl. I was also aware that I was falling in love with her. I had no idea what future, if any, we might have together, but I had the confidence that if we did decide to make a go of it, I would be able to persuade her to leave Belfast and come away with me.

While away in England, I would phone Mairead once or twice a week to keep in touch and to hear her friendly voice. We would never talk for long, however, because I knew she was still keen to keep her relationship with me away from her large family, especially her five brothers. I had the impression that she probably never told her friends, whom I suspected were probably all Catholic girls, sharing the same thoughts and anti-British feelings. I guessed that the last thing she would want to admit to any good Catholic, or any members of her staunch Republican family, was that she was having an affair with a Brit. That was why I never raised the subject, never suggesting that we should ever meet any of her friends and family but that we should keep our affair a secret between the two of us. In that way, we were, of course, peas from the same pod; both living lies, both hiding from reality and both enjoying the passion and intensity of the affair because it was secret — our secret.

When I returned to Belfast in the summer of 1975, I found Mairead looking more beautiful than ever with a big wonderful smile on her face. We met, as usual, at Marino railway station and she jumped into the car with a spring in her step. Before her train arrived, I had taken a good look around the area but saw no one who appeared suspicious. I wondered throughout that date whether Mairead had changed in any way; whether she had decided to take some action and join the IRA or whether she had met someone else, perhaps a good Catholic boy more her age whom she wouldn't have to hide away.

'What you's been doing?' she asked, having given me a quick kiss on the lips. 'Have you missed me?'

'You know I've missed you,' I replied. 'I thought you might have found yourself another boyfriend, you're looking so good.'

'You's being silly,' she chided me. 'My hunk's the only boy for me,' and she squeezed my arm affectionately.

'What do you want to do tonight?' I asked.

'What do you's think?' she replied. 'Can we go to the cottage?'

'Aye,' I replied.

'What are you's waiting for, then?' she said. 'I just want to spend hours with you, totally naked.'

Mairead was wonderful that night. Any thoughts that I may have had about her seeing another fellow were dispelled in the next three hours. She had never been so loving, so affectionate and so passionate. In the two months I had been in England, I had dated the occasional girl but no one competed with my Mairead. I was beginning to realise how fortunate I had been to meet her on that cold, rainy night all those months ago.

'I've missed you so much,' Mairead would say. 'I thought I could enjoy life without you, but I don't think that's possible. It's great to have you back in Ireland.'

She teased me about the 'German' girls, suggesting I had a string of well-built, blonde girlfriends, but I told her that she was talking nonsense and that I had spent all the time working hard and enjoying the strong German beer.

It was during those hours of love-making that night that I told Mairead that I had fallen in love with her.

'That's wonderful news,' she said, kissing me slowly and gently on the lips, 'because I've been wanting to say the same words to you since we met this evening. Do you really love me, Scott?'

I knew it was just another example of Mairead's innocence, asking such a question, but I ignored her naïveté. 'Yes, I do love you Mairead, honestly.'

'That's wonderful,' she said, and threw her arms around my neck and we kissed again and again.

It was the following week when we met again that Mairead confessed that she had something to tell me. I wondered what on earth she was talking about. We were lying on the bed cuddling one another when she decided to tell me. Everything seemed wonderful between us and it had only been a week since she had said she loved me.

'I've got something you's should know,' she said and, somewhat alarmed, I immediately suspected she was pregnant.

'What's that, then?' I said as nonchalantly as possible, kissing the top of her head as she lay curled in my arms.

'It's a secret I've been meaning to tell you for a long time,' she went on.

'And what is it?'

'Well,' she began, 'you know I said that I

worked in an office.'

'Yes,' I replied as she waited for me to say something.

'Well, that wasn't exactly true,' she said.

'Well, where do you work?' I asked, wondering why she was being so evasive about her job.

'I don't,' she said.

'You don't work then,' I said. 'You're a lady of leisure?' And I moved her head so that I could see her eyes.

'Not exactly,' she teased.

'Well, you had better tell me exactly what you do for a living,' I said, pretending to sound stern.

'I've just left school,' she said and she looked at me waiting to see my reaction.

I was lost for words. 'You've what!' I almost exploded. 'You've just left school?'

'Aye,' she replied looking a little sheepish. 'Does that matter?'

'Well, how old are you?' I asked, praying that she wasn't still under 16.

'Eighteen. It was my birthday some months back ... in March.'

'And you've just left school?'

'Aye,' she said. 'I've just taken my 'A' levels. I get the results in August.'

I sat up and shook my head, not sure how to take this surprising piece of news. Now, everything fell into place. I realised why she had been so keen to keep our affair secret and seemed not to want any of her friends to see me or meet me. I could understand everything but, nonetheless, I was gobsmacked.

'Was I the first man you had ever been to bed with?'

'Yes,' she said. 'Couldn't you tell?'

'Well, yes and no,' I replied, not sure which way to answer that question.

'But you told me that I was a natural,' she said. 'Did you mean that?'

I roared out laughing. In one breath, Mairead was mature and understanding; in the next, wonderfully naïve and childlike. I loved her for that. In a nutshell, it summed up her nature and personality to perfection and that was what I found so appealing in her.

'Do you's still want to see me?' she asked, seeking reassurance.

I didn't reply. I turned her on her back and began kissing her and making love to her. When we had finished, I said, 'That's my answer.'

'That's all right, then,' she said, and deliberately dug her fingernails into my chest and slowly dragged them down, tearing the skin. Then she laughed and jumped off the bed, leaving me lying there.

It was some weeks later that Mairead told me that she wanted to go to Queen's University in Belfast, but that her parents said she should first get a job and then plan to go to university later, if she could get a government grant. She was disappointed. She had hoped her parents would agree for her to hang around during the long summer holidays, receive her exam results and then aim to get a place in university. Within days she had found a job, ironically as a clerk in an insurance firm in Belfast. But I could tell she wasn't happy.

She would bring me small presents, '... because,' as she put it, 'I've never been able to buy you anything before 'cos I never had the money,' and I was touched. She bought me a T-shirt, a sweater, a comb for my hair, a travel rug for the car and a set of bath towels for the cottage. And, occasionally, she would insist on buying the drinks on our nights out at the various pubs we visited.

'It's wonderful having money,' she would say, 'but there's never enough of it. After I've given my Mam some housekeeping, it's gone by Tuesday ... and I don't get paid 'til Friday.'

During the autumn of 1975, Mairead and I had many discussions about the Official and the Provisional wings of the IRA. Her father had some years before been a supporter of the Official wing and, understandably, Mairead took his side. But, as she explained, as the political debate degenerated into violence and murder, her father became disenchanted and decided that he wanted no more involvement when almost open warfare developed between the two wings. But not Mairead.

Through all these discussions, I pretended to know little of what she was talking about. In reality, of course, the Paras would receive updates on the war-within-a-war between the two wings of the IRA as they fought each other for supremacy. Mairead was obviously closely following the political and military developments. She knew that

Gerry Adams, who would soon become Commander of the Provos' Belfast Brigade, and Ruari O'Bradigh, the Provos President, as well as the core of the Provos movement, were committed to waging war in the six counties as the sole means of reuniting Ireland. I realised in those weeks that without any qualification, Mairead, along with the great majority of young Provisional IRA supporters and sympathisers, both urban and rural, supported that commitment without hesitation or qualification. That worried me, for it screamed that Mairead was fast becoming more closely involved with the armed struggle, and I feared that I would be put in an impossible position and she might risk the probability of going to jail.

In November 1975, Mairead told me that she had taken part in her first major street demonstration; a spontaneous effort by a couple of hundred Catholic women to bring a halt to the vicious cycle of murder and killings being fought out between the two wings of the IRA.

Mairead had told me, 'The other day, a little Catholic girl of six, six-years-old, was shot dead by gunmen, Provo gunmen, who had gone in search of an Official IRA man. When they had discovered he wasn't at home that night, they shot his six-year-old daughter. That was murder ... worse than murder. No one can get lower than killing an innocent six-year-old. We all got together and said it had to stop. We had a meeting and went out on to the streets and demanded an end to the warfare. Only women, no men. We didn't want men there. We had had enough of killings.'

The ordinary people of West Belfast had had enough of the internecine warfare and, for the first time since the Troubles began, both the Officials and the Provos realised that they had lost the respect and the support of their own people. The gunmen were alienated from the community as they had never been before and the Catholics, especially the women, were disgusted with the gunmen's antics and their slaughter of innocent people. The women demanded an immediate end to the power struggle.

The British Army and the RUC had decided to let the gun battles in West Belfast, some of which took place in broad daylight, continue without hindrance or intervention, happy to see both sides of the Republican movement killing each other. Virtually no arrests were made at that time and no effort was made by the authorities to stop the slaughter.

It was with some joy that Mairead returned to the subject that had so troubled her when we met in late November. 'It's over,' she told me, 'they've agreed a peace. They're not fighting each other any more.'

'Good,' I said, deliberately sounding non-committal, 'let's have a drink.'

But Mairead was on a high that night, excited by the fact that she had played her part in bringing an end to the Republican movement's internecine war. 'But Scott,' she said excitedly, 'you're not listening to me. The fighting stopped and I helped to stop it. You know how I can't bear violence or killings. I could never have anything to do with things like that. That's abhorrent to me ... it's evil. Well, they've finally stopped it. That makes me feel great. Don't you understand?'

Of course I understood, but I didn't want the struggle between the two wings of the IRA to intrude any further into my relationship with Mairead. As far as I was concerned, I was perfectly happy for the Provos and the Officials to go on killing each other, for in that way they would be too preoccupied with each other to concentrate attacks on the security forces or other innocent people. To me, it was not good news that the two wings had sought peace and my heart sank with Mairead's news but I couldn't tell her that. I pretended to be keen for her sake, but when we made love that night, my heart was not in the love-making for the first time since we had met. And I wondered if she had realised that.

I found it strange that Mairead could be so selective in her abhorrence towards killings and bombings. The newspapers had been full of IRA attacks that autumn in London — the bombing of the London Hilton Hotel in which two innocent people died; the killing of an innocent man outside Green Park tube station in Piccadilly when a bomb exploded prematurely; the killing of a medical professor when the IRA planted a bomb under the wrong car. And the atrocities continued with no-warning bomb attacks on fashionable London restaurants, killing a number of people and wounding many more. Mairead made no complaint or, indeed, uttered a single word to me about these appalling atrocities. And I would wonder why.

During the winter months, Mairead and I would sometimes meet in Belfast in the early evening when she finished work. I would be able to meet her at 6.00pm most evenings, although it was often a rush for me to race back to camp, change out of uniform, have a quick shave and shower and be ready to see her. Mairead would never risk being seen with me in public during the lighter evenings, but she was prepared to see me during the dark winter nights. Most evenings we would meet and chat, sometimes even go to a cinema together, but we would ignore each other when the lights went on as though we were two strangers sitting next to each other. During the films, of course, we would hold hands and, usually, our hands would wander and we would want to leave that instant to kiss and make love somewhere. But that would be impossible and we would sit close, our legs pressed together, our hands entwined, the frustration gnawing away inside. Afterwards, however, we would leave the cinema by different exits and would meet some distance away, snatching a kiss and a cuddle in some secluded spot before Mairead would have to catch her bus back home.

Sometimes, we would meet as though by accident in a Belfast pub, pretending we were old friends who hadn't seen each other for months, checking the place out to see that there was no one that she knew or even recognised. Not once, in fact, during that winter did we ever see or meet anyone that Mairead knew. Neither, thank God, did I. However, I knew the pubs that were open to squaddies and those that were out of bounds on the strict orders of the Army.

I knew I was taking a risk by disobeying those orders, for nearly every pub we drank in was out of bounds to Army personnel. I simply took the risk, preferring to spend time with Mairead having a quiet drink and hoping that we never accidentally walked into a hard-line republican hornet's nest. Thank God we never did, but it wasn't only luck for I constantly made enquiries with friends in the Paras and the RUC, checking out the pubs around Belfast which were most likely to be frequented by Provo sympathisers.

I would never let Mairead choose the pubs where we met for I could never forget the occasions when army squaddies, after a night on the beer, had accidentally ended up in a republican pub and taken a bloody beating. At that time in the early 1970s, most escaped with their lives but there were also some horrific beatings from angry, half-pissed Republicans who were itching for a mob attack on a lone British soldier. And there were also those occasions, embedded on every soldier's brain, where the young Catholic girls had been persuaded by IRA thugs to entice soldiers with the promise of a quick shag, only to find themselves caught in a trap, surrounded by ten or more IRA hoodlums who would not only beat the hell out of them but, more often than not, leave them for dead. Some recovered, but others did not.

Throughout the time I dated Mairead, I never dropped my guard, never forgot to keep my eyes peeled, and would make certain I never had too much to drink, just in case she had been compromised in some way, persuaded to lead me, the man she loved, into a trap and a beating, simply because I was a Brit working in Belfast. I trusted Mairead, but never completely, because the more time we spent together, the more I realised that she was becoming enmeshed in, and enthralled by the Republican cause.

It didn't mean, however, that I didn't love her. Many was the time when on duty, with my SLR in the crook of my arm, that I thought dispassionately about my love for Mairead, telling myself time and again that I must be plain bloody stupid to continue to see a girl who was young, impressionable and a sympathiser of the Provos and the violence they stood for.

And yet, whenever I thought of my situation, I convinced myself that she did truly love me and that it was up to me to persuade her, in the not too distant future, to leave Belfast and come and live with me in England; maybe even marry me, if that was what she wanted for her own security and future. I realised there would be many hurdles to overcome but then, in my naïveté and youth, I believed in the saying 'love conquers all'.

Despite the warnings that I should have

recognised, I was thunderstruck when Mairead told me one night in January 1976 that she had become a fully-fledged member of the Provisional IRA.

5

I WAS A WORRIED MAN when I left Mairead that night. I was now aware of information that I knew would be of vital importance to the security forces, especially the RUC Special Branch, British Army Intelligence and MI5. I knew that if I informed them of the correct name and address of an unknown, teenage girl who had confessed to me of having become a member of the Provisional IRA they would be able to monitor and track her movements without her being aware that she was under such surveillance.

I was fairly certain that the Regiment would take a very dim view of my becoming involved with a Catholic girl, a schoolgirl at that, from the most republican part of Belfast, or that I constantly broke the rules governing the places where soldiers were permitted to go at night. I would probably be put on company orders, my pay docked and possibly have my NCO's stripe taken away, reduced once more to the ranks. Such disobedience would be put down on one's army record and I had high hopes of joining the famed SAS one day. With that on my army record, I guessed that I would have no chance of joining the élite force.

I also realised that whatever punishment the Army decreed, I would be pressured, if not ordered, into continuing the relationship with Mairead and pushed into questioning her about people and places to enable the intelligence agencies to monitor her every move and, more importantly, the people with whom she was mixing. To be given such information from an NCO in the Parachute Regiment, who was dating an IRA member, was like manna from heaven to the intelligence agencies.

At the back of my mind, however, I had niggling doubts. The way that Mairead had told me that she had joined the movement made me wonder if she was telling me the whole truth or, perhaps, exaggerating her own importance as many young people are prone to do. I believed Mairead but I didn't know for certain that she had joined, and been accepted by the IRA as a fully-fledged member. Somehow, I doubted it.

I was well aware that throughout its history, the IRA had a reputation for encouraging young people, mainly teenage boys, to become involved with the movement, to take up arms for the struggle to rid Ireland of the English yoke, but I did not know of many schoolgirls who had been recruited and I somehow doubted that Mairead was, in fact, a full member.

There was also another point. I believed absolutely that Mairead had fallen in love with me and I was more than convinced that I, too, had lost my heart to her. While out on patrol I would often think of her, instinctively looking out for her when engaged in street patrols around the Falls not far from her home. I would think of her last thing at night and first thing in the morning, and the nights we managed to stay together were blissful, so full of passion and wild sex and yet moving and loving and genuine. I wondered if it was the simple fact that this affair was dangerous, an impossible love between two people on opposite sides of the divide, an affair that could only end in heartbreak. I was certain, absolutely certain, that Mairead was still unaware of my true identity.

For three days and nights I weighed everything in my mind and decided not to tell the authorities that I was dating a raw IRA recruit. I would keep my eyes and ears open and promised myself that if Mairead told me that she was becoming an active member of the IRA then I would have no option but to give the information to the security forces. I knew in my heart that I would never conceal any information from them which might result in any army personnel or civilians being put at any risk whatsoever. If Mairead did ever tell me that she had become involved in operations with other IRA members, then I knew I would seriously consider passing on the information to the authorities.

I also believed that to stop seeing Mairead, to end the relationship voluntarily, would not be a sensible thing to do. By continuing the affair I believed that I might learn useful information which could be used to their advantage by Intelligence or the security forces and to the detriment of the Provos. What I hadn't yet decided was whom I should inform if Mairead told me something of significance. Of course, I realised that I was no Intelligence officer and knew very little about their ways of working, but until I was convinced that Mairead was in fact an IRA member and indulging in terrorist activities, I decided that my best policy was to wait and see.

It was during the following few weeks, however, that something happened which probably put me in far greater danger than if I had informed the Intelligence boffins of Mairead's alleged commitment to the IRA cause. I was driving Mairead to a country pub that I had heard of, to the north-west of Belfast. We always tried to visit different pubs so that we would never become regulars in one place, because I knew that could lead to danger for both of us. That meant driving most evenings out of the greater Belfast area to some remote place where Mairead would be unlikely to meet anyone she knew and, perhaps more importantly, I would be unlikely to meet any of my Para mates.

I would always fear that one day I would be sitting in a pub with Mairead, the door would open and five or six of my mates would come rolling in for a drink. I would try to pretend to Mairead that I had met them some time before while out drinking, all

Brits enjoying a night out together. But I wasn't sure Mairead would buy that. Such an incident would certainly make her question my credentials as a shipyard welder and maybe, I feared, she would ask her mates in the IRA to check me out. That scenario always worried me.

As Mairead and I were driving back to Belfast one night, we rounded a corner and ran slap bang into an army road-block. For a second, I thought of stopping and turning round but I knew that would be foolish, not only attracting unwanted attention but maybe risking getting shot up by the army patrol manning the road-block. I knew that any vehicle that was stopped at a VCP and then reversed and drove off was asking to be shot at for that was the standard reaction. I had to keep calm and pray that it would all pass off without a hitch. I also hoped that none of the troops on the VCP would recognise me.

I looked at Mairead to see if she had reacted in any way to the presence of the army road-block but she was sitting as passively as ever by my side. As instructed by the Army, I always carried my driving licence with me and, as advised by the Regiment, tucked inside the licence, for just such an eventuality, was my army ID card. I slowed down behind the line of cars, put my hand in my back pocket and took out the licence. There was no way that I could take out the ID card and hide it without Mairead seeing what I was doing. Then, of course, the game would be up.

I hoped that, in the darkness, the troops would not notice the army ID card and would demand that I get out of the car, like every other motorist was ordered to do, and open the bonnet and the boot for inspection. No such bloody luck — they saw the ID card.

'Good evening,' I said.

'OK, mate,' the NCO said, 'carry on.'

I didn't say a word and tried not to look at Mairead, fearing her reaction. She had seen, as I had seen, that every driver before us had been ordered to show his licence and had then been ordered out of the car to open the bonnet and the boot for inspection.

'Why didn't you have to get out the car?' Mairead asked as I pulled gently away from the soldiers.

'I think one of them recognised my English accent,' I lied.

'Oh really?' Mairead said. 'But you hardly said a word.'

'I expect they're just fed up; haven't got their heart in the job. It's the middle of winter, cold and pissing with rain and it wouldn't surprise me if it snowed later,' I said, trying to sound nonchalant, yet convincing.

'Aye,' is all she said, and I hoped the crisis, that had come so close, was over.

Although Mairead may have put the incident to the back of her mind, I most certainly had not. I felt sure that she would have become suspicious of the way the troops treated me at the check-point. I didn't know whether Mairead realised that the only people let through check-points without having to get out of their vehicles were either RUC officers or members of the security forces. And I wasn't sure whether Mairead did, in fact, take any real notice of the licence incident or whether she simply dismissed the matter as lazy troops wanting to get out of the cold and rain and back to the warmth of their barracks.

The matter did, however, put me on my guard and I watched Mairead even more closely than usual in the following few weeks to see whether her attitude towards me had changed in any way. But I could see no discernible difference. She behaved as she always had done, with the same loving and carefree manner, not pressing me with questions or demands but simply enjoying the times we had together and showing me nothing but affection and, most nights, passion. And I sensed no change whatsoever in her love-making, no holding back, nothing that would make me in the least suspicious. I began to relax.

In March 1976, however, something occurred which made me realise that anything could happen at any moment. And it did not necessarily mean that Mairead was in any way responsible or involved.

We had been to the cinema and I had said farewell to her as usual a few hundred yards from the bus station. As I turned and began to walk away, I had the distinct impression that someone was following me. I decided to check whether I had been put under surveillance by some organisation, be it the Army, the RUC, the Special Branch or, more worryingly, the IRA.

I gradually increased my pace, taking a left turn and then two quick left turns, hoping, if anyone was following, to come up behind them.

I was just about to turn the last corner when I

heard one man, with a distinct Belfast accent, say to another, 'Which way did he go?' The other voice, another Irishman, replied, 'Fuck it, he's away.'

Now I knew I had to do something. I could simply keep still and, when they became fed up and disappeared, make my way as usual to the RV. But the fact I had been followed worried me. I decided on alternative action.

I retraced my steps and waited in the shadows around the next corner, on a small piece of derelict ground, out of sight of my pursuers. The fact that the nearest street lighting must have been 30 yards away gave me comfort. I decided to wait to see if they came looking for me or, if they did not show up in a minute or so, I could be pretty certain the whole matter was of no consequence. The two of them might even have been talking about a mate.

I heard the approach of footsteps and could just hear their voices.

'He was definitely on his own,' one said.

'So he should be easy, then,' the other replied.

I waited until they had passed by, some ten yards in front of me, then I walked from my hiding place in the shadows and out into the street.

'Are you looking for someone?' I asked.

The two men turned round and walked towards me. In my bones I somehow knew they weren't security forces, despite the fact that I knew that some of our undercover officers can look pretty scruffy, with long, unkempt hair and rough clothes.

'You're just the man,' one said in a strong Belfast accent.

When both men were a few yards from me, one of them put his hand into his jacket as though to take something out. The other stopped, his hands by his side, ready, it seemed to me, to lash out at a moment's notice. I decided to take the initiative.

With my right fist I smashed the first one straight in the face with all my 15-stone weight behind the punch. As he staggered, knocked backwards by the force of the punch, his mate took a swipe at me. I ducked and hit him as hard as I could in the pit of his stomach, doubling him up with a grunt. As his head came forward, I clasped my two hands together and smashed them with all my strength across his face. He went sideways and sprawled along the ground. His mate came towards me and aimed a full-blooded kick at me. We had been trained for years how to cope with these attacks. I waited till his foot came up towards my stomach, grabbed his ankle and pulled hard, throwing him off balance. As I pulled him past me, the back of his head hit the ground and I kicked him full in the face. Both men lay still and I assumed they were out cold. I didn't care if they were unconscious or not. I knew I hadn't done any real damage. Whoever they were, I knew they would trouble no one else that night.

As a matter of course, I checked their clothing to see if they were armed with any hand-guns or knives. I was taking no chances. I frisked both of them quickly as they lay motionless on the ground. Finding nothing, I left them and walked quickly to the RV, arriving in the nick of time. But I said nothing to any of my mates. They just chided me, suggesting me I had been with a girl that night but didn't want to leave her to return to barracks. I simply smiled, letting them believe whatever they wanted.

As I lay in bed that night, however, I wondered whether those two Irishmen were members of the IRA, detailed to keep Mairead under surveillance or, worse still, whether she had told her IRA commanders that she was dating an Englishman, a welder, and they had decided to check me out. Whatever the case, I had done nothing to suggest that I was Army, but had simply taken care of myself in a fight, a British welder against two Irish blokes who had tried it on. But the incident reminded me that, come what may, I must not let my guard down, ever.

In late March, her parents had wanted to take her out to celebrate her birthday, so we decided to have our own celebration a couple of days before. I bought a birthday cake with icing and 'Happy Birthday' written on it and a bottle of champagne and took them to the cottage. For her present, I gave her a pair of black knickers and suspenders and two pairs of black stockings, but I did not give her, nor did I send her, a birthday card. I knew she would not have wanted a card arriving at her house which her parents, or brothers, would have probably questioned her about, teasing her about a secret lover, making her blush.

Her birthday party in the cottage went wonderfully well and Mairead seemed delighted that I bought a cake and a bottle of bubbly to celebrate. We drank from the tumblers we used for wine or beer but only after we had first made love and were lying naked on the sofa, eating the cake and drinking champagne. It was just sheer fun. She tried on the presents, paraded up and down the room all but naked, swigging from the bottle and pretending to be a decadent tart from the 1920s in some swish London hotel. Then we made love again.

Before I dropped her at Marino station later that night, Mairead said, 'You's been so kind to me, Scott; thanks a million. I've had a wonderful birthday with the only man I wanted to be with.'

'Go on with you,' I said, 'I enjoyed it more than you did, you know that.'

'You know I'm just mad about you, don't you?' she said.

'I think you're a great girl, too, Mairead ... you know that.'

'Aye,' she said.

She gave me one long, slow, warm kiss before running off. But I noted that even on that night, when really happy and a little drunk and celebrating her birthday, Mairead still had the discipline not to look back at me or to wave farewell, but looked straight ahead and kept walking as though she was alone. And I wondered how she maintained that discipline and who, if anyone, was teaching her those counter-surveillance skills.

I would soon find out.

I knew there was something worrying her from the moment I picked her up. I had phoned her at work earlier in the day, asking what she wanted to do that evening and if she could still make our date.

' 'Course I can,' she had said, 'do you's think I

would miss a night of lovin'?'

'No,' I replied. 'Does that mean you don't want to stay in Belfast and have a drink or go to the cinema?'

'I'd like to go to one of our pubs and then back to the cottage.'

'Fine,' I said. 'I'll meet you at the memorial.'

Mairead knew what I meant by that. She would get off the train at Holywood and walk through the underpass to the War Memorial. I would be waiting around one of the corners, sometimes sitting in the car, at other times standing around, having parked the car some distance away.

Ever since she had started work, it had been much easier communicating with her because I never had to phone her home and, as she explained, most of the girls in the insurance office spent hours on the phone chatting to boyfriends. She never wanted to chat for long, however, because she didn't want to arouse any suspicion. And she knew I always called from phone boxes. There was, of course, no question of Mairead phoning me because I was out all day on the shipyards, half-a-mile or so from the nearest telephone. These were the days before mobile phones. At the very start of our relationship, I had explained that I was not only working all day in the shipyards, but that the landlady where I lived didn't even have a phone in the house!

The landlady, of course, was a figment of my imagination. I described her as in her seventies but fit and mentally alert, a widow who had a good reputation among casual workers for running good lodgings with comfortable clean beds and hot running water for baths. But she provided nothing else; no food, not even breakfast. The digs were, however, cheap and she always kept out of the way, minding her own business and not caring what time anyone came home at night. We all had our own keys. I told Mairead there were only two rules: no women were ever allowed to visit and she demanded to be paid on the dot every Friday, in cash.

I knew something was wrong the moment we met that night. As always, I had arrived at the memorial early to see if any suspicious characters were hanging about. I saw nothing suspicious. I watched her leave the station and walk to the memorial, the same measured walk, looking smart in her office clothes with a dark-blue coat over a sweater and a dark-blue, knee-length skirt, the usual office clothing. She looked neither left nor right until she saw me. She followed me for a short distance and only after we had disappeared around the corner, out of sight of any cars passing on the main road in front of the station, did I slow down so she could catch me up and walk next to me, not holding hands, but acting as if we were more friends than lovers.

Even sitting in the car she seemed strangely nervous. She kept looking at me as if suspicious, or unsure about something. It was so unlike the usual bubbly Mairead who always wanted to kiss and cuddle as soon as we were alone and out of sight.

'Would you fancy a drink?' I asked, hoping that might calm her nerves.

'Aye,' she said, 'I'd love one ... it's been a hell of a day.'

'A vodka?' I joked, because when Mairead needed cheering up or felt upset and angry, she always wanted a strong drink to calm her nerves. When she felt really terrible she liked a double vodka, followed by a pint of lager, drunk fast and furiously.

On this occasion, she only sipped her drink while I quickly downed a pint of Guinness.

'Do you fancy another?' I asked, getting up to order myself another pint.

As though miles away, she replied faintly, 'Yes, thanks ... I'll have just half a lager.'

Something was troubling her and I needed to know what. I hoped it was something trivial but I had never seen Mairead in such a reflective mood before, so obviously concerned about something that seemed very personal to her. I didn't think it was some atrocity, some killing, some despicable act on behalf of the Army or the Loyalists because she would always complain bitterly to me in the most strident terms whenever she witnessed something which she found unfair or brutish. I would not have to wait long.

'Shall we go to the cottage?' she said as soon as she took the last swig of her lager.

It seemed that she wanted to talk, to get something off her chest, and I was keen to hear what was troubling her.

We parked the car and walked up the long approach, leaving the green fields on either side. As soon as we walked inside, Mairead turned and kissed me hard on the lips, so unlike her usual kiss.

'That's a funny kiss,' I said when we broke.

'I know,' she said, 'but I just wanted to kiss you before we began talking.'

'What about?' I asked.

'Me,' she replied.

'What's the matter? Are you all right? Is there anything I can do to help?'

'I'm fine,' she said and we sat down on the sofa. She looked away from me towards the fireplace as if gathering her thoughts, choosing exactly the right words.

After a couple of minutes, during which time she had not looked at me once, Mairead announced, 'Scott, I've got to talk to you.'

'I'm all ears,' I said trying to keep the atmosphere light.

'It's really important,' she said.

'Well, what is it?' I asked again, speaking in a more serious tone, trying to coax her to reveal her secret.

'Well,' she began, 'you know I told you's ages ago that I had joined the Provos?'

'Yes,' I said.

Speaking slowly, she said, 'Well, I'm going on an operation. I've been selected to go on a bombing run,' and she turned towards me suddenly, wanting to see my instant reaction.

I must have looked as though I had seen a ghost. 'Christ, Mairead,' I said, 'are you being serious?'

I looked at her hard to see how she would respond. At that moment, she suddenly seemed so pale, her eyes had lost their beautiful dark lustre and she seemed tired, run down, exhausted, nothing like the bright-eyed girl I knew. And yet I hadn't noticed it until that moment when, suddenly, she seemed drained of all her natural energy.

'You are kidding?' I asked in a jokey voice, hoping that my question might raise doubt in her mind, that she might decide to pull out, make some excuse and refuse to go. But the professional side of my brain was also working overtime. I had to discover where and when the intended bombing would take place. For now people's lives were at risk and Mairead, the girl I loved, was going to be responsible.

It seemed difficult to comprehend that the naïve schoolgirl I had known for 18 months had become an IRA activist, a member of an Active Service Unit, who was prepared to bomb innocent people and, ultimately, kill them through her madness.

I looked at her with fresh eyes, examining her face in silence, trying to understand how such a sweet, loving teenager could ever think of behaving in such a violent way towards other human beings.

'What's your target?' I asked.

'The Conway Hotel in Dunmurry,' she said simply.

'And who's idea is that?' I asked with more determination in my voice.

'I don't know,' she said. 'I was called to a meeting the other night and told that I would be a member of a three-man team. I haven't slept a wink since.'

'What are you going to do? I asked.

'There's nothing I can do now,' she said. 'I've got to go through with it. They need a woman as a decoy for one of the lads, pretending we're going to the hotel for a drink. Then we're going to plant the bomb and make a run for it.'

With some aggression and a distinct note of disapproval in my voice, I said, 'And what about the hotel staff and the guests and the people having a drink? What's going to happen to them? Are you happily going to kill all of them, perhaps wound hundreds of innocent people who have done nothing against you or your family? Haven't you given them a thought, Mairead?'

'Of course I have,' she said, warming to our argument. 'We're going to make sure no one's in the hotel,' she explained. 'We'll issue a warning when we plant the bomb ... tell them they've got 15 minutes to clear the place. We won't hurt anyone, I promise. It's just a wonderful, prestigious target, showing the Provos can hit wherever and whenever they want, even the hotels frequented by the rich and powerful.'

'But how do you know no one will be injured or killed?' I asked again.

'We'll make sure that plenty of warning is given,' she said. 'Scott, you know me better than anyone in the world, better even than my own parents. You know how I feel about violence. I abhor it, hate it, I think killing or injuring people is evil, no matter who is responsible. But this is a war we're involved in. You don't understand the feeling among the Catholics of the Falls who feel powerless, victims of the Prods and

105

the British Army, to be used and abused and treated like shit.'

She paused for breath, then continued in the same vein. 'Now I feel like that, too, Scott. I feel that I'm being victimised, treated as second rate because I'm a Catholic and no one should feel second rate ... no one should feel they can be abused by the system. I feel that I should do my bit to help our people throw off the English bastards once and for all. If the Provos want my help then I will happily give it but only on the condition that no one is hurt or killed. They've promised me no one will be hurt ...'

'And you believe them,' I said, butting in, a note of deliberate sarcasm in my voice.

Mairead went to speak but I wouldn't let her. I wanted her to realise some home truths before this nonsense got out of hand. 'And I suppose no one was going to be hurt at Whitecross in South Armagh?' I protested.

'That was a mistake,' she said with indignation. 'I was told it was an accident, a mistake. It was intended that those Prods would only be frightened but they opened fire first. It was their fault.'

'Their fault?' I said, my voice rising with incredulity while I struggled to control my anger. 'Mairead, listen to me before it's too late. At Whitecross in January this year, six masked gunmen held up a minibus carrying workers from nearby villages. They were nothing to do with the Troubles, just innocent, God-fearing men going to work. They ordered the driver and 11 passengers to get out. The 12 men were lined up and asked their names and religion. Eleven of the men said they were Protestants. The twelfth, a Catholic, was told to leave. The gunmen then took aim and opened fire with automatic weapons, killing ten of the Protestants and badly wounding the eleventh. It was a massacre, Mairead, make no mistake, and the men responsible were all members of the Provisional IRA, the same people who want you to go and bomb a hotel where more innocent people could die ...'

Mairead butted in, searching for a way to escape the horrific truth of the Whitecross massacre. 'That's not true ... that's just lies put about by the RUC and the Prods.'

'It isn't, Mairead,' I said quietly. 'And I'll tell you why. Everyone who died at Whitecross that day, all shot down in cold blood, were Protestants. Not one was a Catholic. That's why I know I am speaking the truth and you had better realise it before it's too late.'

Mairead looked away and I could hear her sobbing, trying to put my words behind her because, in her heart, she knew I was telling the truth. I watched her hunched shoulders heaving but I had no intention of comforting her. I wanted her to know, to realise, what appalling crime she was about to commit, and to realise what the consequences of her actions could be.

After some minutes, when her tears had stopped, she turned towards me. 'What do I do, Scott? For God's sake, tell me what I should do? I'm confused and I don't know what the fuck to do.'

'You must sit here and think long and hard of the decision you have taken and whether you believe it is right for you to go and plant a bomb in a hotel, risking innocent people's lives. I thought I knew you, Mairead. I thought you were a decent, honest person who hated violence in all its forms. I cannot understand how you could ever contemplate such an evil as planting a bomb which might kill innocent women and kids ...'

'Stop, stop, for God's sake, stop, will you's?' she said putting her hands to her ears to blot out my words.

I didn't say another word. Now I wanted to leave her alone to think of everything I had said, to make her realise the possible consequences of the evil deed she was about to carry out.

After about five minutes, she said, 'But how can I get out of it? They've told me what I must do and I didn't say I wouldn't do it. They told me that I would be a very important part of the team ... that this would show that I was a true Republican, prepared to fight for the cause like all those poor bastards locked up in Long Kesh and treated like shit. For God's sake, Scott, tell me what should I do?'

'If you want my honest opinion, you should tell them that you can't go through with it ... that you've had second thoughts, that you're not ready for active service. There are loads of excuses you can use ... they'll understand.'

'But that's backing out,' she said, 'that's showing I'm not committed to the cause.'

'Have you told anyone else?' I asked.

'No, of course not, no one.'

'Not even your brothers, your parents, no one?'

'No one,' she said.

I believed her.

'Well, what are you going to do?' I asked, deliberately pushing her to make a decision.

'I don't know,' she said, 'I just don't know. I'm confused.'

'Well, if you can't decide now,' I suggested, 'why don't you go home and sleep on it? And let me know.'

Before Mairead left that evening, however, I knew that I had to obtain one vital piece of information from her, the date of the planned bombing of The Conway.

As we drove back to Holywood station, I asked, 'How long have you got before you need to reach a decision?'

'What do you mean? she asked.

'Well, when's the operation planned for? Do you have a definite date?' I asked. 'I don't know how these things work.'

'No date's been fixed yet,' she said, 'but it will be soon, possibly in the next week or so. They've got all the stuff.'

Before I dropped her near the station, I said, 'Let me know what you decide, won't you, because otherwise I'll worry terribly about you. I don't want anything to happen to you, you must know that. You do understand, Mairead, that I love you more than anyone I've ever loved before. I believe you're a great girl and I couldn't bear to lose you. Now you've told me this, I'll worry about you. I don't want anything terrible to happen to you.'

'I love you, too, Scott,' Mairead said and she

looked into my eyes.

'Do you really?' I said. 'Do you mean that?'

'Of course I do,' she replied. 'Can't you see that when you look at me?' and as she looked up at me, I saw the tears in her eyes.

Mairead wiped her tears away, gave me a quick kiss on the cheek and was gone.

'Take care,' I shouted after her as she ran away.

As I drove away, I knew precisely what I had to do. I knew the information I now had in my possession would have to be forwarded immediately to the authorities so that a 24-hour guard could be put on the The Conway Hotel. I had no intention, however, of telling my Adjutant or my Company Commander because I realised they would demand to know how I had come across the information. I wondered if I could tell them that I had overheard two blokes discussing it in a pub, but that seemed highly improbable. I figured no one would buy that. Ultimately, it would mean that I would have to tell them the truth about my affair with Mairead which would mean the end of our relationship. I knew that if the RUC was informed of Mairead's involvement, as would automatically happen in the constant liaison between the Army and the RUC Special Branch, then she would be traced to her home, picked up and persuaded to confess the names of all her accomplices and the members of the Active Service Unit.

Alternatively, I figured, the Special Branch would try to persuade her to become an informer and that would probably end with the IRA one day discovering her involvement with the RUC. I knew what that meant because I had seen the bloodied, disfigured bodies of two IRA informers after the punishment gangs had done their dirty work. All IRA informers faced appalling torture and, when they finally confessed, they were taken to some lonely spot and executed with a bullet in the back of the head.

Minutes after I dropped Mairead off, I drove to a phone box on the way back to barracks. I called Jimmy Mac, as he was always called, a Detective Sergeant with the RUC, a mate whom I had got to know well as a drinking partner. He knew I was with the Paras. More importantly, I felt I could trust him to keep my name out of the frame, even with such vital information as a planned bombing of a major hotel. He was not at work but the officer said that if the matter was urgent, he would arrange for Jimmy to phone me back within minutes. I gave him the phone box number and waited.

Two minutes later, the phone rang.

'Scott?' the voice enquired.

I recognised Jimmy's voice immediately. 'What's up?'

'I need to see you,' I said.

'Some time tomorrow soon enough?' he asked.

'Could you manage tonight?' I asked. 'It's very important.'

'What have you been up to?' he asked jokingly. Then, somewhat more seriously, 'You're not in trouble, are you?'

'No,' I said, 'I'm not in trouble but I have some information which could be very important.'

When he found out where I was phoning from,

we arranged to meet in a Belfast club we both knew well.

Having met up at the club, Jimmy wasted no time.

'What's up?' he said when I had ordered the drinks.

'Can we talk away from the bar?'

'Aye,' he replied. 'It's serious, isn't it?'

Ten minutes and two pints later I had told Jimmy everything. He let out a low whistle. 'I see what you mean. Do you think she's telling you the truth?'

'Without a doubt. If you had seen her tonight you would have known she was telling the truth. She's only a kid ... she's not up to telling a pack of lies for no reason. She was frightened, confused and unsure what to do.'

'I'll have to pass this on, you know.'

'Of course you will,' I said. 'Why do you think I came to you?'

'I should pass it on now, immediately, just in case it's taking place tonight.'

'I think we're OK tonight,' I told him. 'I'm sure it's not that imminent. But I suppose it could be any time over the next few days.'

'What about you?' he asked.

'Can you keep my name out of it?' I asked. 'It would really open up a hornet's nest if the Paras learned I was involved with an IRA terrorist.'

'I don't see why not,' Jimmy said. 'They don't need to know the source. I can just tell them it was one of my touts gave me a tip-off.'

'Could you?' I asked, sounding worried.

'Yeah, I can fix that,' he said reassuringly. 'But on one condition?'

'What's that?' I asked.

'If you hear anything else about this, you phone me immediately and without fail. OK?'

'You have my word, Jimmy ... you have my word, promise,' and we shook hands.

Early on the afternoon of 6 April 1976, a Ford Escort drove into the grounds of The Conway Hotel in Dunmurry, up through the avenue of trees, passing the Roman-type open-air pool on the right, where police officers would often gather on summer nights for a barbecue and a late-night swim. But the beautiful grounds, with the trees not yet in full leaf, were deserted that day. At the top of the drive, the car stopped outside the iron gates which had been erected to keep out terrorists, for planting bombs in prestigious hotels had become a hallmark of the IRA during that period of the mid-1970s.

The two guards on duty at the wooden gatehouse had no idea what was happening when the door opened suddenly and a young man walked in, a gun in his hand.

'Don't move, Provisional IRA,' said the gunman.

Then he told them to lie on the floor while his accomplice tied their hands and feet together.

'Say nothing and do as you's told,' the young man told them in a broad Belfast accent.

Mairead Farrell and Sean McDermott carried Colt 45s, while Kieron Doherty had a magnum pistol. Kieron, his magnum at the ready, stayed with the guards in the hut while Mairead and Sean carried three suitcases from the boot of the Escort into the hotel. Each suitcase contained a 5lb bomb.

Mairead and Sean walked towards the hotel. As soon as they walked into the foyer, they took their guns from their pockets.

'Provisional IRA,' shouted Sean.

Everyone looked round, stunned by the words. 'Everyone on the floor,' yelled Sean. 'Lie down now ... do as you're told.'

Mairead shouted, 'Do as you're told and no one will get hurt.'

She continued to stand in the hotel foyer, a Colt 45 in her hand, while Sean ran around placing the three suitcases; one upstairs, one in the dining room and one in the lounge. No one panicked, everyone remained calm as they all lay down on the carpeted floor, not daring to move a muscle.

When Sean returned he shouted, 'This is a 15-minute warning. You all have time to get out.'

Then Mairead and Sean fled.

They ran to their car and leapt inside. Then Sean screamed, 'Mairead, it's the cops, run for it.'

She jumped out as a police van pulled up alongside their car. She ran down the slope, away from the hotel towards the swimming pool, dropping her handbag and Colt 45 as she ran through the trees.

'Halt or we'll shoot.'

Mairead heard the officer's voice loud and clear behind her. She knew it was useless to run any further. She stopped in her tracks and turned towards him. The RUC man grabbed her by the back of the neck and marched her towards the police car. She was shoved into the back of the car and the officer climbed in beside her. Then they drove off but stopped outside a house nearby. She saw an ambulance drive up and the police began asking her questions.

But Mairead would follow IRA orders to the letter. She did not utter a word in response to any of the police questions. The police told her later that day that Sean McDermott had been shot dead but she didn't believe them. She learned three days later that Sean and Kieron had raced to a nearby house where they had tried to hijack a car. The two young men had ordered the owner at gunpoint to hand over the car keys. He pretended to get them from his pocket but, instead he drew a gun and had shot McDermott through the heart. He died instantly. Kieron Doherty had immediately surrendered. Unfortunately for Sean McDermott, who was only 21, the car was owned by an off-duty police officer. Mairead had liked Sean, indeed, he had befriended her from the moment she joined the Provisionals and it had been Sean who had asked her whether she wanted to join an ASU to bomb The Conway Hotel.

Mairead Farrell was already in a cell in Dunmurry police station when she heard the three bombs explode a few hundred yards from where she was sitting. She saw the devastation the bombs caused three days later in a newspaper photograph.

She told friends later, 'I said to myself, "that's for you, Sean," for I was deeply upset that he had been killed. We had hurt no one. We had taken great care to make sure everyone was safely out of the hotel before the bombs exploded. But Sean had died, though, on active service. He was a good lad.'

Mairead would spend the following six months in the remand section of Armagh jail. Her trial, on 9 December 1976, was a short, one-day affair at Belfast City Commission. Three witnesses from The Conway Hotel gave evidence of seeing a young woman with two other young men. They said Mairead had worn a long blue-green coat with tan platform shoes and that she carried a Colt 45.

The IRA leadership always demand that any of their sympathisers, members or activists, arrested and charged with any offence relating to the cause, should never speak to the police or accept the authority of the courts. Mairead followed those orders to the letter, refusing to recognise the court, to give evidence or to make any statement about the case. At 5.30pm Judge Chambers, declared her guilty as charged, and imposed a sentence of 14 years, convicting her of causing three explosions, of having had possession of the three bombs with intent, of possessing firearms and ammunition with intent and of being a member of the IRA.

She was permitted exactly five minutes with her parents and then she was led away to start her sentence. She had not spoken a word.

Kieron Doherty also received a stiff jail sentence for his part in the bombing. He would later join the IRA hunger-strikers in the H-block prisons of Long Kesh. The IRA prisoners were protesting against being treated as ordinary criminals and demanded to be allowed to wear their own clothes and be granted

the status of prisoners of war. The British
Government refused their demands and after years of
the 'dirty protest' in the late 1970s, some IRA
prisoners decided that a hunger-strike was the only
way to force the British Government's hand. Doherty
died in jail in August 1981, after fasting for 73 days.

I heard news of The Conway blast the following
morning. Later that day, I heard that one of the
bombers had been shot dead while trying to escape
and that a young man and woman had been arrested
at the scene. I knew immediately that my beloved,
stupid, mixed-up Mairead was the young woman.

I read all the newspapers, trying to find out
every detail of the blast and Mairead's capture. I
could never forgive her for what she had done, but I
gave her credit for one thing. She had told me that no
one would be killed or injured in the explosion. And,
thank God, no one had been.

6

'WHAT THE FUCK WENT WRONG?' I said angrily the
moment I was put through to my mate, Jimmy Mac. 'I
thought the place was being watched round the
clock.'

'Don't ask me,' he replied. 'I passed it through as
information from a highly reliable source the morning
after we spoke. I'll try to find out and let you know.'

'Thanks,' I said, 'but remember our agreement ...
no names, no pack drill, OK?'

'Don't worry,' he replied. 'I didn't tell them
before and there's no reason to tell them now. Relax.'

I could not believe that the RUC had not staked
out The Conway as a major bomb target after my
warning. The IRA had made it plain that all of
Belfast's prime hotels were bomb targets and a
number, including The Europa, had been devastated

in successful attacks during the previous six months. The Conway should also have been high on the RUC's list of priorities because police officers would often use the hotel, particularly in the summer months. The hotel had also been used by politicians and senior civil servants from London who needed to stay in relative safety when visiting Belfast. The hotel's owners had taken stringent precautions, erecting a 6ft-high, steel perimeter fence, closed-circuit television, and employing a 24-hour security watch at the gatehouse.

There was one major plus that emerged from the cock-up, which I had no intention of discussing or even mentioning to Jimmy. The fact that the RUC had not staked out the hotel meant that Mairead would never guess that I had tipped off the authorities about the IRA's attack.

Over a beer two days later, Jimmy Mac told me what had happened. 'They took the warning seriously enough, but because the Conway already employed a 24-hour guard at the gatehouse they didn't consider it necessary to mount complete police surveillance on the hotel until they heard whether the bomb attack was imminent. As you know, Scott, we had no idea when the attack was to take place, just that it had been planned. Sometimes, it can be weeks or months between hearing of a planned IRA bomb attack and the buggers actually carrying it out.'

'Any blame anywhere?' I asked him.

'No,' Jimmy said, 'not on this one. They shot dead one terrorist and captured the other two so it was counted as a highly successful police operation.

And remember, no one got killed or injured either. The only casualty was the hotel, but that can be rebuilt quickly enough. No, the top brass were pleased with that one ... a good result for them.'

I knew that I must now put Mairead behind me and get on with my life. I wanted to go and see her, just to be with her, sit with her and comfort her, but I knew I could never do that and she would go berserk if I showed up and said I wanted to visit her in jail. I realised that if I ever wanted to see her I would have to be checked out, that the authorities would undoubtedly learn that a Para on active service in the Province was visiting a known IRA bomber in jail. The Intelligence officers would have been called in to find out what the hell was going on and I would be questioned non-stop until I confessed to everything that had been going on between Mairead and me over the last 18 months. Without a doubt, that would ruin my army career.

More importantly, I realised that if I did show up to see Mairead, the IRA might learn of what had been going on and Mairead's life inside would have been made hell by the other IRA prisoners. I knew that if the IRA believed that she and I had been lovers at the time the bomb attack was being planned, she would have had to face physical and probably sexual attacks, and frequent beatings from the other prisoners. The odds were that she would probably 'meet with an accident', in other words be murdered by a gang of female inmates working on instructions from the Provo bosses still at large. The last thing I wanted was to put Mairead at that sort of risk just for my own selfish, emotional needs.

I went to the police station where Mairead was being held but not for one minute did I contemplate going inside. I just walked up and down on the other side of the road, wondering which cell she was being held in and hoping that she might have a small window. But then I realised I was behaving stupidly because the RUC would never hold an IRA prisoner in a cell with a window! Somehow, just walking near the building in which she was being held made me feel closer to her. As I walked round the perimeter of the police station, I thought of what I could have done to stop Mairead taking part in the IRA operation and wondered if I should have told her that, in reality, I was a serving Para. It might have prevented her going on this mission, but I knew it would have ended our relationship for ever and would probably have made her more determined to throw in her lot with the Provos. Fed up, miserable and angry with myself for not having been able to stop her, I went for a drink.

I told myself that I was acting like a love-sick teenager and that I had to pull myself together. I knew that she would be found guilty and that could mean ten or fifteen years in jail. We certainly couldn't see each other or write to each other, because that would expose Mairead to retribution from the other inmates. She had always been so strict about keeping my identity away from her friends and family and, thank God, she had. I drank four pints that night and could have drunk eight, and the more I drank the more I realised that our wonderful love affair was over. I was certain that we would never see each other again and I kept thinking of the wonderful times we had together. Maudlin and a little drunk, I went back to barracks that night convinced that my life was completely ruined.

The following day, I read of the details released by the RUC about the Conway bombing and the string of other explosions that had rocked Belfast in a 12-hour blitz bringing mayhem to the city centre. From what Mairead had told me that night in the pub, it was obvious that the Provos employed anyone they could that night, including naïve, untested teenagers like Mairead, in their determination to organise a number of spectacular hits which would devastate hotels, shops, stores and offices in a bombers' day of destruction.

I wished that I could have spoken to Mairead the day after the IRA blitz, to show her to what lengths the Provos would stoop in their campaign to bring Belfast to its knees. From all reports, it appeared that the Provos had used untried teenagers from Republican families, youngsters with no experience and no training whatsoever in covert missions, cannon-fodder for the Provos. Those in power had not risked any of their trained members with knowledge and experience but only naïve youngsters whose minds they had filled with dreams of fighting for the Republican cause. It did not matter to the Provo chiefs whether the kids were killed in the process of planting bombs, or caught and jailed for ten or fifteen years, for the men who organised and planned the IRA missions would be free to recruit more youngsters and continue their war of attrition.

I still find the details of Monday, 5 April 1976 hard to believe. The effect of the IRA's day of madness seemed to be to tear apart a city which was already on its knees, for the sheer scale of the attacks on buildings and property, and the risk to ordinary people's lives, became almost too great to comprehend, never mind justify. Incendiary devices, petrol bombs, hand-guns and hijackings, all were used by the IRA to bring chaos to Belfast and the surrounding area. City inhabitants eventually reached the stage where they didn't know where to run for safety — bombs seemed to be exploding almost every hour, and the targets included factories, pubs, shops, hotels and offices. Workers, residents, customers and casual passers-by ran for their lives as the warnings were phoned in, and the security services tried desperately to beat the deadlines each time. The enormity of their task was made worse by the number of hoax calls, which stretched their resources even further. It seemed that simple luck, and the efforts of a handful of brave members of the public, managed to avoid the carnage that surely would have followed.

The first bomb went off at 2.11pm in the restaurant of the Wellington Park Hotel on the Malone Road, starting a fire which caused extensive damage. The device was left by an armed man and a teenage girl who warned staff that a bomb was about to explode. Courageous employees rushed around the crowded hotel, telling guests and staff to run for the exits because a bomb was about to explode. Only three minutes after the hotel had been cleared, the explosion ripped apart the restaurant and started a fire which caused severe damage.

Only 15 minutes later, at 2.25pm, a second bomb exploded, this one outside the Milky Way café in Royal Avenue near the city's main shopping and business areas. An unknown waitress was the heroine of the hour. She saw a young man walk into the café and leave a bag on the floor, telling the 20 people in the café at the time to get out because the bomb would explode within minutes. Without a thought for herself, the waitress, a woman in her thirties, grabbed hold of the bag, picked it up and walked out of the café, placing the bomb under the café's front window. The area was filled with people shopping and going about their business. Then she shouted at every one to 'get away', screaming 'bomb ... bomb ... bomb'.

Everyone nearby scattered in panic, including those who had been in the café at the time the bomb was planted. Two minutes later, the device exploded with a huge flash and a bang, causing extensive damage to the building. Due to the courage and foresight of the waitress, however, no one was hurt.

Minutes later, at 2.38pm precisely, a fierce fire broke out without warning after a device exploded in Frederick Thomas' toy and pram shop across the street from the Milky Way café. Two youths were seen entering the shop with a plastic bag, leaving it discreetly in the middle of the shop and then walking out. Members of the public later recalled seeing two youths running away down the street. In a matter of minutes, the blaze spread quickly to adjoining shops and at least four premises were completely gutted. Firemen were still standing by 24 hours later, damping down the smouldering ruins.

At 2.59pm, the Headline Shipping Company's offices in Victoria Street were badly damaged by a bomb which was left by two young men who were both carrying hand-guns. One of the youths stood inside the front door while the other took the bomb, contained in a hold-all, into one of the offices, placing it on the floor. They shouted to the staff that the hold-all contained a bomb which was timed to go off within minutes. The office workers screamed to everyone in the building to get out of the place. Police, called to the scene, arrived within minutes and managed to clear everyone away from the immediate area, having checked that the offices had been emptied. As the police were still appealing for pedestrians to keep away, the bomb exploded, ripping through the block. But, fortunately, no one was injured.

The massive Conway Hotel bomb blasts followed shortly after 3.00pm, but they could not be heard in the centre of Belfast which took the brunt of that days bomb outrages.

Back in the city, a huge 15lb bomb was planted in the premises of Robert Steele in Victoria Street at 4.42 pm. As the premises were emptied, the police were called and when the device did not immediately explode, Army bomb disposal experts were called to the scene to inspect the device. They managed to defuse it.

The centre of Belfast that afternoon was thrown into chaos. No one knew where to run for safety. The entire city centre was a cauldron of noise as alarm bells rang out continuously, and screaming sirens from police cars, ambulances and fire engines filled the air as they raced from one emergency to another. Rush-hour traffic in Belfast was brought to a standstill, many people abandoning their cars and making their way by foot away from the danger area. RUC and Army vehicles, fire engines, ambulances and bomb disposal experts desperately tried to carve their way through the congested traffic, making matters worse.

Not only had the IRA planted a number of bombs and incendiary devices which had all gone off, but at least seven hoax calls were also made to the RUC, sending police and fire engines off in the wrong direction, adding to the chaos. The security forces were stretched to the limit. Areas were cordoned off around the city centre and people were urged to keep away as the RUC and troops were called in to seal off streets and bring some calm to the situation. But the sound of sirens and non-stop fire alarms could be heard throughout the afternoon and evening. It had been the Provos' most extensive day of upheaval in the Province.

But they weren't finished yet. Just as the Security forces believed the crisis to have passed, the terror campaign began again.

At 8.00pm, three petrol bombs were thrown into the main factory of Mackies at Springfield Road, Belfast, but although they all exploded on impact, no damage was caused and no one was injured. But the RUC, the fire brigade and the Army still had to check the scene, stretching their depleted services still further.

At the same time, a beige Mini was reported stolen and left at the Protestant end of the city's Halliday Road. The driver told a passer-by that the car contained a bomb. The security forces were called and an army bomb disposal team were brought in when the device failed to explode. Thirty minutes later, a controlled explosion was carried out by the Army, but when the Mini was examined later, no bomb was found.

A 8.17pm, three young, armed men walked into the Village Inn public house at Killyclogher outside Omagh and told everyone to get out. Fifteen men drinking there at the time and the bar staff were all ordered out at gunpoint. The men produced a large cake tin and told everyone it contained a 10lb bomb which they placed behind the bar. When everyone had left the pub, the three gunmen walked out, climbed into a car which they had hijacked earlier that evening, and drove away. Five minutes later, the entire pub exploded in a burst of flames, wrecking the place. But no one was injured.

Shortly after 10.00pm, that same night, a hijacked car was parked outside Belleck RUC station in Fermanagh and three men fled from the scene. The vehicle was checked out by army bomb disposal experts who believed that a massive bomb had been prepared. Police closed off the area and told families in a radius of 400 yards that they were to leave their homes for their own safety, in case the car bomb exploded. Meanwhile, a bomb disposal team worked on the vehicle and when all the families had been cleared from the area, a controlled explosion blew up the car. A 300lb bomb was found to have been inside. RUC chiefs estimated that the police station and many of the homes in the area would have been severely damaged if the bomb had exploded.

In fact, the RUC station was virtually unscathed and only four cars parked near the vehicle were wrecked. No one was hurt. A few minutes after the car bomb was parked, however, staff at a nearby garage, who were just closing for the night, were held up by three armed men. The garage workers were tied up and told not to move. Then the young men took off in another car.

At 10.25pm, soldiers manning an army check-point in Lifford Road, Strabane, heard a man shouting a warning, telling the soldiers that he had just been ordered to park a car bomb outside the army post. The area was immediately cleared and a bomb disposal squad rushed to the scene, but they did not reach the check-point in time. A 200lb bomb exploded, severely damaging the army post and wrecking the man's white Morris Marina. A woman who was passing some distance away was treated for shock in hospital but there were no other injuries. The man explained that his car had been hijacked and he was then ordered to drive it to the Lifford Road check-point, park the vehicle, tell no one and run.

But the man's courage in warning the soldiers meant that no one was injured.

Thirty minutes later, at 11.00pm, a grocer was closing his shop at the junction of Main Street and Tassagh Road in Keady when a car containing two youths slowed down. The young man in the passenger seat threw a bomb into the shop. Those few people present, including a few customers, realised the package must contain a bomb and fled into the street. Seconds later, the shop erupted in flames, devastating the building and all its contents. Forensic scientists believed that a 5lb bomb had caused the damage.

At 11.10pm, a bomb exploded at a Customs post on the Clones Road outside Newtonbutler in Fermanagh, completely destroying the empty building.

And there were other explosions that night. Shortly after midnight, another Customs post at Mullaghduff on the Newtownbutler-Clones road was wrecked by an explosion, but no one was hurt; a boutique in Main Street, Lisnasken, called Tots & Teens was damaged after a bomb was thrown through the window, but again no one was injured; and in the early hours of the morning, snipers opened fire on soldiers manning a check-point near the Donegal border just outside 'Derry. But no one was hit.

And so, by the evening, fires raged across Belfast, and the extent of the damage to buildings, businesses and property was unprecedented. It was a miracle that no one had been killed.

And I had to come to terms with the fact that the woman I loved believed whole-heartedly in these tactics. I simply wondered how Mairead could have become so enthralled with a cause which ordered and carried out indiscriminate bombings and shootings, trying their utmost to wreck people's lives, their shops, their communities and their firms, forcing workers out of their jobs with little or no regard for people's safety. And I wondered why it was that I remained interested, indeed fascinated, in Mairead, someone who was prepared to carry out such evil work.

The following morning, I went for a hard run and a work-out in the gym. Something told me that I had to get my life back on the rails. I was now 28 and had done some years with the Paras. I needed a new life, a new challenge. For some years, I had contemplated having a crack at joining the SAS, the élite troops of the British Army. Hundreds of Paras dreamed of joining the SAS and each year many put themselves forward for selection. Some, of course, passed the rigorous selection course, but far more failed. As a result, there was great rivalry between the two regiments; the Paras are determined to prove that they were the army's crack regiment, the toughest soldiers in the British Army. But the SAS believes that there is no real competition. The troops of the SAS, trained to extraordinary standards of fitness, resilience and daring, know they have no rivals and they are constantly given the chance to prove themselves, usually in secret in some foreign location but, occasionally, in high-profile situations.

There was another reason to try to pass the SAS

selection. It meant that I would escape from Northern Ireland, at least for a while, which would help me to get over Mairead. I knew, of course, that the SAS were used in the Province, especially on the border, but they didn't have to patrol the streets day and night, something which the Paras had to do for several months a year. I knew that if I stayed in the Paras I would, of course, return to Northern Ireland for another tour of duty and, more than likely, be detailed to patrol the Falls area and other places I used to visit with Mairead. I knew that would make it impossible for me to forget her and I needed to wipe her out of my mind. I knew I had to get over her and find someone else. And, of course, the more I thought of Mairead, the more I convinced myself that I would never find another girl like her.

I trained ridiculously hard to get myself fit over the next three months. I talked to other Paras who had tried and failed the SAS selection and they gave me hints about what to expect. They all emphasised that the fitter I was before the course, the greater the chance I would have of passing. And they warned me that throughout the selection, you should never lose heart because the SAS instructors try everything to kill your spirit, to make the applicant give up. And, they warned me to remember that if a soldier at any time gives up even for an instant, then he is immediately RTU'd (returned to unit) and his one chance of joining the SAS is ended for good. I listened to their advice and it made me even more determined to pass.

And I did.

It was tough, far tougher than I had imagined. But when I left Hereford after three weeks of hell, knowing that I had passed the selection course, I felt 10ft tall. It was great to know that the SAS had thrown everything at me and that I had managed to pass one of the most rigorous tests a soldier could ever face. I had no illusions about the forthcoming training course either.

The 14 weeks' continuation training, including jungle training (which was terrible), required grit, stamina and an iron will but it was also a great experience. I knew I had to be hard and disciplined throughout. I also knew that I could not afford one lapse because any soldier could be RTU'd at any time during the course, even during the final phase of combat survival training, the last hurdle before a volunteer is 'badged', the moment when the new recruit receives his SAS sand-coloured beret and cap-badge. Most of the time I actually enjoyed the relentless, testing atmosphere of the training, determined that the long hard, endurance marches with heavy back-packs would not defeat me. It was rough, especially on the feet, but when I was told that I had passed, I felt fantastic.

My first tour of duty with the SAS in the Province was a far cry from the patrols I used to carry out in and around Belfast with the Parachute Regiment. A squadron of SAS men were choppered into Bessbrook Mill in South Armagh to back up a battalion of Royal Highland Fusiliers already stationed there, patrolling the border.

We were given quite a welcome from the local

IRA. On our second night, we were having a drink at the bar when all hell brook loose. We heard the swoosh of several mortars going off one after the other and, within seconds, the shells were landing all around the camp. Some of the younger soldiers ran from the bar until sense prevailed.

'Walk, fucking walk,' came the order from a bellowing Sergeant Major and the soldiers obeyed instantly. We realised that those firing the mortars would be about 200 yards or so from the base, because we presumed they would be using their own handmade mortars which did not have the range of our manufactured, military weapons.

I picked up my hand-gun and SLR and made my way outside with the others, shortly after the powerful arc lights had been directed towards the sound of the mortars. After half-a-dozen rounds had been fired off, of course, the IRA had run from the scene, fearful that we might catch them. But it was night and anyone venturing outside would have been an easy target for a sniper or machine-gunner hiding in the dark. A chopper was scrambled but the terrorists weren't found that night.

Living at Bessbrook was no picnic. Every morning without fail, patrols would have to leave the Mill and check the roads, lanes and paths in the vicinity of the HQ in case the IRA had laid traps, mines or trip wires. The slightest deviation in the earth had to be checked by bomb squad officers and patrols would search the area throughout the hours of daylight.

Usually, the SAS would go out in five- and six-man fighting patrols. Mostly, we would go out under cover of darkness, sometimes on foot patrols and on other occasions in choppers, vans or cars.

Our mission was to intercept IRA patrols, in the area and to pick up volunteers as they crossed the border from south to north. We would usually be out for 48 hours and, more often than not, the conditions would be the same — wet and cold, the ground boggy. We would be carrying Armalites, SLRs, 9mm hand-guns and 7.62mm general purpose machine-guns. We would survive on hard rations so that we would never light a fire and we would take it in turns to sleep, getting perhaps two hours rest during the 48 hours we were on patrol. We must have gone out on nearly 50 patrols but we never took part in a fire-fight. Sometimes, we took over OPs from other SAS units and stayed there, watching for any movement. But the IRA weren't fools. They knew the SAS were patrolling the border and they took no chances. They knew that if they were ever caught in a fire-fight they would be wiped out.

One night, we heard that an IRA patrol of 13 men was moving north from the border. The OC decided to scramble a chopper in the hope of locating them before sending out an SAS fire-fight patrol. The chopper located the patrol, which fired at the helicopter, and then the troops on board realised that the IRA patrol had scattered in all directions making it impossible to track them down. To chase them in those conditions was asking for trouble, and it was decided to do nothing that night. Checks on the ground the following morning revealed nothing. We were all more than annoyed that we had missed the opportunity of confronting a major IRA patrol, because we had trained for just such an eventuality for month after month. But I would get an opportunity later.

In June 1978, I was again in Northern Ireland with troops from 22 Regiment SAS when Intelligence informed us that the Provos were planning major attacks on communications installations in and around Belfast. This was confirmed some days later by an article in the Belfast Provisional newspaper *Republican News*, which stated that the IRA had shifted from the blanket bombing of commercial premises, like shopping centres and office blocks, to 'a more selective campaign against prestige communications and Government targets'.

One of the largest GPO depots was situated at Ballysillen in North Belfast. This depot was a major GPO centre and highly vulnerable to a bomb attack because huge petrol tanks on the premises stored tens of thousands of gallons of fuel for the hundreds of GPO vans based there. If that lot went up, it would not only cause major damage to the GPO headquarters and the houses and flats in the immediate vicinity, it would also be a massive coup for the IRA.

A four-man SAS patrol was detailed to watch the headquarters and we set up an OP outside the perimeter fence where we could see two sides of the depot. We chose this spot as being one of the most likely points an IRA bomb group would select to infiltrate the depot and set off one or more bombs, sparking a massive fireball. We knew that if the fuel storage tanks exploded, residents living within a half-a-mile radius of the depot could be at risk from the flaming debris that would shoot high into the air before falling in flames to the ground.

We had been keeping watch for six or seven days, when we noticed just after midnight one night that three or four men were walking down the lane by the side of the depot, known locally as The Loney. They approached the perimeter fence a few hundred yards from our OP. Someone tugged my sleeve and pointed some distance away. I thought I could see some movement near the fence. I checked with my night sights and could make out four men carrying heavy bags.

The men were behaving as though on a film set. They marched boldly alongside the fence, their army-style boots making a loud noise on the tarmac. I saw one hurl a haversack over the 8ft-high wire-mesh fence, and it hit the ground with quite a thud. All four men appeared to be carrying sports bags and wearing tartan scarves. I looked at another member of my unit who had also been watching through his night sights. He nodded. I was now almost convinced that these were the bombers we had been waiting for. But we had to be sure because they were acting with such bravado, making no attempt to conceal their presence.

The bombers stopped at a certain point and laid their bags on the ground while another seemed to have taken out a pair of large cutters and began slicing his way through the steel fencing. I knew that would take a while, giving us time to creep closer to the group and challenge them.

Without making a sound, we backed out of sight and made our way around the buildings behind us, coming out a few minutes later about 50 yards from the group of four who were still in the same position, two concentrating on the fence while the other two appeared to be preparing the bombs. We spread out and the fourth man from my unit moved back, further away from the bombers, so that he could use his radio to inform HQ what was going on.

Suddenly, a van came round the corner, some 200 yards from the bombers, startling them and us. Not certain what was happening, the four men froze. At first we believed that the van was part of the IRA plan, but it didn't make any sense. It all seemed to be part of a film with the bravado of the bombers and now the van screeching to a halt, drawing attention to the group. We waited to see what would happen. Ten seconds later, the van's engine revved up again; it backed away and sped off. I breathed a sigh of relief. It seemed as though the van had nothing whatsoever to do with the bombers, but I feared that the IRA squad might have thought it was an RUC or army 'Q' vehicle. I guessed the bombers had been shaken by the arrival of the van, so I decided to move forward to confront them.

We were about 20 yards from them, dressed in our dark, camouflage fatigues, with camouflage cream on our faces. We walked out of the shadows, barely visible to the bombers working away in front of us. One turned and looked straight at us and I sensed we had been spotted. All three of us froze but we were ready for any eventuality. We were armed with automatic sub-machine-guns, the safety catches off, the magazines fully charged.

'Halt,' I shouted. 'Army.'

I had no time to say another word when the four men looked towards us. Three turned and ran, the fourth stayed his ground and seemed to be going for a gun.

'Fire,' I shouted and a hail of bullets sprayed towards them. We kept walking slowly towards the men as they tried to run, then walk, then stagger away from us. Each time we emptied our magazines we pushed home another and continued firing as the men ran in every direction, trying to escape the hail of fire power. The man furthest from us made a getaway and I wasn't sure whether he was hit or not; the other three finally went down. We stopped firing, reloaded, and moved towards them slowly, our safety catches still off, the guns still pointing at the men on the ground. We were taking no chances.

I had seen one man run but knew he was going straight towards another member of our squad. Unfortunately our man's rifle had jammed. As the bomber came towards him, the SAS man grabbed the barrel of the rifle and smashed the butt into the bomber's head, breaking his neck.

As we reached the men and checked that all were dead the place was swamped by police cars, Land Rovers, Armoured Personnel Carriers and hundreds of police officers.

'Get everyone out of here,' I shouted. 'Take cover ... there are live bombs here.'

'Get the bomb squad, fast,' I yelled, 'because these bombs will be primed to go off at any moment.'

'Is everyone OK?' someone shouted through the darkness.

'Yes, all OK,' I yelled back, 'but there are three bodies here ... one bastard escaped.'

One of my SAS mates raced off towards the police marshalling point, directing them to where the fourth bomber had fled.

We handed the operation over to the RUC who took control of the area. Armed police tracked the lone bomber to a nearby block of flats. Residents reported that shortly after midnight, having been woken by the noise of heavy machine-gun fire, a man had knocked at the doors of a number of flats, demanding to be let in. But no one had opened their doors and he had run off through the gardens, making good his escape towards the Falls Road.

One woman who lived in the block of nearby flats said, 'All of a sudden, we were woken to the sound of gunfire. Not just one or two shots, but a hail of bullets was being fired. The noise was terrifying. Some of us ran to a flat furthest from the gunfire. One young mother, whose tiny baby was screaming for food, defied the bullets and ran back to her home for the child's bottle.'

Army bomb disposal experts checked the bags left behind by the bombers and ordered police to move nearby residents out of the blocks of flats, fearing for their safety if the high explosive bombs had detonated. The bomb disposal team did not start to tackle the tricky job of de-activating the bombs until all the residents had been moved to safety. The bomb squad were amazed that the IRA bombers had planned to set off their incendiaries just 20 yards from a block of pensioners' flats. No warning had been given.

The following morning, the close-knit community was indignant that the bombers could have risked their lives by planting the bombs so close to the flats. One woman said, 'If those bombs had gone off and set off the fuel storage tanks, all those poor old people wouldn't have stood a chance.'

The Provos had meant to devastate the GPO depot. The bomb squad discovered four 'La Montype' devices, consisting of a charge of explosive attached to a gallon can of petrol. One of the bombs was neutralised with an explosive on the spot, but the rest had to be carefully dismantled before they could be removed safely.

However, police found another man lying dead some distance from where the bombers had been operating, apparently killed by a ricochet. The man, Billy Hanna, a bachelor and a Protestant, had been walking home after drinking in a Shankill pub with mates.

Another man was also caught in the shoot-out, having been shot in the arm while driving his car past the depot as the SAS poured rounds at the fleeing bombers. Police believed that he, too, must have been hit by a ricochet.

The three Provos killed were William John 'Jack' Mealy, from the Ardoyne, Dennis Emmanuel Brown and James Mulvenna from the Catholic Bone district on the Old Park Road. All three were aged 28 and all were married.

The Provisional IRA high command, which said that the three men had been 'volunteers on active service', challenged the official version of events. The Provos maintained that none of the men had been armed and would have been in no position to resist a British Army challenge when called upon to halt. The entire Active Service Unit was surrounded and could only have surrendered.

The statement continued: 'Having effectively captured the men, they were summarily shot in an orgy of British Army and RUC concentrated fire. By their own admission, the Brits have said that over 200 rounds of ammunition were fired. It is obvious that the British forces showed no humanity or mercy. Examination of the bodies would reveal that the men had been mutilated with multiple gunshot wounds.'

The Army pointed out that the conditions of the so-called 'Yellow Card', which outlined the situations in which troops were permitted to open fire, stated that troops may fire at someone with a firearm if they have reason to believe he is about to use it for offensive purposes, if he refuses to halt when called upon to do so, and if there is no other way of stopping him. Another provision allowed troops to open fire when a person is attacking or destroying property if his action is likely to endanger life.

Back at the barracks later that morning, we all enjoyed a bloody good breakfast, a real victory fry-up. We knew that we had not only saved the GPO depot from being destroyed by fire, but we might well have saved innocent local families from being severely burned or, more than likely, killed in the ensuing explosions. We fully realised that if the Provo bombs had set the GPO fuel storage tanks alight, a square mile of Ballysillen would probably have been destroyed and, with it, many lives. That night we celebrated in style in the bar back at camp but none of the other soldiers had any idea why we were all intent on getting wonderfully, happily drunk.

Throughout those years, I would spend time back at Hereford on various training courses and my SAS squadron would also be sent to the Nordic countries practising skiing, parachuting and living rough in appalling conditions — snow, ice and sub-zero temperatures — for days on end. Officially, we were being groomed for a show-down with the Soviet Union when we might well have to fight behind enemy lines in just such conditions.

Most of the time, it was bloody freezing, hard graft and it was impossible to sleep for more than ten minutes, but it had its compensations — the most wonderful skiing, sensational landscapes and, occasionally, meeting some beautiful young women. But although I would happily get drunk and enjoy wonderful parties and the occasional girlfriend, I would never forget Mairead, counting the months and the years she still had to serve and wondering if, on her return to civilian life after so long behind bars, she would be the same wonderful girl I had known before.

In April 1982, however, most of 22 Regiment SAS

found itself back at base in Hereford studying maps of the Falkland Islands. We all knew there was talk of possible action there but we had no idea at that stage that we would be taking part in a small war. At first, we expected the Falklands to be a low-profile, hush-hush operation for the SAS, where we would be expected to take over the island quietly, followed by an announcement from the Foreign Office that after a little local difficulty, some Argentinian soldiers, who had temporarily set up camp on the island, had been persuaded to fly back home, leaving the islanders to get on with their lives.

It would only be some months or years later that the true story would emerge. The SAS had gone in one night under cover of darkness, surprised the sleeping Argentinian troops and, after a short, ferocious fire-fight, had taken back control of the island while the Argentinian forces flew out in silence, leaving their dead behind them. Maybe one or two SAS men might have died in the operation, but their deaths would have been treated by the authorities more as accidents than as courageous troops killed in action. Not everyone would have gone along with that, however, for their mates and their families would have known what really happened.

But this time it would be different.

Forty-eight hours later, D Squadron was flying from Brize Norton to the Ascension Islands where we were told we would be briefed before being flown down to the Falklands.

'What's the weather like there?' someone asked.

'Just like the Brecon Beacons in winter,' came the reply.

'Wet, wintry and 'orrible,' someone added, laughing.

When we arrived in the Ascension Islands, we heard via the BBC World Service that the nearby island of South Georgia, occupied by a couple of hundred Argentine troops, had been recaptured by just 75 SAS and Royal Marines in a lightning operation. We were impressed and wondered if re-taking the Falklands would be just as easy.

From Ascension we sailed south on the aircraft carrier HMS Hermes. On board, we learned how to handle the new, first-class American Stinger hand-held ground-to-air missile, which we would be taking with us on to the Falklands, as well as the 203 multi-barrelled, anti-tank missile. We also tested our usual Armalites and GP machine-guns.

In addition to weapons preparation, we would keep fit by running around the decks, climbing ropes and doing hundreds of press-ups and pull-ups. Every evening, we were given the latest intelligence briefings, updates and what the Regiment called 'prayers', general orders given out daily as a matter of routine. More importantly, perhaps, we would listen to the BBC World Service and eat first-class food. The Royal Navy looked after us really well.

Many of my mates wrote letters to their families and especially to their wives and girlfriends. We knew this would be no picnic, that some of us would probably never return. I would lie awake at night wondering if I should write just one letter to Mairead.

In case I didn't make it back, I wanted her to know that I loved her and had never forgotten her. But I finally saw sense, and decided that to write such a letter would only be selfish. I didn't write but hoped that I would never regret that decision. Instead, I wrote to my parents and to my grandfather with whom I had always been close. I wrote nothing soppy, simply a grown-up letter telling them what was happening and letting them understand that this time we all realised that re-taking the Falklands would be a real battle.

As we headed south, the weather changed from wonderful balmy, sunny days, perfect for sunbathing, to cold, harsh, rainy conditions which we knew we would have to endure once we had been choppered on to the island. A Sea King helicopter took our four-man patrol on to the Falklands and we were dropped before dawn some miles east of Darwin and Goose Green on the East Falklands. We had been informed that a sizeable force of Argentinians, battalion strength, was dug in between Goose Green and Darwin. We were ordered to make our way forward and take up an OP above any enemy positions we came across.

The second the Sea King touched down we leapt from the chopper, taking all our gear with us, and spread out. A minute later, the Sea King rose into the black sky and headed back to Hermes. We all stayed silent, lying on the ground, our weapons at the ready, our eyes getting used to the darkness and we listened to any sound that might suggest we were near the enemy. We stayed in those positions for 15 minutes, hardly moving a muscle. But we heard nothing. Now we we were on our own. The nearest British ground forces were some 3,000 miles distant on sunny Ascension Island. There were no back-up squads, no quick-reaction forces to help our patrol if we should hit any trouble or stumble across an Argentinian outpost.

We were on our own with just our bare essentials — our weapons, ammunition, fragmentation grenades and hard rations. If an Argentine patrol discovered our presence, we only had our 'Gimpy' and our rifles for defence. We all knew that it would be of paramount importance to keep out of sight at all times because, no matter how hard we fought, with only a four-man patrol and limited ammunition, a half-decent Argie company would have not taken long to deal with us. The realisation did not bear thinking about but it was never far from our minds. We had no idea at that stage how long we would be out there, exposed on the side of the mountain in filthy, wet conditions, sending back to base whatever information we could gather.

'Everyone OK?' I whispered, when I was sure that no enemy was in spitting distance of our dropping point.

My three mates, Tom, Bushy and Alan, the joker of the patrol, all hissed a reply that all was OK.

'Remember, this is no dress rehearsal,' I said quietly as we clambered to our feet and prepared to move out. 'This time it's for real.'

'Right on,' said Tom. 'Let's go.'

First, we had to ensure we could carry all our

gear as comfortably as possible. We knew we could
be in for a damn long endurance march and, although
it was not raining, the ground underfoot was both
lumpy and marshy, making the march far tougher
with the amount of equipment we were carrying. We
knew from the map that we had to cover at least 20
miles marching only under cover of darkness with no
idea where or when we might come across enemy
positions. More importantly, there was the constant
fear of mine fields. In one of our briefings,
Intelligence had told us that the Argies had laid
thousands of mines but they could not, of course, tell
us where they all were. Tabbing only under cover of
darkness, the possibility of hitting a minefield was of
far greater concern than accidentally running across
an enemy patrol. Our first priority, however, was to
cover many, many miles in atrocious conditions
within 72 hours. It was going to be tough.

We were wearing camouflage kit and army-issue
camouflage warm hats. I was carrying an Armalite,
plus eight full magazines; six hand-grenades; a 9mm
Browning hand-gun with four magazines containing
20 rounds; the heavy link for the 'Gimpy'; and a
spade, along with hard rations, sleeping bag and a
basic first-aid kit. We were all carrying different loads
for the Falklands environment, approximately 110lb
in weight, 30lb around our waists, and another 80lb
in my big, 100-litre Bergen. The others were carrying
such extras as the radio equipment, spare batteries,
other 'Gimpy' links and a full medic pack.

We set off, knowing that within a couple of hours
we would have to find somewhere to lie up

throughout the hours of daylight. The Falklands was like a billiard table with no natural vegetation and therefore nowhere to hide from the Argentinian spotter planes and helicopters, or from lookouts in OPs who could see movement for miles with their binoculars. Finding somewhere suitable every dawn after a night's hard march would prove to be one of our most difficult tasks.The Falklands had no cover whatsoever; no trees, no bushes, no natural dips where we could hole up for the day. Worse still, the ground beneath the marshy, spongy surface was like rock, so digging a hole big enough to hide in was all but impossible.

We would have to scrape off a thin top layer of surface grass, to perhaps a depth of 15 inches, entwine it in chicken-wire, lie down as though in a coffin and then pull the 'camouflaged' chicken-wire over us. We knew that the Argentinian planes would pick up areas which had been disturbed which they could then examine more closely. If they saw any ground disturbances, they could then send out a patrol or simply send in their Pucara aircraft to strafe the area.

And from day one we were all wet through. The boots we wore were not waterproof so we would try to sleep cold, damp and yet unable to move for fear of dislodging the blanket of heather and grass which covered us. We slept, or rather tried to sleep, in these conditions for about three weeks. Most days we all found we were nodding off for an hour or two at the most, but would be woken shaking with the cold, our teeth chattering and the realisation that the damp had soaked through to our skins.

We would dig our shell scrapes about three to four feet apart — a tactical distance — so that we could be in whispering distance of each other though we hardly ever spoke a word during the hours of daylight. We knew that even whispers can be picked up on the wind in such places and we were in no position to lift our heads to see if any Argies were marching towards us.

On a few occasions, I thought I heard the tramp, tramp of feet and pressed my ear to the ground to see if I was dreaming or if we were in danger of being accidentally discovered by some Argie patrol. But it must have been my nerves working overtime for we were never discovered. Most of the time, it seemed that the Argies preferred to remain in their defensive positions, waiting for an attack and not wishing to risk their troops on patrol, trying to search out and destroy enemy units.

Only once were we in any real danger of being discovered. We had been out about a week and had established a good OP from where we could just see the Argentinian encampment between Goose Green and Darwin. Around 3.00am we heard the noise of what sounded like a vehicle, probably an army jeep, seemingly not far away. Knowing that anyone in the jeep would be unable to hear me, I hissed to the lads.

Two kicked my leg gently, the sign that they had heard my hiss and Alan hissed back.

'Can you all hear the vehicle?' I asked speaking just above a whisper.

Again, I received two light foot taps and a hiss from Alan.

'Anyone see anything?' I asked but there was no reply, meaning a negative.

'Safety catches off?' I whispered. Again two kicks and a hiss.

Then we waited, all of us on edge, waiting for the jeep to come closer. We all knew that we had to lie still, not moving a muscle, until the danger had passed. We also knew that if the Argies came too close and we had no choice but to attack, then we would swing into instant action and let them have whatever was needed to finish them off.

We waited and waited and I strained to see the lights of the jeep approaching. The two lights were bright and piercing in the darkness, which surprised me. Then I suddenly realised that the noise of the engine was not a jeep, but the sound of a helicopter. Still, no one moved a muscle. Now I could tell that there was not one but two choppers coming towards us and closing fast. I guessed the choppers must have been some distance away and I knew they could never have pin-pointed our position. But we weren't taking any risks and we lay still until the two choppers turned away and flew off into the far distance.

'OK, lads,' I whispered and we all got to our feet, re-adjusted our gear and continued the march.

'Thank fuck for that,' said Bushy, taking off his hat and running his hand through his mop of hair. 'I lay so still not trying to move a muscle that I felt as though rigor mortis had set in.'

'I was itching to have a go,' said Tom. 'All we're doing here is living like bloody field mice.'

'Cool it,' said Bushy. 'You'll get a chance soon enough.'

'I fucking hope so,' said Tom, 'all this ammo we're humping around is killing me.'

'Cut it,' I said.

Each evening, we could not wait for dusk to fall as our muscles and our very bones seemed to be aching in the cold and the damp and the 110lb we were each carrying seemed more like a ton. As soon as the light faded sufficiently, we would be up and about, desperately trying to get the circulation moving again in an effort to get some warmth back into our bodies. And there was, of course, no question of ever lighting a fire for it would have been seen miles away by the Argentinian OPs. As a result, of course, we never had any hot food to help keep us warm. Cold rations only throughout the three weeks we spent on the islands. I had a dozen cans of baked beans and spaghetti, hard-tack biscuits, cheese, rich cake, Garibaldi biscuits, porridge oats, chocolate, Mars bars and Rolos.

As the weeks wore on and our rations became rapidly depleted, I would wet my finger and then dip it in the cocoa powder, which was already mixed with sugar, before licking it slowly, trying to get some nourishment into my body. Throughout the time we were on the Falklands, we were marching to different lying-up points most nights but not once was it possible to re-supply us. By the end, we were physically exhausted, our body strength seriously depleted, relying on nervous energy and our training to see us through. I knew we were all in a state of near hypothermia and was worried that, as each day passed, we were having to use all our grit to keep going and hope that our numbed, cold and perpetually wet feet would return to life, however painful the process. If any of us had, in fact, deteriorated to such an extent that hypothermia had set in, we would have had to seek permission for the frozen man and one mate to retire to an RV so he could be evacuated out by chopper.

It was on such occasions that we all realised we had to stick together and look after each other. It is easy in such conditions to let exhaustion and sleeplessness reduce even a super-fit SAS man to wanting to throw in the towel. But not once did I think that because I had three mates who not only helped me keep up my morale, but because I knew I was responsible, as we were all responsible, for making sure our patrol survived and got back in one piece. We also had a vitally important job to carry out, passing back intelligence to headquarters so that they could plan the attack to re-take the islands.

Often we would be lying in our 'coffins' looking up into the sky and through the camouflage of grass we would watch the Argentinian choppers and Pucara aircraft, the rather slow ground-attack jets, which the Argies appeared to be using as spotter planes.

Most days, I would think of Mairead, working out the time difference between Belfast and the Falklands, and then trying to calculate what she would have been doing in Armagh Prison. I would even chuckle to myself because, if ever she thought of me, she would imagine me on some welding job in Belfast or Germany or Scotland, with not the faintest idea that I was lying in a shallow 'grave' in the Falklands, shaking with cold, and dreaming of the wonderful times we had enjoyed together. Most of the time, I would think of Mairead and me in the summer months with the warm sun above us, sometimes lying naked in the grass around the lake or prancing around the hay barn, madly making love at every opportunity.

I would also spend hours wondering if Mairead and I had a future together, whether the years in jail would make her more certain that the IRA cause she supported was really worth ten years of her life or whether those days, weeks, months and years inside would create doubt, uncertainty and disillusionment. I had not the faintest idea but I hoped it might be possible one day in the future to meet her again and perhaps persuade her to forget Belfast, the Provos and her commitment, and come to live with me somewhere on the British mainland. Occasionally, I would believe that there was a chance of persuading her to give up everything and quit Belfast; at other times, I would remember the grit and determination she had shown whenever we discussed the Republican cause.

But reality would bring me to my senses. Mairead had never wanted me to speak to her in public, or anywhere we could be overheard, simply because I spoke with an English rather than an Irish accent. I knew she hated the very fact that I was an Englishman and she would always remind me that under no circumstances must I ever visit her home or speak to any of her family on the phone. And yet, when we were alone together, Mairead was magic, telling me she loved me, never wanting to leave me and acting as if she was in love. She would always be fun, upbeat, smiling and nearly always bubbling with happiness.

Then the cold and the damp of the Falklands would bring me back to earth. Throughout those three weeks in the field, it seemed as though we were on constant 'escape and evasion' exercises back on the Brecon Beacons in mid-winter and sometimes we would have to pinch ourselves to believe that this was for real. We did, however, realise that any mistake on our behalf could bring swift retribution and we knew there was zero chance of anyone ever coming to our rescue. Our job was to take up new LUPs (lying-up points) each day and report back by radio whatever we had seen of enemy positions and enemy movements.

Our final position overlooked the Argentinian base camp. As dawn approached one day, we came over the brow of the hill and in the distance, about three miles away, we could see lights. They were obviously the lights of an Argie camp. We back-tracked and rested up on the reverse side of the slope and decided to build as deep a hole as possible under cover of darkness the following night. In that way, we hoped it would be possible for one of us to take up the OP throughout the following day, obtaining what we hoped would be valuable intelligence.

Everything turned out brilliantly. With difficulty,

we managed to dig out a big enough dip, and after Tom had burrowed down we covered him with chicken-wire before replacing the moss and tufts of marshy grass. That night, when Tom crawled back to our side of the hill, he reported seeing the camp, with an estimated two to three hundred Argie soldiers, some on guard duty, others digging trenches and some digging latrines outside the immediate camp area. Through the powerful binoculars he had been able to see the fuel storage tanks and many of the Argie army vehicles and jeeps as well as three army helicopters. We reported all this intelligence back to base.

We were ordered to stay in the same position and try to determine if any re-supplying of men and materials was taking place, day or night. That meant splitting stags (shifts) so Tom and I worked together and Alan and Bushy, always great mates, took the following 12-hour shift.

At the change-over we would huddle together and discuss in whispers what had been seen that day and decide what should be radioed back to Intelligence. Sometimes, we prayed for a beautiful clear sky with a full moon, which made it easier to see each other and write notes; on other occasions, we feared the moon because of the brilliant light it gave out, making us far more conspicuous to any enemy look-out or sorties. It seemed to us, however, that no foot patrols were being made outside the camp during the hours of daylight, but that did not mean that Argie patrols weren't out at night. We would never know if they were or not, but we never saw any sign of them.

We would prepare our coded radio signal under a waterproof poncho. Alan and I would get under the poncho, fix some paper with a pin-prick over the flash bulb and put the torch very close to the paper to write the report. We knew that any light, even a pin prick, can be seen hundreds of yards away and great care had to be taken not to give away any of our LUPs. Then we would send everything over by morse code and receive any messages in the same way. Sometimes, Intelligence might have information they wanted to pass on or questions they wanted answered.

We never saw action but we knew that the intelligence we had provided would make the assault by the Paras at Goose Green a more straightforward attack.

We had been tabbing on and off for nearly three weeks, living in our damp hell holes for 12 hours a day, and we were feeling low. We were still hauling 110lb of equipment each and we all felt shattered. Finally, the order came to make our way to a new RV for the pick up. We examined the map. It was still a two-night tab away, a hell of a distance when you're feeling so low, your boots are rubbing and your feet are covered in blisters. The last thing any of us felt like doing was another two nights forced march with heavy packs. Yet it had to be done.

It was during the final night, just before dawn, that we heard our 21-inch naval guns open up on the Goose Green camp we had had under observation. We could see the flashes in the distance and that sight and that sound warmed our hearts. Suddenly, it all seemed worthwhile and we strode on to the RV happier than we had been for days.

A Sea King chopper picked us up within 30 minutes of our arrival at the RV and ferried us back to Bluff Cove and the Royal Naval Auxiliary Resource. We dumped our kit as soon as we hit the deck, thankful at last to be rid of the weight that had caused us so much hardship. We unloaded our weapons and stowed them away before going below deck to be debriefed. We went down to the mess looking forward to a wonderful slap-up nosh but, of course, our stomachs had shrunk so much we could eat very little. Instead, we drank hot, strong, sweet cocoa which helped build up our sugar level and warmed us wonderfully, before taking a long hot shower, a shave and a close examination of our cracked feet.

Alan and I were suffering from 'trench foot', the disease which had affected the soldiers of the First World War when they had to live for weeks on end in appalling, wet conditions in water-logged trenches.

Within hours of getting back to the ship, however, our joy at returning unscathed was shattered when we heard of the Sea King tragedy.

On 19 May, two days before D-day — and the day we were ordered to return to base — a Sea King helicopter took off at about 9.30pm, two hours after dusk, on a five-minute flight from Hermes to the assault ship Intrepid. All in all, when she went down, the SAS and support specialists who were lost on board numbered twenty men. The ten survivors who clung to an upturned dinghy were fortunate to be rescued alive for they had been in the sea for 30 minutes, far beyond the time anyone could rationally expect to survive in those icy waters. In fact, they all came within minutes of death. At first, in the chaos that followed the accident, no one on board Intrepid or Hermes could spot the survivors and a rescue helicopter had missed them. By chance, a small rescue craft from HMS Brilliant passed by, saw the survivors clinging to the dinghy, and somehow hauled the exhausted, dazed and nearly unconscious men aboard. Most of the survivors would wake up on board Brilliant, totally unaware that they had been rescued, or how.

The precise cause of the Sea King crash will never be known but experts believe that a giant petrel, with a wingspan of 6ft, was the likely cause. Flocks of petrels fly from the Falklands, following ships in search of food.

I felt gutted when I heard the news. I had known five or six of the victims really well, they were mates with whom I had been out on patrol, with whom I had enjoyed nights out on the town and whom I respected as damn good soldiers. It seemed so cruel that they should have been killed in a helicopter crash. We all expect to lose one or two men on active service but not 20 men, snatched like that, their lives somehow wasted.

As a result, there was no jubilation among the SAS men, even after the Union Jack was raised at Stanley three weeks later. The deaths of all those mates had knocked the stuffing out of us. We stayed

on board Hermes recovering our strength and our
appetite and thinking about what had happened to
our mates. When we had set out from Hereford, we
knew there was a distinct possibility that one or two
of us might 'buy' it, but none of us were prepared for
a chopper to fall out of the sky, killing so many in
such a horrendous way. Somehow, we all felt that we
wanted an end to this war, to get back home to
comfort the wives and kids who had lost loved ones.
Only then did we feel we could start to live again.

I was on board with the other lads when we
heard that the Argentinians had capitulated some
three weeks after we finished our task near Goose
Green. And yet we didn't feel like celebrating.

We were choppered to Port Stanley and took a
look around the town. The Argie prisoners looked
terrible, dejected, miserable and most seemed barely
out of their teens. That didn't help morale. It didn't
seem fair, somehow, that the élite of the British Army
had been brought to bear on a few hundred Argie
teenagers who seemed lost and perplexed by the
whole war. Some were in quite a bad shape as well,
suffering from burns and wounds. Our medics
treated them as best they could but, understandably,
all they wanted to do was get back home as soon as
possible and forget about their bloody awful baptism
of fire. I could see that none of them seemed to have
the stomach for a fight and I couldn't blame them.
They were kids who had been sent to do a man's job.

We flew by Hercules back home to Britain,
landing at Brize Norton before being taken on to
Hereford. It seemed good to be back but the

atmosphere in camp was depressing and grim, with everyone still recovering from the news of the Sea King crash and the loss of life. There was no jubilation over a job well done after this SAS involvement. And I felt the same. Usually, there is a mood among the SAS, that the loss of life is an accepted risk of the job, and those fortunate to survive must look forward and forget the deaths of the mates who didn't make it. But the Falklands War was different. So many had died that everyone knew at least one close mate who had died in the chopper, affecting the entire Regiment.

Even the decorations that were awarded later — the South Atlantic Medal, with a Rosette for those who took an active part — meant little to most of us because of the toll the war had taken on the Regiment. We knew that, one day, we would have to forget those mates who died in the South Atlantic, but we all knew it would be bloody difficult.

7

AT FIRST SIGHT, SHE reminded me of Mairead — dark haired, not more than 5ft 3in tall and with a lovely smile. From the first moment I saw her, my pulse quickened. She wasn't as lovely as Mairead and yet she seemed to have the same sparkle in her dark eyes. I was standing at the bar in a Belfast pub with a couple of mates when I noticed her walk in with a group of young people. They sat around a table, the blokes drinking pints of lager and Guinness, the girls halves of lager.

As I looked at her, it all seemed too much of a coincidence. I had first met Mairead in a Belfast city centre pub and, from the moment our eyes met, we both knew there was a fatal attraction. So far, this girl had not looked at me and our eyes hadn't met, but we were both in a Belfast city pub. I wondered what I should do. Part of me thought of leaving immediately, not wanting to look at her, or talk to her, fearing that to do so would be a betrayal of my love for Mairead.

'Don't be so daft,' I told myself, but the feeling of betrayal wouldn't go away. Mairead was still in prison with at least another four years to go and here was I, enjoying a drink, and finding myself fascinated and attracted to another girl, a stranger, but someone who could have been Mairead's sister. I looked at her more closely, examining her in more detail, comparing her face, her eyes, her hair, her body to Mairead. The more I looked, of course, the more my memory played tricks and the more I realised that this girl was someone who did closely resemble Mairead, but nothing more.

That realisation made me feel more relaxed and I had another beer, ate a couple of peanuts and a packet of crisps and had a third pint as I continued to watch her, fascinated. When she left to go to the lavatory with two other girls, I noticed she was a little taller than Mairead and with a fuller figure and judged her to be 24 or 25 years of age. As I took a deep draught of my pint I wondered what she would be like in bed. That brought back memories of Mairead and I felt like a bastard.

I could not bring myself to say a word to the mystery girl that night and preferred instead to leave any possible meeting in the lap of the Gods. So I left but returned to the pub at the same time the following week. Once more she arrived with a group of young people and they sat and drank, chatted and laughed together. I tried to work out if she was, in fact, with any of the young guys at the table, but I noticed no discernible involvement between her and any of the lads. This evening, however, I had arrived alone and I managed to catch her eye and we exchanged a smile.

An hour later, she left the room alone and I waited. When she returned, she walked back via the bar.

'Hello,' she said, 'how are you tonight?'

Somewhat taken aback, I said, 'Fine thanks, and you?'

'Yes,' she replied, 'I'm fine. I saw you here last week but you were with mates.'

'That's right,' I said, a little embarrassed, knowing she would have guessed that I had returned just to see her.

'Are you waiting for anyone?' she asked.

'No,' I said, 'just enjoying a quiet pint and surveying the scene. Would you like a drink?'

'Thanks, but no,' she said, 'as you can see, I'm with friends.'

'Do you come here any other night?' I asked.

'No,' she said, 'but I could.' And she looked me straight in the eye.

'Tomorrow?' I asked.

'OK, tomorrow,' she said. 'At about the same time?'

'I'll be here by eight,' I said. 'Is that OK with you?'

'Yep, fine. Bye,' and she held out her hand and I took it. But she only grasped my hand for a split-second before turning and walking back to her friends. I didn't want to remain any longer because that could have been embarrassing, so I downed my pint and left, smiling briefly at her before disappearing through the door.

The next morning, I went for a long hard run and spent almost two hours in the gym, climbing the ropes and doing hundreds of press-ups and sit-ups. I felt good and wanted to feel fit for the evening, and I knew that burning off excess energy would help me to relax. As I had done with Mairead, I felt that I was going to get on with this girl, although she was more pushy and more confident than my lovely Mairead.

It was the first time in seven years that I had felt like this with another girl. Of course, I had enjoyed some flirtatious times with other girls and, on a few occasions, gone to bed with a few young women, but I had never felt about any of them as I had felt towards Mairead. Now, this girl had aroused an interest in me which had remained dormant for so long and I didn't want to mess it up.

I arrived at the pub — The Four Winds in Saintfields Road, in Protestant East Belfast — well before 8.00pm. I checked out the area before going inside, making sure there were no likely lads sitting in cars or waiting suspiciously on street corners. The Army's warnings about honey traps still rang in my ears, even more so after my months of SAS training.

She walked into the bar on her own ten minutes after 8.00pm and I admired her timing. She was dressed in a short plaid, darkish woollen skirt and yellow shirt and wearing a short, black leather jacket.

Top left: Mairead in her younger days.

Top right and Bottom: Revisiting old memories – the lane from the station to the pub, and the lake where we would lie in the grass together.

Top: Marino Station, where I used to meet Mairead.

Bottom: The Cultra Inn – a country pub, where we could chat and drink in safety.

Top: The rundown cottage where we spent some magical times.

Bottom: Redburn Square in Holywood. I used to park here and wait for Mairead, so as not to arouse suspicion.

Top: Loughgall – Some of the gunmen took cover behind this van. The evidence speaks for itself.

Bottom: Destruction at the RUC station, Loughgall. Luckily my unit had the station under surveillance.

Top: The IRA gunmen killed in action by my SAS unit at Loughgall.

Bottom: The dust settles after the gun battle.

The crowds take to the streets of Belfast for the funeral of Mairead and her accomplices.

Top: Gerry Adams helps with Mairead's coffin having draped it with the Irish Tricolour in recognition of her sacrifice.

Bottom: Fellow IRA members Sean Savage (left) and Danny McCann (right) who were shot with Mairead in Gibralter.

Her hair was dark and shiny and cut quite short. She looked younger than I recalled and, in that instant, I realised that I fancied her strongly.

Once again, I was standing at the bar enjoying a Guinness. She smiled broadly.

'Hi,' she said and shook my hand. 'How are you?'

I smiled, rather liking her businesslike approach to a casual drink with a stranger.

'I'm great,' I replied. 'What would you like to drink?'

'Well, as you probably know, I usually drink lager when I'm with my friends but I would like a rum and Coke if that's all right with you?'

'That's fine with me,' I said. 'A single or a double rum?'

'I think I had better just have the single,' she said. 'Here we are having just met, and you're trying to get me drunk.'

'No, I'm not,' I said, 'just helping to loosen your tongue, only I don't think you need that sort of assistance.'

'I'm Jackie,' she said, 'What's your name?'

'Scott,' I replied, 'Scott Graham.'

'And what do you's do for a living then, 'cos I can tell you're not Irish, not with that accent? You must be from the mainland.'

I smiled, hearing the way she said 'you's' in exactly the same way that Mairead had always done, slurring the phrase into one word. To me, that idiom had always reminded me of Mairead, wherever I heard it, and still did.

I knew before I met Jackie that I would not lie about my job the way I had done to Mairead. But I also knew that I could not and would not tell her the whole truth. I guessed that Jackie was probably a Prod for she obviously used The Four Winds, a Prod pub, fairly regularly. She would not be surprised to find that I was in the British Army, but I had no intention of revealing that I was with the SAS.

'You're right,' I said. 'I am from the mainland, from London originally, and I'll let you guess what I do for a living.'

'You're in the Army,' she replied immediately.

'You've got it in one,' I said.

'And what regiment?'

'I'm an army cook,' I lied. 'Now it's my turn. What do you do for a living?'

'I work in a bank, clerking,' she answered somewhat disconsolately. 'I'm afraid it's a bit boring, but it's a job and it brings me in some money every week.'

'What would you like to do?' I asked, genuinely interested in her ambitions, her dreams.

'An international courier for a well-known company like American Express,' she said. 'Then I could travel the world and get away from this place.'

'You're not happy living here?' I asked.

'You can say that again,' she said, 'with all the bombs and the Troubles and the road-blocks and you people all over the place,' and she playfully poked my stomach with her finger.

'My goodness,' she said, 'that's like steel. Are you fit or super fit?' and she prodded my stomach again, pressing harder this time.

'I try to keep fit,' I said.

'You can say that again,' she said. 'I like that in a man.'

'Good,' I said.

'I thought all cooks were fat and overweight,' she said, 'not built like muscle men.'

'I try to be different,' I said and smiled at her, knowingly.

We left the bar and went and sat at a small table where we could chat without being overheard by others. We sat opposite each other and, the more we talked, the more eye contact we exchanged. Deliberately, from years of practice, I had taken the seat in the corner with my back to the wall, so that I could see if any trouble came our way.

For two hours, we talked about everything. I discovered that she lived with her parents in Bloomfield. Her father had been in the RUC but had left the service early and now worked as a security officer. Jackie, an only child, had left school at 16 having passed six GCSEs and had trained as a shorthand typist. She had worked in a couple of small offices before starting work for the bank 18 months before. She was 24.

Shortly after 10.00pm, and quite a few drinks each, Jackie said she had to be away. I asked whether I could drive her home but she declined.

'Perhaps another time,' she said. By way of explanation, she continued, 'Don't worry, the bus stop's only a short distance from my house. In any case, most nights I take a taxi. I'll be home in 20 minutes.'

'Could I have a phone number?' I asked.

'Of course you can,' she said. 'I'll give you my home and the office if you like.'

As she was writing them down, she asked, 'Will you's be phoning me, then?'

'Yes,' I said, 'if you would like another drink one night.'

'I would that,' she said, getting up to leave. 'Thanks for tonight, I really enjoyed myself,' and she gave me a kiss on the cheek.

'When did you's say you'd phone?' she asked.

'I didn't,' I said. 'When are you free?'

'Phone me and ask me and I'll probably be free,' she said, a big smile crossing her face. 'See you,' she added, and was gone.

Within two weeks, Jackie and I were lovers. After that first date we both knew that we wanted to see more of each other and I knew that I was keen, hoping Jackie thought the same way. Fortunately for me, she did and I asked whether she wanted to spend a weekend away. I had a weekend pass for R & R, and thought we could go to a small hotel outside Belfast.

'I'd love to,' she said. 'Are you inviting me?'

'Of course I am,' I said. 'Is that a "yes"?'

'It is, it is!' Jackie said, and threw her arms around me and gave me a kiss on the lips. I picked her off the ground and held her close for a minute or more while we kissed.

That evening was special. She told me that she had been engaged for 18 months to an RUC officer but the two of them had decided to split a couple of months ago. Since then she had not had serious boyfriends. I told her that I had been involved with a girl for some years but that it had ended some time ago.

The weekend break was wonderful. We drank too much and ate too much and made love time and time again. It had been the first time since Mairead and I had been together in the cottage before The Conway bombing that I felt so relaxed and enjoyed myself so much with someone. Of course the thought of Mairead occasionally raced through my mind and I tried to forget her.

Jackie was fun to be with and she loved to laugh. She also had a wonderfully wicked sense of humour which appealed to me. That weekend, she was particularly cruel in her comments about some of the other guests at the hotel but it was all quite harmless. She made me laugh.

After that weekend, Jackie and I became an item, seeing each other two or three times a week. The only problem was that I had to spend time on patrol in the border area for weeks at a time and then I would be recalled to Hereford on a training course, spending weeks away. Jackie didn't like that but there was nothing I could do about it.

To some extent, I was happy that we should be parted because I believed Jackie was becoming too keen, too quickly. She wanted me to go and stay at her parents' home for the weekend but I didn't want to do that because I felt that I might be committing myself. There was always something at the back of my mind, something stopping me from totally giving my heart and soul to Jackie. And I knew that, deep down, I had not been able to forget Mairead. It wasn't that I felt responsible for her or that I believed I could have acted differently as the circumstances unfolded. And yet I did feel guilty that she was imprisoned and I still wanted to see her again and talk to her.

It was during one of my training schedules in the early 1980s at Hereford that I first met Peter O'Kane, a Sergeant with the RUC who had been sent to what was then called Bradbury Lines (later Stirling Lines) with 39 other RUC officers who had been selected to join the Special Support Group, a new crack unit, which was later named the Headquarters Mobile Support Unit, HMSU for short. The RUC officers, hand-picked men in their late twenties and early thirties, were selected on the same basic principles as those soldiers seeking to join the SAS, including dedication to the job combined with self-discipline, independence of mind, stamina, patience and an ability to work under pressure and unsupervised. They trained for ten weeks at the School of Counter-Revolutionary Warfare at Hereford.

The HMSU lads lived during the week at a disused Territorial Army training camp and they would travel the 70 miles to Hereford each day in two or three vans. 'Operation C' — the computer name given to the exercise — involved training by qualified SAS experts in sniping, house combat, house assault and all methods of covert operations.

I met Peter O'Kane on one of the Special Project teams. He was about my age, an RUC officer who had seen most of the horrors of the Troubles in the

Province and who had been mainly involved in tracking the hard men of both the IRA and the Protestant Loyalists. We met during his training course at Hereford and had a few beers together. We got on famously and, like me, he was also a bachelor who enjoyed himself immensely when not working. He also had a small house in Belfast.

That house would become a focal point of the months I spent in Northern Ireland throughout my years with the SAS. He would invite me to stay during my 72-hour leaves and whenever I had a weekend off duty. We threw a number of great parties where the drink would flow 'til the early hours of the morning, the music would blare non-stop and the young men would let their hair down, relax, get drunk and have wonderful flings with the girls who enjoyed the carefree atmosphere.

In Northern Ireland, those involved in the day-to-day hard stress of working in dangerous situations, facing the trauma of bomb outrages, shootings and the mayhem of policing daily troubles and mini-riots, needed to release their pent up energies and go wild for a few hours. And it seemed young people in particular needed that release, to recharge their batteries for the problems and dangers they constantly faced on the streets.

I introduced Jackie to Peter a few weeks after we began going out and he immediately invited her to one of his parties. I wasn't so sure, however, because those parties were quite wild affairs and I had no idea how Jackie would react to them. I did not know whether she had lived a sheltered life with her fiancé or whether they had attended such parties together, for we had never discussed things like that. And I did not wish to shock her. People not only became very drunk over those wild weekends but the sexual antics some of them enjoyed were sometimes quite outrageous and often far too revealing. The situation would sometimes arise in the early hours of the morning when the young men and women present, all happily boozed, would be cheering on a couple making passionate love in front of everyone. No one seemed to mind or, if they did, they never accepted another invitation to a party.

'What do you think?' I asked Peter later.

'What do you mean?' he retorted.

'About Jackie?'

'What about Jackie?' he asked.

'I'm worried that she might be a bit shy for one of your parties,' I explained. 'I don't know how experienced she really is or whether she might be shocked by the goings-on.'

'Well, bring her along and we'll see soon enough.'

'But I don't want to lose her,' I said. 'You don't think she might see what goes on and then disappear for good? She's bound to think that I've been behaving like that as well.'

'Aye,' said Peter, 'and she would be right. You have been,' and he roared with laughter at my predicament.

He went on, 'If you're really worried then you shouldn't bring her along. Talk to her about it, tell her what goes on and let her be the judge. In any case, she's probably seen it all before, you know, my house isn't the only place with wild parties.'

So I talked to Jackie one night after a few drinks. I thought it might be better to let her relax with a couple of rum and Cokes before telling her the intimate, sordid details.

'What's on your mind?' she asked after only a couple of drinks.

'What do you mean?' I asked, feigning surprise.

'Well, I know when you's got something on your mind and you have tonight.'

I decided to come to the point. 'You've met Peter, Peter O'Kane, my cop friend?'

'The fella who invited me to one of his raves?'

'Yes, that's him,' I said.

'Well?' she asked.

'He just thought I ought to warn you that they are pretty wild affairs and he didn't know if you would like that sort of thing, that's all.'

'Have you been to them?' she asked.

'Yes, of course,' I said. 'Remember, we're mates. We have been for a few years now.'

'And did you find the parties too wild?'

'Well, some people do get carried away,' I warned, testing her reaction.

'Scott,' she said, sounding very down to earth, 'let's get down to facts. Are you talking about booze, drugs, sex or all three?'

'No drugs,' I replied honestly. 'Well, I've never seen any drugs.'

'And the sex and the booze?' she asked, pressing me.

'Yes,' I said, 'that would be right. Lots of booze.'

'And sex?' she went on, 'Do you mean these are orgies with everyone banging away at each other?'

I was in a quandary. She was exaggerating and yet, to some people, the wild sex could have been interpreted as orgies.

'No, not exactly,' I said, 'but some people do get carried away.'

'Sounds exciting!' she said. 'When's the next one?'

'Are you sure you would like to go?' I asked.

'Try and stop me,' she replied.

'Have you been to these sort of parties before then?' I enquired, wanting more than anything to discover a side of Jackie which I hadn't realised existed.

'I've had my moments,' she said with a laugh, 'but I've never been to an orgy or even seen one on video. But I'd love to see what goes on ... it sounds great.'

'All right, then,' I said, sounding like an elder brother trying to protect the morals of his more innocent sister.

'Am I going to meet old girlfriends of yours?' Jackie asked. 'Is that why you don't want me to go?'

'No,' I replied, 'not that I know of,' and laughed off the suggestion.

The party went well, despite the fact that I was full of trepidation. For most of the evening, I watched Jackie's face, checking her reaction to the goings-on. At Peter's suggestion, I also made sure that Jackie's glass was kept topped up most of the time. She started with a few rum and Cokes and, when she began dancing, she switched to cans of lager. Peter proved a mate, keeping an eye on her as well and making her feel at home. Most of the other people present that night, and there must have been more than 20, had been before and knew that sometime after midnight when everyone was fairly pissed, the fun would probably begin. And it did.

At first, I noticed one or two couples becoming rather amorous whilst dancing and smooching and they discreetly disappeared upstairs. Jackie noticed, too, and she wanted to smooch and kiss and cuddle, which was lovely. Sometime after 1.00am, when the party was still in full swing, one couple decided they wanted to make love on the sofa in the living room where others were drinking and chatting. The couple remained partly dressed while they had sex and no one took much notice.

Jackie, however, was fascinated.

'I've never seen anyone else do it before in public,' she whispered to me as we cuddled, 'It seems funny watching others do it.'

'Do you think so?' I asked.

'Do we look like that?' she wondered aloud, giggling as the couple reached orgasm.

'I've no idea,' I said honestly. 'I suppose so.'

'Scott,' Jackie whispered in my ear, 'I'm so turned on, can we go and screw somewhere?'

'Here?' I joked.

'No,' she said, punching me playfully in the stomach. 'Is there anywhere private we could go?'

'Come on,' I said and we made our way upstairs.

I popped my head around the two bedroom doors and saw they were occupied by couples.

'Can I have a look?' Jackie said.

'Yes, if you want to,' I said and Jackie put her head round one door and watched for a few seconds before gently closing it. The couple took not the slightest notice.

'Can we go outside then?' she said and we almost ran down the stairs and out into the small back garden.

Twenty minutes later, we returned. 'That feels better,' Jackie said, kissing me, 'but if I see any others screwing I'll want more. I hope you're feeling strong tonight.'

An hour later, as more couples became adventurous, Jackie whispered that she was becoming so horny she wanted to make love again.

'Here?' I asked again, jokingly.

'No, definitely not,' she said, 'I'd be too embarrassed ... take me outside again.'

At 3.00am, as the party began to wind down, I decided it was time to take Jackie home. 'I've arranged to stay out the night,' she said. 'I've told my parents I'm staying at a girlfriend's house so I can't go home now, not at this hour.'

I spoke to Peter who was with his girlfriend and just planning to go to bed. 'Stay here,' he said. 'I don't know who's stopping or who's going but I'll get you a blanket and you two can bed down on the floor for the night. You could have the other bedroom, only a mate and his girl booked it days ago. OK?'

'Fine,' I said and Jackie and I bedded down on

the floor behind the sofa which another couple had 'booked' for what remained of the night. Thirty minutes later, after succumbing once more to Jackie's demands, we fell asleep.

'Well,' I said, when we met for a drink a few days later, 'did you enjoy the party?'

'I could never have done what some of those girls did in public,' she said. 'But I did enjoy the party and it was fascinating to see others doing it. I never knew people did it like that in public. Don't they get embarrassed?'

'They didn't look embarrassed,' I said.

The more time we spent together, the more I found myself falling for Jackie. Our affair had begun while I was still dazed and confused about Mairead, and the feeling of having lost her, both to prison and to the IRA, was hard to cope with. Jackie initially satisfied my need for companionship and the warmth of a woman's touch, but she soon became a vital part of my life and I craved her company and her sense of fun and willingness to explore new experiences. We often spent time going out with her friends or with army mates of mine, and my memories of those times centre on the laughter and the jokes, and the feeling that we really enjoyed each other's company, and that we had become a contented couple.

Peter's party seemed to have unlocked Jackie's sexual awareness and sense of adventure, and she became a willing and liberated partner, prepared to try almost anything, anywhere. She seemed to have lurched from one extreme to another — at first, shy and almost embarrassed and, now, daring to the point of recklessness, demanding that I satisfy her in cinemas, in a park and even on a staircase in an office block. It seemed as though we had found ourselves in each other, and we both had the sense that this was now the norm, that, together, we had the whole of our lives to look forward to.

In the summer of 1985, however, tragedy struck. Jackie and I had planned to holiday together in Spain but two weeks before we were due to fly out to Marbella, I was ordered to Germany on an SAS exercise. There was no way I could get out of this one and although I put in a request for leave, it was turned down. Jackie and I had booked a hotel and so rather than waste the money, and the holiday, she decided to go with a girlfriend instead. I would have loved to have had two weeks with Jackie enjoying the summer sun in Spain, but it was not to be.

It was only when I returned to Hereford and phoned her home that I learned of the tragedy. While on holiday, Jackie had been killed in a car accident. When her father told me the news, I could not believe it. I was stunned that anything could have happened to her. I felt guilty that I hadn't pushed harder for my leave, and guilty that if I had been with her, she would never have died, even though I knew none of the details. I even began to feel guilty that if I had loved her more perhaps things would have worked out differently and she would never have been at the scene of the accident at that time.

It seemed that every serious relationship I entered into went wrong, horribly, terribly wrong and I suspected that I was to blame. I had always chastised myself for not working harder to persuade Mairead to quit the IRA; now another girl with whom I was closely and intimately involved had actually died. And once again I hadn't been there to save her. I kept asking myself what was wrong with me. It seemed that I could take part in gun battles against the IRA and survive, take an active role in the Falklands war and survive, and yet a number of my mates had died in the Falklands Sea King disaster and of the two people who had been closest to me, one had died in a car crash and the other was languishing in prison.

I believe that the death of Jackie drove me closer than ever to Mairead and I was determined to see her when she finally left prison. I had heard that she was likely to be freed in 1986 or 1987 depending, of course, on her behaviour, and I had no idea whether she had been a model prisoner or not. But I vowed to wait and see her before getting involved with anyone else.

8

PETER O'KANE PROVED A true friend over the death of Jackie. He knew nothing whatsoever of my relationship with Mairead and, of course, I never mentioned it to him. I didn't know him that well and he was not only a member of the RUC but a Protestant and an HMSU élite officer whose job was to trace, track down and arrest or kill IRA gunmen and bombers. I realised that if he had known of my relationship with Mairead, he would have been duty bound to inform his superior officers.

But he had, of course, known about Jackie and he had encouraged the two of us because he believed we made a good couple. After Jackie's initiation at his party, he would invite the two of us to use the bedroom in his house whenever we wanted it. And Jackie and I would often go for a few beers together

183

with Peter and his then girlfriend Angie, or have a meal at his house. We all got on well together. And Jackie and I did attend two or three more of Peter's wild parties and each time Jackie found herself becoming really turned on by all the sexual antics of the various couples. But she never wanted to take part herself, always preferring that we went somewhere quietly so that we could be alone.

Following Jackie's death, however, I became depressed and introverted and Peter would take me out for long, quiet drinks or walks in the country and we would talk about anything and everything. He knew I needed help in those months and he was prepared to see me through it. As a result, of course, we became close and we would exchange details of the counter-terrorist work we were both involved in. I would tell him details of the work I was carrying out patrolling the border country with the SAS, and he would chat to me about the work the HMSU groups were detailed to undergo in their war of attrition against the terrorist elements of both the IRA and the Ulster paramilitaries.

Throughout those years following the Falklands War, I would spend many months a year, taking it in turns with other SAS Squadrons, patrolling the border areas for weeks at a time in both covert patrols and in uniform. Some of the time, of course, we would be engaged patrolling in and around Belfast and 'Derry, but most of the time the bandit country south of Armagh was our prime responsibility.

For some months after Jackie's death, however, I felt my heart wasn't in soldiering, that I had lost my keenness and appetite for the job as though the stuffing had been knocked out of me. I felt I was going about my duties like an automaton rather than a dedicated trooper. I had always taken pride in being a member of the SAS, the élite of the British forces, and now I sometimes didn't even feel like getting out of bed in the morning, let alone going out spending days and nights living in atrocious conditions while waiting patiently for a fire-fight with a bunch of terrorists. I even allowed myself to become somewhat unfit. I couldn't find the energy to train, to shin up and down ropes or do hundreds of sit-ups each day. Nothing seemed worth the effort.

But Peter found a way of bringing me out of the doldrums and renewing my interest in life and the SAS. He would seek my advice, phoning me and saying he needed to talk to me about some problem, or that he needed some help, or needed my experience. His enthusiasm and his line of approach encouraged me to react to his requests and I found myself, once again, becoming interested in everything around me, including the Regiment. At the time, however, I didn't realise that in his subtle way, he was encouraging me to start living life to the full again.

By the middle of the 1980s, the HMSU was earning itself a reputation, searching out, following and tracking suspects and, more importantly, bringing terrorists to justice. Sometimes they managed to arrest an IRA man or a Loyalist paramilitary, but on some occasions their quarry would resort to a shoot-out. Without exception, those terrorists prepared to take on the HMSU in fire-fights ended up on the losing side.

Peter told me of some of the major missions in which the HMSU had been actively involved, operations very similar to those I had conducted with the SAS, and in which the terrorists had ended up dead.

In early October 1982, officers from E4A had been tipped off that a large load of home-made explosives was to be shipped into the North. They followed a hay lorry from the border to a hayshed off the Ballynery Road, outside Lurgan, called Kitty's Barn, a ramshackle, breeze-block and corrugated iron building owned by Kitty Kearns, a woman in her seventies, who cared for aged greyhounds. The farmhouse and barn lay close to a housing estate on the outskirts of Lurgan occupied by staunch Republicans. Kitty Kearns was a local character, the widow of an old-time Republican whose husband had died some years before.

Officers from E4A watched from a distance one night as six men took seven hours to unload the hay lorry. When the officers checked the barn later, they discovered 1,000lb of explosives and some old-fashioned guns behind the hay stacks. Officers from MI5, trained in counter-terrorist operations, were called to the scene and installed sophisticated listening devices in the roof of the barn, set to pick up not only conversations but also any noise of the explosives or arms being removed.

An SOP, manned during the hours of darkness by officers on shifts, was set up to keep a close eye on the barn. By day, officers in cars would drive past the barn checking for any activity. From sources inside the IRA, the TCG learned that the explosives had been brought in to launch an attack on the security forces but they had no idea where or when the attack was due to take place.

On October 27, an anonymous phonecall, allegedly from a member of the public, was received at Lurgan police station informing officers that a motorcycle appeared to have been abandoned on a dirt track road named Kinnego Embankment. Three uniformed officers, Sergeant Sean Quinn and Constables Paul Hamilton and Alan McCloy, were detailed to check out the motorbike but no one thought of informing the HMSU or the TCG before asking the officers to check. Ten minutes later, a huge explosion rocked the area and the three officers were blown to pieces.

Explosives experts called to the scene found that the bombers had planted a booby-trap bomb in a culvert beneath the Embankment which had exploded when the officers walked over it. The forensic experts also discovered that the explosives used on Kinnego Embankment had come from the 1,000lb hidden in Kitty's Barn.

There had been two tragic turns of events. Two or three men had made their way, unnoticed, to the barn in a vehicle, loaded up a large amount of explosives, and had then driven away. A van had been seen at Kitty's Barn the previous day but no one had had the vehicle tailed, checked or searched, nor had anyone checked whether any of the explosives in the barn had been removed.

The next problem was that the listening device, fitted in the eaves of the roof by MI5 experts, had been affected by the wind and rain and no longer worked. The device was so sophisticated that it should have picked up any conversation in the barn or the noise of people walking around inside. As a result, those listening to the device back at base had heard nothing, assuming that no one had been inside the barn. A new listening device was immediately set up in the barn, this time in the handle of the door, where it would be unaffected by weather conditions.

In early November, E4A learned that the two men responsible for planting the Kinnego bomb, Sean Burns and Eugene Toman, both 21 and from Lurgan, had returned secretly to the Province. They had been on the run for the attempted murder of a police patrol some months earlier. Now, after killing three innocent police officers, they were seen as being among the most dangerous IRA activists and, as a consequence, became a prime target for the security forces.

On 11 November, E4A traced the two men to the home of a known Provo sympathiser, James Jervais McKerr, 31, who lived in Avondale Green, near Lurgan. TCG was informed and an HMSU patrol was immediately despatched to the area.

The HMSU patrol had only just arrived at the scene when, minutes later, E4A radioed that Burns and Toman were leaving the house in a car driven by McKerr. When the HMSU patrol learned in which direction the men were travelling, they set up an impromptu check-point near a T-junction.

As the car containing the three IRA men

approached the T-junction, the HMSU vehicle was blocking the left side of the narrow road while one officer stood on the right side waving a red light, advising the approaching car to stop. The IRA car, a green Ford Escort, slowed down almost to a halt and then accelerated fast, forcing the officer to leap out of the way as the Provos' car raced past. The officer did, however, manage to fire off five shots from his Ruger mini 14 rifle, shooting out the car's rear window and hitting the man sitting in the back. He also managed to puncture a rear tyre. As the car sped off, swerving all over the road, with one flat tyre, the HMSU officers gave chase.

As they raced along in pursuit, the HMSU officers grabbed their Stirling sub-machine-guns and opened fire, Chicago-style, leaning out of the windows and firing into the back of the getaway car. As the Provos' car approached a roundabout a few hundred yards down the road, the driver tried to turn right but lost control and careered off the road and down an embankment.

The HMSU car stopped and the three officers leapt out and opened fire, pouring 117 rounds into the Provos' car. When the firing stopped and they examined the bodies, all three Provos were shot to pieces, riddled with bullets. They were virtually unrecognisable. But police found no weapons in the car.

The deaths of those three men caused a furore. Their families denied that any of them were members of the Provisional IRA, and claimed that all three could have been picked up by police from their homes at any time.

Eugene Toman's brother said, 'My brother was a plasterer who lived at home. If they had wanted him, they could have come to his home. It's just plain murder and it only fuels the hatred of the RUC.'

Sinn Fein, the political wing of the IRA, claimed that the shooting had been a 'summary execution' by police and suggested that the road-block had been set up only after the shooting had taken place. However, days later, the three men were all given paramilitary-style funerals and the North Armagh Brigade of the IRA said that the three men were members of the organisation. Black berets, gloves and tricolours were placed on their coffins and, at the graveside, a single shot was fired over the coffins by a masked man.

Though the explosives had been taken away from Kitty's Barn, the TCG decided to leave the rifles they had found there and keep a 24-hour watch over the building to see if any other IRA members knew of their existence and would come to retrieve them.

Some days later, at about 4.30pm on 18 November 1982, the listening device in Kitty's Barn indicated that someone was tampering with the rifles that had been left there. This time there were no mistakes; the HMSU raced to the scene to investigate.

All was quiet as the officers, dressed in their traditional dark-green uniforms, armed with sub-machine-guns and wearing flak-jackets, cautiously approached the barn while other officers surrounded the area, in case the intruders made a break for it. The officers had no idea of the identity of the men inside, nor how many there were, but they had picked up conversations on the listening device and knew there must at least be two. Inside, two young men were holding the rifles, and examining them closely for they were almost antiques. In fact, both were bolt-action weapons from the First World War. Two were German Mausers and the third of Italian or Spanish origin. Arms experts believed they were probably manufactured before 1914. Forensic experts would later contend that all three rifles were in working order and capable of being fired, but ammunition for such weapons would have been difficult to come by. In fact, no ammunition was ever found at the barn.

One HMSU officer, a Sergeant, opened up, spraying the entire side of the barn with rounds from his Stirling sub-machine-gun, making a terrible racket as the rounds spattered into the corrugated iron building.

In the barn, the two teenagers, Michael Tighe, 17, and Martin McCauley, 19, must have wondered what the hell was going on for they had no idea that anyone was outside, let alone armed police. They fled to the back of the barn taking the weapons with them and hid behind the hay stacks. Then the door opened and in strode the three armed officers.

'Right, come on out,' shouted one officer.

In the chaos that ensued, two bursts of machine-gun fire hit them, killing Tighe instantly and seriously injuring McCauley. Both young men were hit by three shots.

Another burst of machine-gun fire followed. Then the three officers walked to the back of the barn, grabbed hold of McCauley and dragged him out.

Having lost a lot of blood and on the verge of consciousness, McCauley could not speak and fainted.

Every word that occurred that evening in the barn was picked up by the listening device concealed in the door handle of the barn. It worked perfectly. But no one would ever know exactly what happened for the tape disappeared immediately after the shootings and was never produced at the subsequent inquiry. Indeed, the RUC failed to hand over the tape.

Understandably, these shootings also caused a wave of anger among the republicans of Lurgan who were incensed that two young men should have been shot down in cold blood without any warning whatsoever. And police were never able to produce any evidence suggesting that either teenager was a member of the IRA. The search for information showed that neither Tighe nor McCauley had a security record or any criminal convictions. Tighe was a fresh-faced 17-year-old and his death had been a bewildering tragedy for his parents. They told police that Michael had never shown the slightest interest in politics or terrorist activity. He lived at home quietly and was a good and considerate son who had a number of friends of a similar background, including Martin McCauley, who was two years older.

The parents of the two boys told police that their sons had gone to the barn to feed the dogs because Kitty Kearns had gone away for the day and she had asked them to do so.

Later, McCauley appeared at Belfast Crown Court charged with possessing the three old rifles that had been found in the barn without ammunition. In his judgment, Lord Justice Kelly expressed doubts about the police evidence, especially about the true position of police officers when the shots were fired, and whether they had ever seen Tighe and McCauley actually holding rifles. Nevertheless, Lord Justice Kelly found McCauley guilty of being in possession of one of the old rifles and imposed a suspended prison sentence of two years.

The third incident occurred only three weeks later, on Sunday, 12 December 1982, when two leading members of the INLA, Peter James Grew, 31, known to all as Seamus, from Mullacreavie Park, Armagh, and Roderick Martin Carroll, 22, from Callanbridge Park, Armagh, were shot dead by the HMSU. Their deaths would become known as 'The Mullacreavie Park Massacre'.

Grew had been a member of the IRA and later the INLA for 11 years and was jailed for 14 years in 1975 for attempting to murder a policeman. He had only been released from jail eight months earlier and, during that time, police maintained that he was the chief suspect in a number of murders and attempted murders in the Armagh district.

Grew and Carroll had been visiting friends in the Irish Republic and drove northwards across the border in torrential rain. Keeping them under constant surveillance were three police vehicles, an HMSU car, a 'Det' surveillance team car and an unmarked Ford Cortina. The HMSU car stopped and the 'Det' car skidded on the wet road and crashed into the back of it. The third car arrived on the scene, stopped and then watched as the orange Austin Allegro containing the two INLA suspects casually drove on, unaware that the three vehicles contained members of the security forces.

The official police statement read, 'A car approached and was signalled to stop with a red light. It accelerated through the road check knocking down a police officer. Police at the scene radioed another police vehicle in the area which moved to give assistance. It gave chase to the escaping vehicle which by then had been identified as belonging to a known leading terrorist. The police vehicle which was attempting to cut off the escaping car had followed it at speed for some distance when it turned into Mullacreavie Park. The police vehicle forced the escaping car to stop. The car then reversed at speed with its headlights full on, clearly identifying the police in full uniform who had dismounted from their vehicle and were calling on the occupants of the car to halt. The driver of the car jumped out. The police, believing they were about to be fired on, themselves opened fire. Both occupants of the vehicle were shot.'

The police statement went on, 'No weapons were found at the scene. A search along the route of the chase was carried out but nothing was found.'

Within 24 hours of the incident, the INLA vowed to avenge with 'unmerciful ferocity' the deaths of the two men and troops and police were put on full alert as security chiefs prepared for a terrorist onslaught. 'These well-paid executioners have now left themselves open to any form of attack and can prepare to suffer the consequences of their action. The

INLA will avenge the two men's deaths.'

The three separate incidents in which terrorists were shot dead in such unusual and dramatic circumstances led to charges that the British Government was implementing a shoot-to-kill policy. But the then Secretary of State, James Prior, totally denied that such a policy was operating within the RUC. The Minister admitted that special units were operating throughout the Province, specifically aimed at combatting terrorism, but no new orders relating to shoot-to-kill had been issued.

Mr Prior said, 'I am satisfied that the Chief Constable, Sir John Hermon, wholly understands the importance of maintaining the impartiality of the police force and the need for impartial inquiries into the recent incidents in the South Armagh area. If there are people bent on committing crimes there will be incidents of this nature. I know there is a certain amount of public disquiet about certain police activities, and it is very important that the public should have full confidence in the police force.'

Three days after the deaths of Grew and Carroll, an INLA unit, dressed in the traditional black boiler suits of republican gunmen at these funeral ceremonies, fired shots over their coffins with police watching only 100 yards away. The ceremonial farewell pistol shots occurred at the corner of Cathedral Road, Armagh, when the funeral cortèges of the two men joined up on their way to St Patrick's Cathedral. The hearses carrying the coffins, which were draped with the Irish tricolour, stopped about 100 yards from a dozen RUC Land Rovers.

The mourners, some wearing hoods, formed a circle around the two hearses. There was a hushed silence from the 200 people as an INLA firing party, including two girls, suddenly appeared out of the crowd. All the INLA party, dressed in black uniforms and wearing black hoods, stood alongside the coffins before one of the men gave the order to fire. One of the party fired three shots into the air from a handgun. When the shots rang out, the crowd began cheering and clapping, illustrating their defiance of the police. As quickly as the firing party appeared, they melted into the crowd. And the police made no attempt to intervene.

Those three incidents formed the basis for the famous Stalker Enquiry when the Deputy Chief Constable of the Greater Manchester Police Force, John Stalker, was asked to undertake an enquiry into the deaths of the six men which took place during that five-week period in late 1982. He was asked to investigate allegations that the RUC had a secret but official 'shoot-to-kill' policy against suspected members of the IRA.

As his investigation developed, John Stalker met increasing resistance from members of the RUC at all levels from the Chief Constable, Sir John Hermon, down. The investigation should have been completed within nine months but remained open after two years, at which point John Stalker was dramatically relieved of his duties — at the very moment he was about to gain access to the missing tape recording. He believed that tape would be highly embarrassing to the RUC.

As Stalker investigated the killings, he became more convinced that he was looking at possible murder, or unlawful killing, in all three cases. If that were so, then the road could lead in only one direction: the question of whether senior police officers were involved in the formulation of any deliberate policies of shooting to kill.

I discussed all these cases with Peter O'Kane and we would relate them to the training we had both received at Hereford with the SAS. Both of us were living similar lives, involved with tracing, arresting and, sometimes, killing IRA suspects, gunmen and bombers. We both realised that in the heat of the moment nerves become frayed, mistakes are made and even highly trained soldiers can mistake someone's movements as threatening. Our training spells out precisely how an SAS soldier must react if he believes, for one moment, that he is about to be shot — it is his duty to make sure he shoots first.

No chances can be taken in Northern Ireland by SAS or police engaged in a ruthless war against men prepared to kill. I had learned that already. In the not too distant future, I would see the whole scenario from the victim's standpoint. And I would never forget it.

9

It was around 11.00am on a bright, warm August day in 1986 when I first received the message. We had been training at the army firing range at Ballykinlar and I remember the trees swaying in the gentle breeze, ruffling the leaves, and I wondered as I studied the trees what effect that wind-speed might have on my target practice and whether I would need to compensate to make sure those rounds kept hitting the bull. I had just finished practising with my Heckler & Koch when the pager bleeped and I wondered who was calling me at that time of day.

'Call Derek,' it said and nothing more.

Derek, I thought, Derek. Then I remembered. Derek was my RUC mate whose tumble-down cottage I had borrowed so frequently back in the mid-1970s before Mairead bombed The Conway.

I was somewhat perplexed that he should be trying to contact me. After the bombing, I hadn't seen so much of Derek although I had no reason to suppose that he knew Mairead was the girl I had been taking to his cottage during those 18 months. I had never told him the name of the girl, nor had I told him that it had been Mairead who had informed me that The Conway was to be bombed. I had always wondered if he had put two-and-two together. Somehow, I doubted it because he would have wanted to pump me for information about her if he had believed she was my steady girlfriend.

I phoned Derek back at lunchtime. I didn't want to appear too eager to contact him because we hadn't spoken for two or three years at least and, before then, we had only spoken occasionally since Mairead had gone down.

'Hi,' I said, 'It's Scott. You called me on my pager. What can I do for you?'

'Oh, nothing,' he said. 'In fact, I've forgotten why I wanted to speak to you.'

'So it wasn't that important,' I said, a little annoyed that he had wanted me for no reason at all. 'Give me a call when you remember,' I added.

I was about to put down the receiver when Derek said, 'Hold on, I remember now. Listen.'

'I'm listening,' I said, gentle sarcasm in my voice.

'You know that girl that went down for The Conway bomb job?' he said.

'Yes,' I said, 'I remember it.'

'Well,' said Derek, 'she's out.'

'Out?' I said raising my voice with some surprise.

'I thought she got 14 years ... she can't be out yet, can she?'

'She can and she is,' he said.

'Are you sure?' I asked again, unable to believe that Mairead was actually free.

'Certain,' he said. 'Positive. I suppose it must have been good behaviour.'

'I suppose so,' I said, deliberately trying not to sound excited at the prospect of seeing Mairead once again.

'What are you going to do about it?' he asked, as though trying to encourage me to see her.

'What do you mean?' I asked. 'Why should I do anything about it?'

'Just thought you might get back in touch,' he added enigmatically.

'Nothing to do with me,' I said, quick to distance myself as much as possible from a convicted IRA bomber. I knew that I would be out of the Regiment in double-quick time if the SAS found out I had been dating someone like Mairead.

'Just thought you'd like to know,' Derek said. 'Take care.'

'Thanks,' I said, 'thanks a lot. I'll be in touch ... perhaps we could have a beer together like the old days.'

'Give us a call some time,' said Derek, and he was gone.

Derek's suggestion that I knew Mairead troubled me. I was sure that I had never suggested that I ever knew Mairead Farrell and yet he had assumed from that brief conversation that I had known her. 'Get back in touch,' were the exact words Derek used which screamed that he must have known that I had had contact with her before The Conway bombing. I could not believe that he would simply make a wild guess, chancing his arm, wondering if I might make a mistake and admit that I had known Mairead well and that it had been her who had tipped me off about The Conway bomb.

His news, however, thrilled me. I knew instantly that I would see Mairead again; I knew that I wanted to see her. Derek's hint made me realise that if I did then we would have to take extraordinary care not to be seen, by anyone. And that included the RUC, the Intelligence services, the security services and anyone else whom I realised would become immediately suspicious of me if they ever realised that we had been lovers all those years ago.

'Shit!' I thought to myself, 'shit, shit, shit.'

All that week I waited patiently to see her, hardly able to sleep at night, wondering whether she had changed during ten years inside, hoping that she might still remember me and praying to God that she still felt something for me after such a long time away from the real world. I had decided to borrow a car the following weekend and to cruise around Andersonstown in the hope of seeing her. Of course, I still had the phone number of her parents' home and I presumed she had moved back there. But to phone her there would have been stupendously naïve because I presumed the Intelligence services would have put a tap on her calls to see if any of her former IRA mates called to welcome her back. The thought even crossed my mind that the RUC might be checking to see whether I phoned. I had no reason to suppose so but I couldn't be totally sure.

I borrowed a car the following weekend and made my way along the Falls Road towards Andersonstown Road. This was republican West Belfast where the Nationalist flag flew proudly from many houses and atop many high walls. I had travelled down this road many times in Army Land Rovers, armoured vehicles capable of withstanding machine-gun fire or a bomb thrown beneath the wheels. But it had been some time since I had driven in broad daylight and alone into the IRA heartland.

The Falls Road at that time was not a pretty sight. It looked unkempt and untidy as though the local authorities had not bothered to clean the roads too well. Down the side roads I could see burned-out cars, scruffy houses which didn't look as though they had seen a lick of paint for years and the people seemed to have lost the spirit I remembered from the 1970s. Many were walking down the road slowly, heads bowed, shoulders bent, as though they had the troubles of the world on their shoulders. The kids, too, seemed to have lost that sparkle of youth, though a few groups were kicking footballs around, and I wondered how much of a toll 15 years of bitterness and desperation had really had on the Catholic community.

There were mobile army and RUC patrols around that Saturday but no foot patrols, as though the security forces didn't want to risk causing strife among the locals on a Saturday, preferring to let them enjoy their weekend without having to face the armed patrols they so hated and, in some cases, feared.

I drove on down the Falls knowing full well that many people would consider me mad taking such a risk. I was well built, physically fit and alone and must have looked like a British Army Para or an off-duty PTI. I knew that if I was stopped and asked to hand over some identification, I would have been unable to do so. Deliberately, I had gone out that day with nothing declaring the fact that I was a member of the British Army — no ID card, no driving licence, no credit cards, nothing. I was also travelling without a weapon. Not even a knife. And I also believed that if I was confronted by just one or two yobs, I would be able to hold my own and make my escape. The only trouble I feared was being stopped at lights, my car surrounded by a gang of yobs and people beginning to ask questions. But it was a Saturday morning and most of the people seemed to be in a fairly relaxed frame of mind.

'Fuck it,' I thought, 'I'll be OK.'

I passed the end of her road driving slowly and looked across to see if I could spot her. I knew the odds of actually seeing Mairead were perhaps 50 to 1; the odds of talking to her were probably double that! And yet, I knew there must be a chance. Suddenly, a thought struck me; maybe she had changed so much I wouldn't recognise her and she might not recognise me. I smiled and told myself not to be so stupid.

Four times I drove past the end of her road, slowing down each time and having a damn good look, while at the same time trying not to draw attention to myself, driving around as though lost, not knowing where to go. I knew that was taking a risk, for if anyone had been paying attention to me and my driving, they would have believed I was a stranger in that republican area of town. And strangers are not only unwelcome in Nationalist areas, the locals are always deadly suspicious. If anyone was paying attention, it would be quite usual for a stranger in an unknown car to be stopped and questioned. Any doubts whatsoever would mean being dragged from the car, taken to someone's house and grilled and cross-questioned until the IRA were satisfied. If, for one moment, the IRA interrogators believed the man was Army or Intelligence, he would be unlikely to survive the torture that would follow. I knew from my SAS training that if ever an SAS man is captured by the IRA, he would be executed with a bullet in the back of the head within minutes of confessing and his killing hailed as a magnificent victory for the IRA Intelligence unit. And yet, here I was, driving back and forth in the vain hope of seeing Mairead.

I decided to take one final look before forgetting the whole idea and driving back to barracks. I was about 200 yards from her road when I saw a woman coming out of a mini-supermarket with a carrier bag in her hand. I must have been 50 or 60 yards from her. She didn't look up but kept her head down as she walked away from me. Her hair was dark, but short; she seemed a little over 5ft tall and I looked at her body to see if I could tell whether it was Mairead. I felt sure it wasn't ... and yet ...

I drove along a little and stopped in front of the young woman and looked back towards her. Though she appeared to be looking at the ground and taking no notice of people around her, I felt sure it was Mairead although I couldn't see her face properly. Gently, I tapped the nearside passenger window to attract her attention and she looked up. It was her and my heart missed a beat. The moment she saw me, it was as though she had seen a ghost; a shocked look crossed her face and she immediately looked away and then straight back at me, trying to convince herself that it was me in the car. She looked up and down the street as though checking that no one was looking and I wondered whom she thought would be watching her. I had no idea. She must have thought I was out of my mind driving to see her when she had always pleaded with me, making me promise that I would never surprise her by coming anywhere near her home.

With her right forefinger, Mairead pointed to the left indicating for me to take the next left turn. I drove off when there was a gap in the traffic, turned left 200 yards down the road, stopped a short distance from the main road, and waited. In a minute or so, I saw her walking towards me, dressed in jeans and a white shirt, looking strained and anxious. She had a dull look to her skin as though she had been sheltered from the sun for a long time and I suddenly realised that was the colour of everyone who had spent years in jail, their skin hardly ever exposed to direct sunlight. But the pallor of her skin made her eyes look even darker, like black coals staring from a white sheet.

As she walked up to the car, I leant over and wound down the passenger window.

'What you's doing here?' were her first words

after more than ten years.

'I've come to welcome you home,' I said.

'You's must be mad coming here,' she said, reprimanding me. 'You know's I told you never to come around these parts.'

'I know, I know,' I said, 'but I had no other way of meeting you. I didn't want to use the phone ... you never know who might be listening.'

'What do you want?' she said.

'I want to see you,' I said. 'It's been a long time.'

'Don't I know it,' she said, with some venom in her voice, 'don't I know it.'

'Can I see you?' I asked, looking at her straight in the eyes. In that second, I realised she had aged, matured, seemingly more worldly-wise, more astute, more adult, and I saw that lines had appeared around her eyes that had never been there before. Once again, she suddenly appeared vulnerable.

'Do you's want to?' she asked, 'after everything that happened?'

'Aye, that's why I'm here,' I replied.

'The War Memorial as usual,' she said. 'Can you make tomorrow? No, not tomorrow, that's Sunday. Can you make it Tuesday night?'

'Eight o'clock?' I asked.

'Aye.'

She had put one hand on the window and I put my hand on hers and pressed gently.

'Not here, for God's sake,' she said and quickly took her hand away. And she was gone, walking away from the car without ever looking back.

Before pulling away from the kerb, I checked to

see if a car was coming, but actually I was making a sweep of the whole area, particularly back towards the main road to see if anyone had been watching our reunion. I was fairly sure that no one was but I was taking no chances. I made a slow, deliberate three-point turn in the road as though I was a stranger, trying to behave as though I had only been seeking directions from a girl walking along the street. At the same time, I checked the houses to see if any prying eyes had been watching us as I drove back to the main road, turning left towards the Falls and Belfast. I made two or three deliberate turns on the way back, checking to see whether a car was following, but I was certain no one was trailing me.

That weekend passed very slowly. I wanted to tell my mate Peter O'Kane, but never for one moment did I really ever contemplate telling anyone. I went out with mates drinking at night and spent most of the time in the gym or going for runs. And I couldn't possibly tell any of my SAS mates. I always got on well with them but never shared my innermost thoughts with anyone. I had my drinking mates and those with whom I would often go out on patrol. But I had always been a loner, never wanting to share my private life.

Some of my mates would boast about their conquests, show off their latest girlfriends and brag about how many times a night they had made love and how many women they had laid. I would say nothing and sometimes, when drunk, they would take the piss out of me. I never wanted to train with them either. I much preferred to go to the gym alone, go on long, endurance runs on my own and compete against the stop-watch or myself. I suppose I had always been like that since I was a teenager, because if I ever got into a fight as a kid, I would get into trouble for punching too hard or attacking someone too ferociously. So I learned to keep away from people but at the same time to keep myself really fit. I didn't smoke; I never smoked. But I did like a pint. I could handle that and I knew my body could, too, because the following day I would go and sweat it out of my system, proving myself against the clock.

That weekend, we were off-duty having spent the best part of a month on patrol in the border region. We had seen nothing and done nothing but the weather had been quite good and although bored with no action whatsoever, I had quite enjoyed the peace and tranquillity of the lovely countryside with its small fields, low brick walls and green, green landscape, dotted with trees and hedgerows under which we would often sleep.

That Tuesday, I went to the gym and worked out really hard. I sweated out all the pints of Guinness and lager I had consumed during the past 72 hours and after a kip and a shower in the early evening I felt on good form. And I splashed on quite a lot of aftershave. In total, there would have been about 40 soldiers stationed at my quarters, 20 SAS men and 20 made up of 14 Intelligence Unit and the Det, the men and women seconded to carry out undercover Intelligence work in Northern Ireland. We were all involved in Intelligence and surveillance patrols, of one type or another, the vast majority of our work focusing on the IRA. I smiled as I shaved, wondering what the lads would say if they knew that I was going on a date with a known IRA bomber.

As I drove towards Holywood, I told myself that if Mairead and I began dating seriously again, I would make sure that I kept my eyes and ears open, checking whether she was still involved with any cell or terrorist activity. I wondered whether her ten long years in jail had changed her ideas or had, in fact, hardened them. I would soon find out.

One point worried me. Now I was a member of the SAS, we were entitled to use admin cars that we could take out at night, mainly for our own security. Of course, we always had to book the cars and get permission to take them for an evening or a weekend trip away from Belfast. If we were taking one for the night, we didn't have to state exactly where we would be travelling but if we took one for a weekend then we would have to say where we intended to visit and stay. All these cars appeared to be ordinary, normal four-door saloons, like Ford Sierras, Vauxhall Cavaliers, Ford Escorts, Montegos or Maestros. But, in reality, all were kept in perfect condition and all were armour-plated. The armour was built into the doors and into the backs of the seats, both back and front. We knew these cars were different, the seats were that bit more rigid and unyielding, but anyone taken for a ride in one was meant to be unable to detect the armour plating. I wondered whether Mairead would guess. If she did suspect, then I knew my cover as a shipyard welder would be blown.

When I first saw her walking towards me it seemed she had not changed one jot. She walked in the same way as she had done before, leaving from the railway station, walking through the underpass beneath the dual carriageway towards the Memorial, looking around to see where I was waiting. I had been sitting in my car some distance away, taking even more precautions than I had done ten years ago. The SAS training throughout those years had taught me to be extra vigilant and to leave nothing whatsoever to chance. Usually, one was a member of a four or five-man patrol, all trained to watch out for each other, but now I was totally alone and my training had taught me well.

I had driven around the area twice, checking that no one was waiting in any of the parked cars in the surrounding roads with a view of the War Memorial. The Memorial itself was quite exposed in the middle of a square and only yards from the main road, but I realised that an ambush could have been staged in one or two of the side-streets leading from the Memorial.

I stepped from the car, leaving the engine running, waved to Mairead and immediately got back in. I was taking no chances. I had no idea what Mairead had been doing during her ten years inside, surrounded by other IRA women, but I knew it would be foolish to run any risks. For all I knew, Mairead might have been followed, either by IRA sympathisers, Loyalist paramilitaries or one of our lot. I realised full well that if anyone caught us together, it would be curtains for one or, more likely, both of us.

From inside the car, I opened the passenger door as she approached. She was looking serious and still pale.

I smiled, trying to reassure her. 'Nice to see you again,' I said.

'Just hold me,' she said and Mairead threw herself into my arms and I could feel her body shaking.

Her tears and emotion shook her body as I held her closely and Mairead let herself weep, unable to control the relief she obviously felt. As I wrapped my arms around her small body, I checked to see if anyone was approaching the car but the area seemed deserted. I looked in the rear view mirror but no one was about.

After a few minutes, Mairead began repeating through her tears, 'Jesus, Holy Mary, Joseph ... Jesus, Holy Mary, Joseph ... it's wonderful to see you again, Scott. I have dreamed for ten years of being with you again in your arms and, now I'm here, I can't cope.' And she broke down again and the tears returned.

I had never expected this reaction and I felt somewhat unnerved. I had never been very confident of how to handle girlfriends when they broke down in tears. On this occasion, however, I had other things on my mind as well. I kept watching the street, checking the rear-view mirror but, thankfully, no one was about. I began to relax as Mairead stopped shaking, though she lay in my arms with her head buried in my shoulder so that I could not see her face. I guessed she didn't want me to see her in this state with her face smeared with tears and whatever make-up she was wearing and so I let her be, waiting for her to come to terms with her feelings about our meeting. But it was still broad daylight and I didn't want to wait around the Memorial for too long.

After perhaps four or five minutes, Mairead took

some tissues from her handbag and wiped her face and eyes and then blew her nose. 'I'm so sorry,' she kept repeating, 'I'm so sorry ... I was so looking forward to seeing you again and yet I never expected to see you again, ever. It was such a surprise to see you in the car the other day. I didn't believe it was you at first.'

'Everything's fine now,' I said. 'It is me, I promise,' and I tried to sound cheerful in an effort to defuse the heightened tension in the car.

'Could you manage a drink?' I asked, hoping she hadn't lost her thirst for the occasional vodka or half of lager.

'Could I?' she said, sounding like someone dying of thirst. 'I could kill a pint of lager. But I must look frightful, awful,' and she took a hand-mirror from her handbag to check.

'Jesus, I look terrible,' she said.

'Don't be silly,' I said, 'you look lovely.'

'Don't you's say things like that to me when I know I look like I've been dragged through a hedge backwards,' she said and looked at me, a weak smile across her lips.

That weak, vulnerable smile made me feel so tender towards her. I hadn't seen her for ten years and yet it felt as though I had seen her only a few days before. It seemed as though we hadn't been parted for a decade and all the feelings of love and tenderness that I had felt towards her came back to me. All she had done was to plant a bomb for the cause she believed in, making sure in the process that no one had been killed, wounded or injured. And I asked myself whether that was such a terrible crime.

'Shall we go to the Cultra, like the good old days?' I suggested.

'Will you give me a few minutes to get this face of mine respectable to be seen in public?' she asked and the smile seemed to grow stronger.

'That's better,' I said, 'that's more like the girl I knew.'

'Girl,' Mairead said interrupting. 'I'm more like an old woman now after ten years in that hole.'

'No, you're not at all,' I said, 'you're just as lovely as you always were.'

'Get away with you's,' she said, 'I'll have none of your nonsense.'

I grabbed hold of her and kissed her long and hard on the mouth until we realised that we were becoming absorbed in the sensation, a feeling so passionate and wild that we both wanted to have sex there and then, in the car in the middle of a street in broad daylight.

'I think we had better stop,' I said. 'That was wonderful.'

'Jesus, Scott,' she said, 'I had forgotten what it was like. Do you need a drink now?'

'Let's go,' I said and we drove off towards the country.

One hour later, having made love twice in the car in a country lane, hardly stopping to take breath, we drove towards the Cultra Inn.

'Do you think everyone will realise what we've been doing?' said Mairead as I stopped the car and leaned over to give her one more kiss. 'I must look terrible.'

'You look lovely,' I said, 'and the sparkle's coming back to your eyes.'

'You's a terrible man,' she said, and she got out of the car and adjusted her shirt, sweater and jeans once more, checking that she looked respectable enough and feeling guilty that the customers might realise that she had been making love in the back of a car.

'Do you think anyone will recognise me?' she said.

'I doubt it very much,' I said. 'I never saw your photo in any of the papers and that was ten years ago.'

'You're right,' she said, 'I must be getting paranoid in my old age.'

'Old age?' I tutted, and smacked her bottom quite hard as we walked together into the pub.

'I still love your muscles,' she said with a sexy look in her eye.

'And I still love your body,' I said.

'Ssshh,' she said, 'none of that in here ... people will start talking.'

Within three minutes, we had both emptied our pints of lager and I ordered two more.

'Jesus, that's better,' Mairead said, 'it tastes wonderful.'

'Is that your first since ...' but I deliberately didn't complete the sentence.

'No,' she said, 'I had a couple last week with my brothers to celebrate. But I needed this one more tonight.'

'Why was that?' I enquired.

'Because last week I hadn't just been screwed,' she whispered in my ear, giving it a gentle bite, 'and now I have.'

'And did you enjoy it?' I asked jokingly.

'Jesus,' Mairead replied, 'I thought I was going to lose my mind. If you's had gone on much longer I'd have passed out.'

'I will next time,' I joked.

'You bastard,' she said. And then she stopped. 'Would you really?'

'Would you like me to?' I asked.

'Yes, I think that would be fantastic,' she said and squeezed my thigh. 'I'm dying to spend a day or a night in bed with you again,' she said, 'so that I can see all those muscles while you's screwing me.'

'Soon,' I said, 'I promise you.'

I arranged to have a long weekend and booked an admin car for two days. Mairead said she would love to spend a few days away in a small hotel somewhere and so I fixed an out-of-the-way place, a pub with food and accommodation, where I knew we would be very unlikely to run across any of the lads enjoying a dirty weekend. Many of my SAS mates took their wives or girlfriends to stay in various pubs and small hotels all over Northern Ireland, but we were always encouraged to stick to pubs that were well known to the security forces, pubs where the landlord could be trusted. And, of course, we always went in civvies, making sure we never wore any clothes suggesting we were in the Army.

It was to be a weekend that I would never forget.

The sex, of course, was wonderful, as it always had been with Mairead. But now it was truly sensational and wild. Mairead was almost insatiable and the 72 hours became a round of drinking, eating and making love. Before and after every meal, we would go to our room and stay there for hours, spending afternoons in bed and then back in our room by 10.00pm each night after a few pints and a meal.

'I need you, Scott,' Mairead would say every time we began to screw. 'I need your muscles ... I need you body and soul ... I want you's to screw me and never to stop. I want you to do whatever you want. Use me ... use my body ... abuse me in anyway way you want ... fuck me and screw me everywhere and take no notice when I plead with you to stop.'

And, from her actions, it seemed that she meant every word. Never before had she spoken like that to me and I wondered what had happened to her during her time away.

I was now becoming aware that this was not the Mairead who had left my life ten years ago. Although our feelings for each other seemed to be as strong as ever, and possibly even heightened, the Mairead lying next to me was far from the naïve schoolgirl who talked passionately of the nationalist struggle as though it was her personal adventure. I had hoped to have Mairead back, and pick up the relationship we once had, but the subtle shifts in our response to each other awakened an unease in me, and they were not only apparent in Mairead's approach to love-making and her comments during it. I knew that she must be scarred mentally from her time inside, and I could vaguely perceive the extent of that scarring, and the effect it might have on our time together.

Later, when we lay together and chatted, I asked

her whether she knew what she had been saying to me in those moments of extreme passion.

'Yes,' she would say quietly, 'I know exactly what I'm saying.'

'Why?' I would ask her. 'Why do you want me to treat you like that? You weren't like that before.'

'I know, Scott,' she would say, speaking gently and, at the same time, caressing my legs, my arms or my chest and stomach. 'But I've changed in the last ten years. You don't know what I've been through.'

'What do you mean?' I asked, wanting to learn what had happened to her.

'Inside,' she said, 'you don't know what it's like in a women's prison.'

At first, Mairead didn't want to talk to me about her experiences, but by the end of the weekend, when she began to feel more confident and more relaxed, she began to open up.

'Remember, Scott, I was a wee innocent girl of 18 when I went inside. We had made love lots of times but always in a loving, gentle way although it was passionate between us. But some of those women in there had been inside without a man for years and whenever someone like me, young and innocent, came inside, we were like lambs to the slaughter.'

I knew that she wanted to continue, and I was naïve enough to wonder what she meant. I decided that Mairead clearly needed to talk, whether I wanted to hear about her experiences or not. I had not had much experience in handling situations like this, but it seemed that the best thing for me to do would be to give her the space she needed to get the last ten years out of her system — and that meant being as good a listener as I could be. And if I could go some way to understanding the horrors of the past ten years, we might then achieve a sort of equality, and perhaps we might be able to move on together, stronger than we were before. I asked her what she meant by 'lambs to the slaughter'.

'At first they were gentle and encouraging. Five or six different women approached me and wanted to become my protector, but I was so very innocent I didn't understand. I thought that I wouldn't need protecting because there were only the jailers and the prisoners ... there were no men to be seen. I wanted to be left alone but that soon became impossible. They told me that if I wouldn't accept a protector then one of the women would take me by force instead. They told me that people had been playing cards for me but I didn't believe a word they said.

'I asked them what they meant by playing cards for me. And the women, the prisoners, laughed at my innocence and then told me that people played cards for the right to have sex with a particular prisoner and because I was young and seemed so innocent I was particularly attractive to them as a sexual object.

'I wondered what they meant, telling them that I believed only men thought of women as sexual objects. At that they all laughed and told me that I would soon learn.'

I kept quiet, not daring to ask questions, and believing that Mairead wanted to tell me everything in her own way, in her own time.

As she related the story to me, she didn't look at

me but rather looked away as though talking to a stranger. She went on, 'One night, another young girl in her early twenties came to me and began to talk to me. She seemed frightened and told me she was doing six years for hitting a policeman. She told me that for my own protection I should choose one of the women prisoners who would protect me. "If you don't," she said, "then they will just take it in turns to rape you until you agree. They won't leave you alone. There was another girl who refused and they spent nights taking it in turns to rape her until she became a physical, nervous wreck. She was held down and assaulted repeatedly, until she felt like an animal. Except that no animal would ever treat another in such a despicable way."'

She told me that she had a protector with whom she slept most nights and who would do whatever she wanted with her.

'My new girlfriend, Anne, seemed to want me as a friend, not in a sexual way but as someone who was also young and innocent. She introduced me to another girl, a little older who was pretty and good looking with short dark hair and seemingly quite tough, but with a good figure. This girl had been gang banged a number of times because she had refused to co-operate. She told me that six of them would get hold of her and rape her for three or four hours until they had had enough. She was left badly bruised and bleeding, her breasts and stomach and inner thighs bitten, and it had taken weeks for the bruises to heal and the bite marks to fade. Then they would come for her again. In the end, she had to get a protector, too. It was the only way to survive.

'I hoped that I could remain on my own, leading my own life and so I said "No" to any requests to stay in someone else's cell. Most of the time in Armagh, we were allowed to sleep in whichever cell we wanted, with little or no restrictions, so long as we returned to our own cells by the morning. Some of the women who had special girlfriends worked things so they shared cells with their girls because the screws wanted to keep some of the more powerful women happy. In that way, the screws reckoned the place remained happier and there was less trouble. The screws wanted an easy life.'

Mairead told me that on one occasion two powerful women subjected her to a terrible sexual attack. 'I talked to my friend Anne, told her what had happened and asked her advice. She told me that the women would probably return, taking it in turns to rape me and I would become a wreck, not knowing when they were coming for me, unable to sleep for fear of what would happen. She asked me if I had thought any more of taking a protector, or if I could fancy any of the women who had approached me, but I just shook my head. I asked her whether I should complain to the Governor and she said that if I did that, my life would be made hell for the 14 years I was due to stay inside. She urged me to keep quiet and never to complain because, if I did so, I would be lucky to leave the place alive or sane.'

Again, I asked Mairead, 'So what happened?'

'Anne told me that because I was young and considered attractive, many of the butch women wanted me to be their girl. She told me that other young girls were worried they might be thrown over in favour of me and some were out to get me, considering whether they should scratch my face, throw boiling water over me or find some other way to make me less attractive. They contemplated stirring up trouble for me with the screws. You's have no idea, Scott, what the atmosphere is like in a women's prison. Many women there are so bitchy, so horrible, some of them are openly vicious, evil women. They're poisonous. It was like that in Armagh for the whole time I was there. Maybe it's not so bad in prisons where women are only detained for a short while, or are on remand. But in our section at Armagh, we were all there for a long time and that seemed to make the women more bitchy and violent because they had nothing to lose.'

Mairead then went on to tell me how she managed to cope with all the abuse, and how she finally found her way of getting through the next few years.

It became clear that sexual aggression and the release of sexual tension preoccupied many of the long-term prisoners, and that, if you were relatively young and attractive, you would be a permanent target for the most dangerous and violent inmates and screws. So you had to work within the system if you were going to survive, and that meant finding a benevolent protector. Mairead's first friend inside, Anne, helped her to find just such a protector. She was called Marie-Therese. I asked Mairead how she felt about their first meeting.

'Marie-Therese came to see me. She was about 28 and had dark brown hair down to her shoulders. She had been convicted of being a member of the IRA and having a gun and had been given ten years. She had been a married woman but had no kids. She was taller than me and more powerfully built but, although she looked hard, I sensed she might also have a gentle side. Anne told me that Marie-Therese didn't have a reputation for treating her lovers badly, but she was the jealous type who usually protected her girls. She had been inside for five years and had won the respect of many other prisoners because she was a member of the IRA and considered intelligent.

'She told me she would look after me and told me to tell her if anything happened to me. We would take meals together and go out in the exercise yard together. I became her girlfriend and that was understood by everyone. The tense atmosphere stopped and people began to ignore me. Before, as well as making obscene remarks to me, they would also make it obvious they were talking about me, pointing at me, deliberately bumping into me, making me feel nervous and uneasy.

'Now, I knew that I could rely on Marie-Therese to protect me, but I was nervous about how she would treat me herself. Initially, she was very demanding, but Anne helped me to come to terms with the routine, suggesting that I should try to feel more open to Marie-Therese, to find qualities that I liked in her, and so begin to enjoy our time together if at all possible. After three months, I began to take a more active role instead of the passive victim I had played so far, and I found that it helped. I took more control of my destiny, and it went beyond our personal relationship, enabling me to feel far more confident within the prison environment generally.'

'It must have been awful, terrible for you,' I said. 'How did you cope?'

'I coped because I had to. I had no alternative. People don't realise how hellish life can be inside. I was a kid, Scott, when I went inside. I knew nothing of life. Now I know the very worst of life ... how awful and totally selfish people can be.'

After a year or so, Mairead and Marie-Therese fell out, but by that time, Mairead had become more actively involved with the IRA movement within her wing at Armagh, and had already set up an IRA cell with the help of Marie-Therese. They would hold meetings, discuss matters, talk about the political situation in London, Dublin and Stormont, and encourage others to join in. She also began to appreciate that close friends, real friends, could be made in prison, and like-minded Republican prisoners could become a strong and respected force if they stood together. Mairead realised that she could maintain her active involvement in the nationalist cause despite being incarcerated, and her energies and passions could now be successfully directed exclusively to that end.

10

TEN DAYS LATER, I MET Mairead again, this time at
Marino railway station, one stop down the line from
Holywood. As I stood on the old stone bridge
overlooking the tiny station, I wondered at the life she
had led in Armagh. Ever since that weekend together,
I was amazed how she had endured such a gruelling
time. As she alighted from the train and walked along
the platform, through the wooden gate and up the
steep slope to the road, it seemed extraordinary that
this girl, who had seemed so young and
inexperienced, had managed to survive the ordeal.
Looking petite and vulnerable as she walked alone
along the platform, my heart went out to her for the
bloody awful time she had experienced in jail and I
wanted to bring some laughter, fun and happiness
back to her. She had spent ten of the best years of her

young life in jail and it seemed such a waste.

Her face dissolved into a wonderful beaming smile when I opened the passenger door for her to climb in. She leant over and gave me a big kiss on the lips and I marvelled how anyone who had been through such trauma for so long could be so together and, seemingly, so relaxed and happy.

'You look wonderful,' I told her, and I meant every word.

'Thanks,' she said.

'What have you been doing?' I asked.

'This and that,' she replied in a non-committal manner, apparently wanting to avoid a direct answer.

'Go on, give me a clue,' I said, deliberately probing.

'It's a long story,' Mairead explained. 'I'll tell you another time. I'm not sure what I should do but I think I should concentrate on my education. I've had ten years to reach a decision and now I'm out I don't know which way to turn. Isn't that silly?'

To me, education had been a terrible bore and I could never understand why people wanted to leave school and then continue studying for three more years at technical college or university. I knew that I could rely on the Army to further my education.

But I replied, 'No, that's not silly, that's life. Education is wonderful but don't you want to find a job?' I had assumed that she would return to being a clerk or working in some capacity in an office.

'No,' she said. 'I did a lot of thinking inside and I knew I wanted to improve my education so that I can find a really good, worthwhile job. I don't want to be somebody's secretary, to be ordered around, told what to do. I had enough of that inside. Now I'm out I want to make the decisions affecting my life by myself with no one dictating to me.'

That made sense to me. In a flash, I realised something that I hadn't even considered before. Prison was obviously worse than the Army. In the Army, I had spent my life obeying orders to the letter but I always had the option to quit if I really wanted to. Mairead never had that option and that was why it must have been so galling to be ordered to do everything from first thing in the morning to last thing at night.

I said, 'That makes sense ... I understand.'

'Do you really understand, Scott?' Mairead asked, turning on me, raising her voice, sounding far more serious and challenging than she had ever been since leaving jail.

I turned and looked at her. 'I think I do,' I said, 'I think it must be a bit like the Army or the police I suppose, always having to obey orders.'

'No it's not,' she said, her voice raised in anger. 'It's nothing like the Army at all. In prison you can't make any decisions for yourself, ever. I haven't been able to decide when I brush my teeth for ten fucking years, Scott. They told me when I could get up, walk out of my cell, have breakfast, dinner and tea. They told me when I could have a bath or a shower. They told me when I could go to the fucking lavatory. Can you imagine? Can you imagine, Scott, what that life's really like?'

'I see,' I replied, somewhat taken aback by her

onslaught and anger.

'No you don't, Scott,' she said, continuing her attack. 'If you haven't been to jail, you never know how fucking awful it is having no life of your own. It's terrible, Scott, it's degrading, demeaning, humiliating. The screws try to make you feel so small, so insignificant, Scott. They make you feel like shit. And, no matter how you try to rise above it, you can't because they always have the whip hand. You're putty in their hands and they know it. If you get on the wrong side of a bitch screw, your life is made hell for weeks until she decides she's had enough fun riding you and she'll go on to some other poor bitch.'

I knew that Mairead wasn't really attacking me for my lack of understanding and I told myself to stay calm and listen and try not to argue with her. She had the experience of prison and I had never been inside, so I thought it best to let her get the whole awful business out of her system. I also wondered how I would have reacted if I had been banged up for ten years and the thought sent a shudder through me. I knew that I would have been able to look after myself inside. There would have been no risk of other prisoners challenging me or trying to fuck me about because I would have given them a bloody hard thumping.

'I can't really understand the hell you've been through, Mairead,' I told her. 'But if I can help, then please let me know what I can do.'

'I know,' she said, temporarily deflated, sounding as if she had managed to rid herself of the angst she had been feeling.

'If you want to let your anger out, do,' I said. 'I'm quite a good punch-bag.'

'I'm sorry,' she said. 'It's just that, sometimes, when I think how I was treated inside, especially during the first couple of years, I feel so insecure and insignificant. And that's what makes me so angry and frustrated.'

'So it did get better?' I asked, hopefully.

'Yeah,' she said in a resigned voice. 'But only because I took control of my own destiny.'

'What do you mean?' I asked.

'Are you going to take me for a drink or a bite to eat or what?' she said, changing the subject. 'Or are we going to sit here outside the station and talk all night until it's time for me to go back home?'

'Let's go and eat something,' I said, starting the car. 'I could do with a steak and a pint of Guinness. How about you?'

'Done,' she said and, as we drove off, Mairead put her hand on my thigh and gently rubbed it up and down as though gaining some inner strength from the contact.

'That's nice,' I said and put my hand on her thigh.

'Later,' she said, 'we're eating first. I'm hungry and thirsty.'

We went to another country pub some miles from the railway station, a place I had been told about by some mates from the Regiment who had just spent four months in Holywood Barracks. They had told me the place was quite deserted and the food was good. I just hoped none of the lads were there that night, but I doubted it because they usually only went out that far from barracks on Friday or Saturday nights.

Thank God the place was virtually deserted and, as I went to the bar to buy the drinks and pick up a menu, Mairead went to a corner table furthest from the bar.

Mairead needed a drink that night and I didn't blame her. Two pints of lager and a good meal later, Mairead began to unwind and settle back in her chair, wanting to hold my hand and relax. The drink had obviously done her the power of good for she smiled and appeared contented, planning when we could spend another weekend together in some small country hotel miles away from Belfast and the Troubles.

As we sat and talked, I felt guilty that I was still masquerading as a welder, allegedly plying my trade in Belfast, Scotland and Germany when, in reality, I was a proud member of a great Regiment whose main job during the years I had been involved was to patrol the border between Northern Ireland and the Republic, tracking, arresting and killing IRA gunmen, bombers and sympathisers who only wanted to fight for what they saw as their right to a united Ireland. And Mairead, the girl who had been prepared to go to jail for ten years for fighting for that same right, would open her heart to me, little realising that, in reality, I was one of the unnamed, inconspicuous enemies that she so hated.

We left with 15 minutes to spare before her train was due and we managed to have sex, a quickie in the car, before racing off to the station.

On other occasions that autumn, Mairead

confessed to what else had happened in jail and how her views had changed from being someone with an interest in Republicanism and Nationalism to becoming a totally committed member of the Provisional IRA.

During the winter of 1986–87, I had arranged to rent an apartment in Belfast from an RUC mate who had been sent on a three-month course to London. He only wanted a small rent for the place, someone to care for the flat during the winter. It suited Mairead and me perfectly. I would meet her at the bus station and we would drive to the flat off the Beersbridge Road in Ballymacarrett in East Belfast and spend the evening there, and sometimes the entire night or weekend, enjoying life as a couple who never spent enough time together. They were great times.

We managed to see each other at least once a week, and sometimes more, and whenever we arrived at the flat we would make love before we did anything else at all.

'You's terrible,' Mairead would say as I would start to undress her before we had walked into the flat. Sometimes we wouldn't get further than the hallway, so keen were we both to see each other again. Mairead hardly ever wanted to venture outside, afraid that we might be seen together despite the fact that we were in the middle of Protestant Belfast and at least a mile or more from where Catholics would ever be seen. But she didn't want to take any chances.

Understandably, I, too, was perfectly happy for our relationship to continue like this because the last thing I wanted was to be seen by my SAS mates with a girl they had never seen before, although I was confident that they would have not the faintest idea that Mairead was a convicted IRA bomber. But the problem would have arisen when Mairead would have questioned me afterwards, intrigued as to how I came to have such good friends in the British Army. Thank goodness, the problem never arose.

Most evenings, I would have bought a couple of bottles of wine or a couple of six packs and we would cook a frozen meal bought from a supermarket or pick up a take-away. I always ate well at Holywood Barracks and these nightly dishes were snacks to keep Mairead company. She seemed to enjoy them greatly, particularly after a few drinks. I soon discovered that after a drink and an hour or so in bed, Mairead loved to talk and I let her do so, wanting to learn more of her life in jail as well as learning as much as I could about any interests she might still nurture towards the Provisionals. Sometimes, I wondered whether my SAS training was getting the better of me or whether I was simply curious to know whether Mairead, having served ten years in jail for Republicanism, still harboured the same determination to help the cause. From the way she had spoken on our first date, pouring out her emotions and her fears, I thought that she would never do anything to risk being sent back to jail.

But I was wrong.

Mairead would talk to me about her IRA activities inside Armagh. I was amazed and appalled when she told me that she was one of only a few women who had taken an active part in the dirty protest at Armagh jail. I had believed that it was only the men in the Long Kesh H-blocks who had organised dirty protests, refusing to empty their chamber pots, to take baths or to shave.

She told me, 'We followed what the Republican inmates were doing at Long Kesh. They demanded that they should be treated as prisoners of war and not as ordinary criminals, and we demanded the same rights. The screws told us that we would never be given such rights in a hundred years.

'The screws also warned us that if we adopted the same dirty protest, then we would be the losers. "Anything you can do we can make much worse," they would tell us. It didn't make the slightest difference. Through friends outside, we were in constant contact with our colleagues in the H-blocks who were demanding an end to criminalisation.

'The British Government said that the men on the dirty protest were nothing more than "violent convicts"and insisted that the rules of the jail would have to be obeyed no matter how sickening or shocking the situation became.

'The screws would come into our cells and somehow the chamber pots would be accidentally knocked over. Then they would give us buckets and mops and order us to clean up the mess. At first, we did as we were told, and then we decided we had had enough of this treatment and refused, telling the screws to clean up the mess themselves. That may have been a mistake.

'They would take us out, one at a time, make us strip naked in the showers and scrub us clean, leaving scratches, cuts, abrasions and bruises all over our bodies. When they had finished scrubbing us with hard bristle brushes and carbolic soap, they would hose us down with strong, cold water jets. Then they would paint us with disinfectant and we would be returned to our cells, the blood oozing from scratches all over our bodies from the vigorous brushing.'

Mairead told me that conditions steadily grew worse. The women decided to follow the men's example and smear the walls of their cells with excrement, while the floors became pools of urine. The continued support that the protesters gave each other did little to help them cope with the stench, filth and sense of degradation.

They took strength and some satisfaction from the fact that the screws hated the conditions, although the repercussions were inevitable. Undeterred, though, the dozen or so women would sit covered by a blanket each, caked in filth and determined to see the protest out to the bitter end.

I was amazed that Mairead had found the strength to join these protests and to persevere with them, and particularly that she seemed to be growing in status within the prison hierarchy itself. Mairead had become one of the leading lights of the nationalist cause within the prison, and her stature within the organisation as a whole was becoming apparent, too. I asked how they could possibly continue with such a demoralising and degrading protest, never knowing how or when it would resolve itself.

'It became a matter of will power,' she replied, 'and we managed that by keeping our spirits up by singing republican songs, shouting encouragement to each other, teaching each other the Irish language and learning Irish history. We'd concentrate on the appalling crimes perpetrated by the British politicians and troops over the centuries, and we'd cheer any news of other Provo mates' victories over the security forces or prison officers in other jails. The screws hated that, and we'd bait them further by telling them that they'd be next on the death list. We knew that, eventually, the British Government would be branded as barbaric and that public pressure, particularly from the United States, would force them to back down, and grant us prisoner-of-war status.

'As punishment, we were forbidden little luxuries like newspapers or TV, and we even had exercise rights removed, but we kept abreast of protests in other prisons through the grapevine. Knowing that our mates in the Maze were still resolute helped us enormously, and we knew that our determination was helping them as well. It's just amazing how you can survive in such conditions, Scott. I suppose it's just down to the human spirit.

'Did you never feel like caving in?' I asked, wondering how the hell anyone could live in those conditions for so long.

'Yes, sometimes,' she confessed. 'Usually when they put me in solitary.'

'They put you in solitary as well?' I asked, surprised.

'Did they, Jesus!' she said, 'That was awful, 'cos you's was cut off from your mates and you's support. I hated solitary. They would leave me in there for a week at a time, seeing no one, talking to no one, unable to hear anyone. Just sitting in a tiny, bare cell with a naked light on the ceiling so you could never sleep. And just one blanket to hide your nakedness. I wasn't allowed clothes to wear or anything because I was on the dirty protest. So that's what they gave me, one fucking blanket.'

'I don't know how I survived. Sometimes I would cry through the night because I felt so lonely and so helpless. But I never let the screws hear me or see me crying. I would hold the blanket tight to my mouth so they couldn't hear but, shit, Scott, I felt terribly lonely.'

She looked at me with tears welling in her eyes and put out her hand and touched my lips.

'Sometimes I would think of you, of us, together, as we were before. I wondered if we would ever see each other again and I wondered where you were in the world and what you were doing. And I would cry even more when I wondered if you ever, ever thought of me. I presumed after The Conway bomb that you had just walked away. I understood that most people would just forget about someone who could plant a bomb and wreck a hotel. But I just hoped you realised that I hadn't killed anyone. Not a soul. Nor was anyone injured. I just hoped that you had realised that and that gave me hope that you might sometimes think of me. But, Jesus, Scott, I wanted you. I never needed anyone like I needed you then. I thought of your strong arms and you's muscles and I wanted you's to be there with me. Sometimes, I wondered like a young child whether you would come along and rescue me and take me away and that would make me feel pathetic and silly and childish and I would pinch myself and tell myself that I had got myself into the mess and I had to get myself out of it. But, Scott, I was terribly, terribly lonely. I just wanted you to love me and I felt that no one did. That I was totally alone.'

Reliving her experiences that night, however, finally took its toll on Mairead and she broke down and cried and wanted to be cuddled and comforted like a child who felt lonely and unloved. I understood that and cradled her in my arms until the tears stopped. Sometimes, I felt she wanted to talk of her prison experiences; at other times, she wanted to banish them from her mind.

As a result, I resolved never to raise the subject again, letting her tell me of her experiences only if and when she wanted to, but never asking her any of the details, letting her tell me only as much as she wanted, because I felt the trauma of those times was so strong that she had problems coming to terms with what had happened. But I would wonder what else she had suffered that I didn't know about, and whether she was, in fact, holding back even more horrific details.

Some weeks later, when we were once again spending a weekend in the flat together, Mairead began talking about her hunger-strike. We had just finished a meal, a take-away curry which she always enjoyed, from a shop near Belfast city centre.

'That was delicious,' she said, 'I really enjoyed that meal tonight.'

'It was great,' I said, 'but you always say that, every time we have one. Have you always liked curry?'

'No,' she said, 'but I used to dream about it in Armagh. The curries we were given inside were awful, wishy-washy things. I like proper curries with garlic and real spices, preferably cooked by Indians. Did you know I was on hunger-strike?' she asked, as though discussing the weather.

'Hunger-strike?' I said, astonished. 'You never told me you were on hunger-strike!'

'Yes,' she said. 'It was after we stopped the dirty protest. In December 1980, two other girls, Mary Doyle and Mairead Nugent, and myself went on hunger-strike. There were a number of lads on hunger-strike at the Maze and we decided that we should follow their example. We had a meeting, the Provos that is, and we asked for volunteers. I put up my hand and so did Mary and the other Mairead, and we agreed there and then to go on hunger-strike, refusing all food but just taking a little water.'

'Did the authorities know?' I asked.

'Of course they knew. We told the screws and we knew the governor would be told within minutes. We knew they didn't want us to go on hunger-strike because they feared we would carry on until we starved ourselves to death. And the British didn't want any Fenian martyrs on their hands. They knew that if any IRA prisoner died on hunger-strike the whole of West Belfast would erupt in mayhem. The women of Armagh prison had shown in the dirty protest that we could take a hell of a lot of punishment and degradation without giving in, and I think they were shit-scared that we might die.

'The three of us didn't eat a thing and within

days we were moved to hospital so that our health could be monitored by medical experts. We all felt dreadful, our strength ebbing away and we felt we wouldn't last too long. But I never dreamed of giving in and accepting food. We knew that the last accusation the British Government would want to face was the charge that a prisoner had been left to die in a cell without proper medical supervision.'

'What happened to you?' I asked.

'I don't remember much about it after I was moved to hospital,' Mairead told me. 'I felt terribly weak, as though I had no energy whatsoever. I didn't even have the strength to get out of bed. They kept offering food at first and I refused to eat anything. I would just say "water" and nothing else. Once or twice I detected sugar and salt in the water, which they'd added in an effort to give me some nourishment, but on those occasions the water tasted funny so I spat it out and asked for plain water. Doctors and nurses seemed to be there whenever I opened my eyes, but I was getting weaker and weaker.'

I wasn't sure if she wanted to go on, but I knew that I should give her the chance if she did.

'How did the hunger-strike end?' I asked.

'One day, a doctor came in and said there was someone to talk to me and one of my Provo inmates came in. Everyone left the room and she sat on the bed and asked if I could understand if she spoke to me. I remember trying to mouth "Yes" but my lips wouldn't open and my tongue felt big and bloated and I couldn't speak. So I nodded. She told me that word had come from outside, from Sinn Fein headquarters, that everyone in Belfast was following my condition and they all thought me very, very brave but that things had changed on the political front. Sinn Fein had apparently secured some political concessions, and they told me to end my hunger-strike. As a good soldier, they knew I would obey orders. I nodded to her and tried to smile and before she left she wished me good luck.'

'Did you get into trouble?' I asked.

'No, not at all,' she said. 'I stayed at the hospital for a few days and everyone was terribly kind to me. They gave me everything to eat and drink that I wanted. At first, they told me that I must take things very gently and eat very little so that my stomach and my body would have time to adjust to accepting food once again. At first they gave me baby food, or something like that, which was easy to digest. And they gave me water with sugar in an effort to get my blood sugar content back to normal. It was after I recovered and felt stronger that I developed this yearning for curry and rice but they never gave me that.'

'And how quickly did you get over it?'

'I don't know, Scott. I began to feel better within a week I suppose. But it took me a month before I felt I had recovered my old energy. The women prisoners, my friends, kept telling me that I was looking better each day, but when I checked in the mirror I still looked pale and thin. I was beginning to feel strong again when I heard that the concessions which the British had hinted at to make us end our hunger-strike had been withdrawn. A week before, I felt I would die for something in which I really believed, but it had all been in vain. I cried that night as I had never cried before. I felt cheated and angry and hated everything about Britain.'

Those words alarmed me but I tried not to show Mairead. From that moment, I became convinced that my lovely Mairead was still a full member of the Provisionals, only now it wasn't that she was a Republican who believed Ireland should be united, but a young woman with hatred in her heart for Britain and everything British.

Throughout the following week, I thought long and hard about what Mairead had said and I understood how she was feeling and why she felt such hatred. I knew that if I had experienced exactly the same circumstances and had been treated in the same way, I, too, would have sought revenge against the people I saw as my oppressors, the British Government and, of course, their military wing, the British Army.

I wondered whether I should stop seeing Mairead, make an excuse that I had to go and work in Germany once more and leave her, forget her and find someone else. I kept wondering whether I was kidding myself about how much I loved her and whether I could love any young woman who so hated Britain. The arguments went back and forth in my mind and I wanted to discuss the whole issue with someone, talk to someone who would understand. Yet I knew in my heart that there was no one to whom I could turn, for if I confessed my love for Mairead

Farrell, a Provo bomber, to anyone, I knew they would immediately inform the authorities. And that would mean not only the end of my relationship with Mairead, but my career with the SAS and the Army.

I loved my work with the SAS; the training, the exercises and the occasional opportunity to carry out some real soldiering, as we had done in the Falklands. In fact, that had been a most terrible experience, something I had no wish to repeat again anywhere in the world. We had nearly frozen to death for three weeks in dreadful conditions and had not even had the satisfaction of getting involved in a fire-fight. Ironically, the only gunfights I had ever been involved in had taken place in Ireland and I expected there might be others to come. For though this was a dirty, internecine war with the enemy masquerading as ordinary citizens going about their business, I felt it was a challenge. Any time of the day or night, on duty or off duty, I knew that I could be shot in the back and killed by a total stranger, man or woman. It was my duty to keep my wits about me and now, unbelievably, I found myself with a once-in-a-lifetime opportunity, living and loving a woman who was totally involved with the enemy, and who had already proved she was perfectly capable of taking an active part in a spectacular bombing.

I had no idea at this time whether Mairead was still an active Provo or not. But most of the time I was with her after her release, I accepted that she was probably still working for them. I had no idea, of course, whether she was personally engaged as a member of an Active Service Unit, or a Provo cell, or whether she was only committed to the cause. It seemed to me that the Provos would leave her alone for some months after her release, simply because of the fear that she could be tailed by one of the security services as a prime suspect.

But I also knew that if I learned anything from her, any hint of a planned attack, a bombing or a shooting, I would do as I had done before and tell someone immediately. I began to feel that I could perhaps help to prevent some outrage by learning something vital from her. That gave me a fresh reason to stay with her, to watch her, to see what I could learn from her. In a way, I wondered if this now meant that I was an Intelligence officer working inside the IRA and the thought made me smile, for two reasons — I was now involved in an inside, undercover job and I had found a reason to continue my affair with Mairead.

I would examine my conscience time and time again, telling myself on the one hand that I was totally and completely stupid to continue the relationship, but knowing that I loved the girl and, the more she told me of the life she had led inside jail, the more I admired her and her courage. I knew my relationships with women had never before been so deep and so meaningful, but now I had found someone who dazzled me with her simplicity and her honesty. And her passion. Whenever I thought of her, I wanted to make love to her. And when I did, it was like magic, a feeling, a buzz I had never felt with anyone else.

And yet, and yet ...

I knew that if we ever came face to face in a life or death situation, I would have to kill her. If I stood between her and the murder of someone or the bombing of innocent people, I believed that I would have the guts, the strength of character, to pull the trigger. Maybe it would have been the SAS training or my sense of right and wrong. I don't know. But I kept thinking of possible scenarios, wondering if I could ever kill her, even if my own life was in danger. And I would wake suddenly at night in my bed in the barracks, sweating from the reality of my dreams, not knowing what I would do if such a situation arose. Sometimes I doubted my own resolve, at others I believed that I would kill her if the circumstances merited it. But in my heart I knew that I would do everything to avoid killing her. I knew I was good, bloody good, at unarmed combat, capable of taking guns or knives off people within seconds. I knew that in any emergency I might face with Mairead, I would resolve to disarm her rather than kill her. As a result of those dreams, I would work out with more gusto and determination than ever before, concentrating on unarmed combat, honing my skills. And that thought gave me the strength to continue my relationship with her.

But I was leaving nothing to chance. She had already proved that she was quite capable of carrying out terrorist acts, even though she had tried to ensure that no one would be injured or killed. With the involved conversations we were now having from time to time, I thought it highly probable that Mairead had committed herself once again to the Republican cause, happy to help the Provos in any way to rid the Province of British troops. I also found myself asking more questions, probing her lifestyle, trying to discover whether she was still working with the Provos, and, more importantly, what she was doing. As before, I hoped that she would still discuss with me any mission that had been planned. But I wasn't counting on that because I feared she might be more professional than ever, especially after ten years' hard training in Armagh jail.

During another wonderful night together, Mairead told me how she had spent her time in jail when she wasn't involved with the dirty protest or refusing food.

She told me as we lay together on the bed after making love, 'It must have taken me two years or more to get my head together and decide that I had to make my time in prison a useful period of my life, rather than living the life of so many of the no-hopers who spent their time bitching and arguing over petty, unimportant rubbish.'

When Mairead talked of life in Armagh, she would always adopt the same position, nestling close into the crook of my arm as though seeking protection. Yet she would hardly ever look at me, but spent the time looking up at the ceiling, as though that helped her recall with accuracy everything that had occurred. It seemed she never wanted to look me in the eye, but needed me there as her support, her protector. I felt that I had become her father confessor, her confidant and her counsellor, and that she needed me in that role so that she could talk through all the horrid incidents of her time inside. And I was happy to do that.

'I deliberately sought out all the hard-line Republicans, particularly those who were doing time, as I was, for being involved with the Provos, either simply as a member or as someone who had carried out missions as I had. It did not take long for there to be a nucleus of perhaps 20 of us, mostly women in their twenties and thirties, who had seen the treatment meted out to friends and families in the Catholic areas by the RUC and the Army.

'All of us had been touched by the Troubles. All of us knew people whose lives had been shattered in one way or another by standing up against the police, the Army or the Loyalists. There were many whose husbands, brothers or boyfriends had been arrested, beaten up and convicted, many on trumped-up charges.

'You just can't understand, Scott, what it is to be a Catholic in Belfast, where all the power lies with the Protestants and the police and where no one will ever believe the word of a Catholic just because he or she is a Catholic. We don't trust anyone in authority any more because they will simply lie or cheat. The only people we trust are the Provos. If anyone is robbed we go to the Provos to sort it out, not the RUC. If anyone is burgled it will be the local Provos who will find and punish the culprit, not the police. They don't want to know about us; they only want to care for their own, the Prods.'

I had to intervene. 'But does everyone think like that?' I asked, somewhat taken aback that all Catholics would think in that way, having no faith or trust in authority.

'I tell you, Scott, I promise you, everyone thinks like that nowadays,' she said, sounding exasperated that I doubted her word. 'The RUC and the Army treat the Catholics like shit all the time and then the politicians in Westminster wonder why the Troubles won't die down and fade away. Scott, you must understand that we have to win this fight, otherwise we will be put down for another 50 years, given the lousy jobs that no Prod will do, given lousy housing, no sports facilities, nowhere for the old people to go because everything is given to the Protestants.

'Drive around the Catholic areas of Belfast and then drive around the Prod areas and you will see the difference. It's as plain as a pike-staff. We see the difference between the two communities and that's why we fight for justice, to be treated as equals, to be offered decent, well-paid jobs like the Prods are offered. The politicians talk about equality of opportunity. It's bullshit, Scott, it's crap; it's lies and they know it's lies. They have kept us down as second-class citizens for centuries and they want that to continue.'

Mairead was becoming more furious and I could see the strong line of her jaw and hear the suppressed anger in her voice. And the more she talked the more sense she made.

'Now you can understand why I joined the Provos and why thousands like me are so determined to win. If we give up the fight now do you really think anyone would give the Catholics anything? Of course they wouldn't. It would be back to the status quo, back to the 'them and us' and we would be subjected to living a second-class life once again.

'Well, Scott, let me tell you. No more. I'm only a young woman but I will do my utmost to overthrow this present system where the Catholics are treated disgracefully compared to the Prods. The time has come for us to stand and fight and we will continue to do so. In Armagh jail, we were all absolutely resolute in our determination to support the Provos and do everything in our power to bring about social change.'

Mairead seemed to calm a little and I asked her whether being a member of the republican group in Armagh had helped pass the time.

She smiled at that. 'Yes, definitely,' she said. 'It was great therapy for me. It also gave me tremendous inner strength and from that time on I had not the slightest trouble or bother from any of the butch bitches or the screws. It was like magic, Scott. Everyone began to be nice to me, polite, helpful, everything. They were charming to all of us who had decided to have our own Provo cell in the jail. But we would only allow those women to join who had been convicted of some offence connected with the Troubles, even if they had not been fully-fledged members of the IRA. Others wanted to join because they knew we had power outside the jail, people who would support us, but we refused to permit it.'

'What did you do?' I asked.

'We held meetings, we discussed matters, we decided how we would behave towards the screws and the prison authorities. And the screws began to treat us as if we really had power, as if we were more important than they were. All of a sudden, they became apprehensive of us, even the bitches who had hurt me and others. From that time on, none of the screws even hinted at beating me. They sensed we had real power and they didn't want to cross our path. We were given little privileges, offered the best food, given the best seats in the TV room and people would clear a space for us at mealtimes. It was great.'

'And you had no more trouble?' I asked.

'Not really. But that only happened in the last three years after all the dirty protest was over and done with. We would have gone on hunger-strike again but we were told not to by the Provos on the outside. They were worried that we might take all the headlines and they wanted to concentrate on other matters. Bobby Sands had stolen the limelight for so long that the Republican leaders became fearful that hunger-strikes could be exceedingly dangerous and unreliable weapons.'

Mairead was once more in full flow, sure of her argument. 'Whenever a hunger-strike was undertaken, the credibility and political direction of the entire movement became dependent on the will power of one individual or a small group of isolated inmates who were out of direct contact with the political leadership. We were considering further hunger-strikes but were told in no uncertain terms that the leadership was tactically, strategically, physically and morally opposed to a hunger-strike.'

'So what else could you do inside?' I asked.

'We never forgot the day that Bobby Sands died. When the news came through some time after midnight on Tuesday, 5 May, 1981, the entire block erupted. Word flashed through the cell block in seconds with people shouting that Bobby Sands, our hero, the Member of Parliament for Fermanagh, South Tyrone, had died of starvation in the Maze prison. In fact, he had died in the H-block hospital after refusing food for 66 days. We had followed every day of his hunger-strike. We knew of all the demands made on the Thatcher government, we knew of all the parades and the street disturbances made in his name. And we had known for days that his death was imminent and we were prepared to yell and scream and make as much din as possible when we heard the news of his murder. Because Scott, believe me, it was murder of an innocent Nationalist by the British Government's régime of brutality towards all Republican prisoners.'

Mairead continued, her voice a combination of anger and pride, 'I would have given my right arm to attend his funeral, but of course, that was impossible. But our hearts were with the 100,000 people who followed his coffin as the hearse carried his body from the family home on the Twinbrook estate through West Belfast to the cemetery.

'As you know, Scott, other deaths followed in the next few weeks, but still the Thatcher Government refused to permit our right to be treated as special prisoners. There was special legislation to deal with Republicans, special courts to hear cases against Republicans and yet, surprise, surprise, we were not to be treated as special prisoners. Totally unfair and unreasonable. So we protested in the only way we could while being banged up. Every time a Republican died as a result of a hunger-strike, we created as much noise and mayhem as possible. The screws would race round the block trying to shut us up but we would take not a blind bit of notice and they could do nothing to stop us. They knew we had a right to protest at people dying from hunger but they still tried to stop our demonstrations. We would hear the news that riots throughout Belfast followed the death of every Republican hunger-striker and the thousands of people who attended their funerals showed the whole world that the vast majority of the Catholic population were solidly behind Sinn Fein and the IRA.

'We would hold our own funeral services in the jail, showing that their deaths were as much a celebration of solidarity between the people and the Provos as they were a solemn show of respect for the martyred volunteer. The ritual displays at the cemetery, when hand-guns were fired over the coffins, were both an expression of genuine communal grief at the loss of a fighter and a reaffirmation of mass support for "The People's Army".'

'Did you get any support from the other prisoners?' I asked.

'Did we?' Mairead said, raising her voice. 'It was fantastic! The prisoners treated us like heroes because we led the demonstrations inside. Many other women decided to join the Provos as a result of those hunger-strikes, exactly the opposite of what the Thatcher Government wanted. We were all proud to be Republicans, Nationalists and Provos and we would sing Irish nationalist songs late into the night which annoyed the screws and the prison authorities

SCOTT GRAHAM

intensely who were all Prods. It was great, Scott, it was great.'

Whenever she spoke of such events, I could see a light in Mairead's eye, a gleam of enthusiasm and, I believed, absolute dedication to the Republican cause. That, of course, worried me and yet part of me admired her for having such belief and absolute faith in the right of her cause, a united Ireland.

'Did you know that I was nearly an MP?' she asked cheekily.

'An MP?' I queried, surprised. 'What do you mean?'

'I mean,' she said, 'that I stood for Parliament, the Irish Parliament. You know, the Dail, the Irish Parliament and all that.'

'When did you do that?' I asked confused and somewhat taken aback.

'The trouble with you's, Scott, is that you's don't read the newspapers.'

'What do you mean?' I replied. 'I do.'

'Aye,' she said, 'probably the fuckin' *Sun*; that's not a newspaper, it's just Thatcher's Tory rag.'

'Well, tell me ... what's this about being an MP?'

'It was decided in 1981, during the hunger-strikes, that I should stand for Parliament in the same way as Kieron Doherty, a hunger-striker who died. He was serving time in the Maze and he was elected to the Dail as the Sinn Fein candidate for Cavan-Monaghan and Bobby Sands stood for the British Parliament. My name was put forward by Sinn Fein to represent Cork, North Central and I was adopted as their candidate. And that was it. I didn't get many votes but I could have been an MP and that would have been sensational.'

'Would you have liked that?' I asked.

'Liked it? Jesus, I would have loved it, though I could never take my seat. But it would have given me so much to do inside. The time would have gone like lightning. And it would have given me a career for when I came out.'

I smiled. 'Bad luck,' I said. 'Now you're out, don't you want to have another go?'

'I would, yes,' she replied. 'I'd love it but I'm not sure whether the Provos want people to stand for Parliament any more.'

On only one occasion during these conversations did Mairead ask me if I wanted to become involved in the cause. And I had to think quickly.

I told her, 'If I had been born a Catholic in West Belfast I am sure I would have the same dedication and enthusiasm for the cause as you do. But I just believe that there must be another way of achieving political ends rather than bombing and killing people.'

But Mairead wanted to argue. 'But they won't give in to any of our demands unless we fight them, wage war, kill them,' she said.

'But there must be another way, Mairead,' I stressed. 'You cannot be in favour of killing innocent people for a political cause.'

'Listen, Scott,' she said, squaring up to me and looking me straight in the eye. 'If there was another way, we would do it that way. But there is no other way. The only time the British Government has given in to anything in Ireland is as a direct result of force.

The British have never given anything away unless under pressure. We have no alternative ... we have to fight. Don't you understand?'

'I understand what you're saying, Mairead,' I replied, 'but I can't go along with killing innocent people. Why don't the Republicans adopt the same political weapon as Gandhi in India, passive resistance? That was brilliant. It worked and the British Government gave them the independence they demanded.'

'But those days are past,' she said. 'Now, in the modern world, passive resistance wouldn't work. It's terrorism that works today, guns and bullets are what counts and that's the way we must fight for our freedom.'

I knew there was no point in continuing the argument and I didn't want to fall out with Mairead. I admired her but I believed in my heart that she was totally wrong, her mind warped by ten years in jail, surrounded by Provo propaganda and Provo beliefs. I understood. Being a member of the Provos had given Mairead status inside the jail and she enjoyed the respect of the other prisoners that had taken some years to achieve. She had gone through some hard times in Armagh but her membership of the Provisional IRA had raised her status until, I presumed, she was one of the leaders inside the jail.

I wanted to change the subject and I asked Mairead how she had passed the time in those years following the hunger-strikes. I also wanted to discover whether she was still a rabid Republican or whether her enthusiasm for the cause had waned the longer she spent behind bars.

'I really did two things after I got my act together,' she said with enthusiasm. 'I became more politically involved and I would chair republican meetings, sort out any problems in our block, and during the last few years I was the person everyone came to for advice and help. I tried to stamp out the bitchiness but that was impossible. I did help to stop the gang bangs and bullying, though not entirely. And the screws would come to me to help sort out any problems, too. I instilled some discipline, telling all the IRA woman that we were part of an army and that we should show an example to the rest of the women by behaving in a disciplined manner.'

For a second, she stopped and then, her voice filled with enthusiasm and some pride, went on, 'You's would have been proud of me, Scott ... it worked. I managed to create discipline in that hell hole and I won their respect.'

But Mairead hadn't finished yet. 'And I had my work.'

'What work?' I asked. 'What do you mean, work?'

'My education,' she replied.

'What education?' I replied. 'You've never told me anything about education.'

'Didn't I?' she asked. 'I thought I had. Well, I decided that I wanted to educate myself, properly. I had done quite well at school and then I heard of the Open University ... you know, where you can educate yourself, wherever you live, by taking a postal course. I took a course in politics and economics and I passed.

It took me three years. It was great for me, Scott. The course took up hours of my time and I not only enjoyed it, but I also learned lots of things I had no idea about. I learned everything about the Republican cause, its history, the heroes, the politicians, the political arguments. Now I'm half-educated and I'm hoping to go to Queen's in Belfast to continue my studies and gain another degree. After that, who knows what will lie ahead?'

'That's great,' I said, 'better than planting bombs.'

'Perhaps,' she said, 'the two careers go together. I haven't decided yet.'

'Decided what to do?'

'No,' she said, 'maybe politics and bombing go together.'

'But you don't want to go back inside do you?'

'Jesus, Scott,' she said, 'that's the last place I want to go. I've done ten years of my life there ... I never want to go back.'

'So?' I said, demanding an answer.

'So, I don't know yet, Scott, I really don't know.'

11

THROUGHOUT THOSE MONTHS IN 1987 when Mairead was studying for her degree and spending time with me, life became hectic. My SAS squadron was on almost constant patrol, not only on the Irish border but in other areas as well. Sometimes, we would spend two weeks or more out in the country, more often than not protecting Loyalists who had been targeted by the Provos, under 24-hour surveillance. On those occasions, our duty was not only to ensure the safety of the targets, but also their wives and children and, at the same time, have contingency plans ready in case a Provo Active Service Unit turned up on the scene.

We would be sent along to a potential target, someone high on the Provo hit list, whom Intelligence had discovered to be particularly vulnerable. We would be introduced to the man and would then discuss what level of security he wanted, and how much we could offer. Mostly, we would be a straightforward four-man patrol, and we might stay with the man and his family for a couple of weeks or so before being relieved by another SAS patrol.

Often, we would live in the man's garage or a barn, keeping strictly to ourselves and not sharing in the family's life. We would be totally self-contained, not even taking a meal or a cup of coffee with the family, and never taking a bath or shower or even a wash in their house. To enter the house would constitute a risk because we could never be 100 per cent sure that the IRA weren't keeping the place under long-distance surveillance, using 'bins' hundreds of yards away. If one or two of us were seen hanging about a farm or a house, it would be immediately obvious that we were SAS or an RUC unit, brought in to guard a target.

These tasks were mostly boring and a complete waste of time. Nothing would ever happen. And yet we had to maintain a 24-hour, round-the-clock guard, taking it in turns to sleep and rest and eat, while the others stayed alert. We were always armed, usually with hand-guns and sub-machine-guns, and always ready for immediate action. But when nothing ever happens it is very difficult to maintain interest and morale. We would need to tell each other that discipline was essential and we would try to pass the time by playing cards, telling jokes and preparing meals. But, no matter what time of the night or day, we would always be on guard duty.

During these duties, when it would be impossible to see or even talk to Mairead, I would have to resort to telling her a succession of white lies; that I had been posted somewhere at a moment's notice to carry out an emergency welding job in Scotland, Liverpool or Newcastle or wherever. I think she believed me because I had never changed my story or my lifestyle ever since we had met. It seemed as though I was a straightforward, boring welder, who spent his life travelling from one well-paid job to another with no interest in the politics of Ireland.

There were times when I wondered whether Mairead had another boyfriend, and I once asked her if she had met anyone else. When I raised the question she laughed. 'Well,' she began 'you know I have nobody else in my life apart from you, but you remember Sean McDermott, the young lad that was shot dead by the off-duty peeler after The Conway — well, the Provos wanted him to be my boyfriend. He told me nearly everything I knew about the Provos, and it was Sean who wanted me as part of his ASU. That's why I went, really. But there was nothing between us.'

'Nothing?' I asked.

She smiled at me fondly, and replied 'Nothing. Cross my heart. What you's got to understand is that the Provos like to keep everyone in the family. They encourage girls like me, keen members, only to go around with other IRA people, to mix together, go to all the same republican clubs and gatherings; they want us to find boyfriends in the organisation. It makes sense, of course. It also means that the commanders can keep tabs on us — they know who we are seeing, meeting, dating, sleeping with. Pillow talk is kept within the organisation and secrecy is very, very important. The

IRA suspects everybody is a traitor. Sometimes, they'll make out that one of their members is going out with a girl who has been imprisoned so that the authorities will permit him to visit her as her boyfriend. Sometimes they hardly even know each other, but it gives them both a chance to prove that they are both committed to the IRA, and also provides a ready-made access for prison visits which is always useful for passing information in and out of jails.'

Sometimes, when we were alone together, Mairead would ask me whether I was married, asking me if every time I went away I was really returning to my wife in England. And she would constantly demand to know if I had any other secret girlfriends, hidden somewhere on the mainland.

'You must have ... you must have,' she would joke whenever she raised the subject.

'Well, I don't have anyone but you,' I would answer truthfully.

'Are you's sure?' she would demand, and I would tell her once again that she was the only girl in my life.

'I just don't believe you's,' she would say, 'a beautiful hunk of a man like you and you've only got one girlfriend?'

'You're enough of a handful for any man,' I would tell her and she loved hearing that.

'Am I really a handful?' she would ask teasingly.

'What do you think?' I would reply.

'Well, if you mean can I ever get enough of you, the answer's "no",' she would say.

'Don't you get your fair share?'

'When I'm with you's I do,' she would reply, 'but

when I'm not with you's, I miss you and I want you so much my whole body aches.'

'You're just over-sexed,' I would reply.

And when those conversations came to that point, Mairead would demand that we have sex once more, there and then, even if we were running late or had only just finished making love. Usually, on those occasions, Mairead would want passionate, wild sex, wanting me to bite her hard all over her body, and she would orgasm uncontrollably.

I would sometimes wonder when we were making love so violently how she could ever sustain her interest in the Provisional IRA and the nationalist cause. Politics would seem a million miles from her life as an Irish woman with a family, a boyfriend and a possible career. And I would wonder whether the passion she showed me in our love-making was matched by the passion she showed her IRA colleagues as they went about their deadly business.

Sometimes, too, the SAS took an active part in that deadly business.

Only on very rare occasions was the SAS given such excellent prior notice of intended Provo targets as we received before the Ballysillen shoot-out, enabling us to set up first-class OPs so that we could keep round-the-clock surveillance on a particular target. Unfortunately, the level of information passed to us was nowhere near that calibre, but we understood that anyone targeted by the IRA had to be protected. The number of occasions when SAS troops laid in wait for Provo gunmen and bombers and managed to catch them red-handed were very few and far between throughout the 1980s. I was fortunate, however, to be involved in one other major fire-fight with the Provos, this one bigger, more dramatic, more challenging and, fortunately for many innocent men, women and children, brilliantly successful.

The gun battle, which cost the IRA its highest number of casualties in an exchange with the security forces, occurred during the early evening of Friday, 8 May, 1987, in the village of Loughgall, a lovely Irish beauty spot on the back road between Portadown and Armagh. Loughgall was a perfect target for an IRA bombing spectacular for the village, with a population of only 250, is a founding centre of Orangemen and the population is almost exclusively Protestant.

I was one of the 20 SAS men detailed to watch the Loughgall police station. We had been tipped off by Intelligence that a major attack had been planned. From the beginning of 1987, the IRA had been targeting police stations and security bases, trying to bomb them out of existence. The attack on Loughgall was the twelfth that year and the seventh during the previous fortnight. Most of the earlier attacks had been with home-made mortars and though the police stations and bases were hit no one had been injured and little structural damage had occurred. Only this time, we were waiting for them.

Unfortunately, Intelligence did not know the precise time or date of the expected attack but they were confident it was planned as a major, high-profile hit. We had been in position for 48 hours, keeping the police station under round-the-clock surveillance while maintaining a low profile in the surrounding fields which provided adequate cover. Only a few villagers knew of our presence because we had moved in under cover of darkness, setting up OPs well screened from any access routes. Orders had been given to vacate the police station when we moved into position because Intelligence told us the Provos intended to destroy the entire place with one huge bomb. Worried that they were operating in a well-guarded, high-profile Protestant village where strangers would be instantly spotted, Intelligence reports indicated that the Provos would use a large squad of well-armed men in case the bombers ran into trouble. It was exactly the scenario the SAS loved — setting a trap for a load of unsuspecting killers.

We knew they would be well armed possibly with sub-machine-guns, AK-47 assault rifles and hand-guns. We were well armed, too.

After taking a meal break, my four man unit had just moved back into position in the hedgerow across the road from the deserted police station. Behind us was a football pitch. Other SAS units were hidden in hedgerows to the left and right of us and on the other side of the road. It was still light when I heard the unmistakable rumble of a tractor or mechanical digger a few hundred yards away. One of the patrol tapped my foot at the same time as I saw the digger slowly making its way down the main village street towards the police station and, more importantly right into the trap we had set. I quietly pushed forward the safety catch of my GPMG and waited. I looked at my mates and saw they were also ready for action, their rifles and sub-machine-guns cocked, no one moving a muscle as their eyes watched the approaching digger.

I could see the driver of the digger and standing either side of him were two men dressed in dark boiler suits, their faces covered with masks. They both appeared to be carrying what I presumed were rifles. Now I was certain — this was it.

I felt my body tense and knew we were about to see some real action. It seemed that we had trained for this moment for ever and I wondered if I would be able to carry out all the procedures which I had practised a thousand times before. I knew what I had to do and I hoped everyone felt as confident.

Suddenly, my attention was drawn away from the digger by the sound of a car or van coming towards us from the same direction, some 20 or 30 yards behind the slow-moving digger. By now, the lumbering yellow digger was little more than 50 yards from the police station and I was certain the three men on board were IRA.

'Shit,' I thought to myself, 'fuck the van. If that van gets between us and the digger we will have to hold our fire. And that could provide an escape for the bombers.'

The blue Hiace van overtook the digger and came to a halt smack opposite the police station. Now I was watching both the van and the digger, wondering what the hell was going on. The digger driver slowed down and turned towards the entrance of the deserted police station, and, with the three men still riding on board, smashed through the wire perimeter fence and trundled on towards the two-storey white building. Seconds before the digger crashed into the building, the three men jumped from the vehicle and began to run back towards the road through the gap in the fence the digger had made.

But my attention was suddenly drawn to the Hiace van. The rear doors opened and half-a-dozen men, also dressed in dark boiler suits and wearing masks, jumped out. All were carrying guns, some were rifles, others hand-guns. This was it.

'Fire!' someone shouted and we opened up. As I aimed and emptied a full magazine at the gunmen in the street, I noticed the digger driver and his two mates running towards the van. But when they heard the sound of non-stop firing, they must have realised they were under serious attack and they darted away, running flat out up the road.

As I reloaded for a second time, an almighty explosion rent the air and the entire roof of the police station lifted off, hurling thousands of bits of masonry, tiles and wood into the sky before they came crashing down around us. As the noise of the explosion abated, the sound of the gun battle took over once again. The Provos from the van were not running this time, but standing their ground and firing back at us. They took up positions behind the vehicle and kept up sustained shooting. The crescendo grew as both sides traded gunfire but the Provos were difficult to hit, though the van took a hammering from our non-stop onslaught. Some SAS men were detailed to drop back and circle round so they could take up positions from where they could pick off the gunmen. A few minutes later, I saw three or four IRA men go down, but it didn't stop the fire-fight.

One or two of the Provos, realising that their

position was rapidly becoming hopeless, decided to make a break for it, legging it up the road. But they didn't get far. I knew that more SAS men were in position to cut off their retreat and I heard them open up as the Provo gunmen ran towards them. In quick succession, the IRA men were gunned down.

'Cease fire!' someone shouted and in an instant there was a near-silence. Slowly, a few SAS men moved forward towards the men lying in the road around the van. But no one was taking any chances. Some troops advanced to examine the bodies while others moved with them, their rifles at their shoulders, ready to open fire in a split-second if any Provo should be so foolish as to try one last shot. No one did. All were dead. The fire-fight had lasted nearly ten minutes.

Moments later, a shout went up and we hit the ground. Two suspects had been seen crawling along a ditch in a field by the side of the road. I heard two orders bark out and then the sound of two magazines being emptied ... then silence once again.

That silence was broken by the sound of Army Land Rovers and Army trucks driving at speed into the village. Overhead, I could hear the whirring sound of a chopper homing in on the village, searching for any possible survivors trying to make their escape. Within minutes, Loughgall village had been sealed off as RUC personnel were brought in to take over control of the situation. But SAS commanders on the scene weren't happy that all the gunmen had been accounted for. The initial body count showed eight dead, but conflicting reports pointed to the possibility of one or two other gunmen who might have escaped the trap.

A little later, another helicopter was scrambled and searched the area with a spotlight, providing light for SAS and RUC personnel to comb the entire area where the gunmen were last seen, just in case others were found. Dogs were also drafted in to check the area but two hours after the last round was fired, the search for other gunmen was called off. All were satisfied that a mistake had been made and no IRA man had escaped the net. When the body count was finally announced eight IRA men were dead and, unfortunately, one innocent passing motorist had been killed, caught in cross-fire.

The killing of eight well-armed IRA gunmen also provided the RUC with details of the importance of the dead men or, more specifically, the weapons they had been carrying that night. Police forensic examination revealed that the weapons used by the Provos had been used before in seven killings and nine attempted killings. One .357 Luger magnum revolver had been taken from the body of a part-time RUC constable who had been shot dead during a gun and bomb attack on the RUC station at Ballygawley, County Tyrone, in December 1985. The same Luger had also been used in three further killings and an attempted murder. Other weapons recovered, which had all been used previously by the IRA in other killings, included three Heckler & Koch rifles, an FN rifle, two .223 FN rifles and a 12-bore shotgun.

Among the Provos killed that night were two of their most prominent members, Jim Lynagh, 32, who had been a Sinn Fein councillor for Monaghan, and Pat Kelly, 30, a married man with three children, and the

Commanding Officer of the East Tyrone Brigade. IRA sympathisers spoke of the 'devastating loss of two of the most dedicated men to the Republican cause'.

Indeed, the East Tyrone Brigade had been one of the most active IRA cells in the Province for nearly ten years. They began the campaign to destroy local police stations throughout Tyrone and then would intimidate builders engaged in reconstructing the buildings, threatening the men that if they continued to help re-build premises blown up by the IRA then they and their families would be killed. Understandably, such threats worked and local men were never invited to take part in any re-building work. Instead, skilled workers from other parts of the Province would be drafted in, men unknown to the locals. Even these strangers had to keep a low profile and would be ferried back and forth in windowless vans. If building work had to be carried out in south Armagh, much of which was a no-go area to the security forces, the builders would be brought in and taken home each day by helicopter.

There had also been another particularly evil and sinister side to the East Tyrone Brigade. For some years they had been deliberately targeting and killing lone Protestant farmers and farming families with only one son. Several unarmed farmers whose families had lived in the area for generations had been shot at their doors and in front of their families by the Brigade, leading some Unionists to claim that the IRA was waging a genocidal campaign against Protestants.

In the previous ten years, the East Tyrone Brigade had been responsible for killing 50 Protestant civilians, mainly farmers. They had also murdered about 50 RUC personnel and more than 60 UDR soldiers. Before the SAS were brought in to try to stem the slaughter, it seems that the IRA had a free run throughout the border area for much of the previous decade.

Back at barracks that night, we were all in a jubilant mood and the beer flowed freely until well after midnight. I deliberately ate a damn good meal after 48 hours on surveillance duty, and the next few hours were magic and we relived the incident time and again. Over the years, the SAS had taken a lot of stick, mainly because we hadn't arrested or shot enough Provos. But tonight we had done everything right and eight of their top gunmen were dead.

We always felt that the politicians in London made us fight the IRA with one hand tied behind our backs. And we were certain that if the authorities had given the SAS a free rein in the Province, we would have finished off the IRA years before. But we weren't allowed to fight the way we could have done, with no rules. We had to obey the rules, keep to the stupid 'yellow card', and were never permitted to take the initiative. We had been taught that 'all's fair in love and war'. Not in this war it wasn't. The IRA could play as dirty as they wanted while we had to play by the bloody rules.

After that success, I would wonder how Mairead and I could ever have a life together. She seemed so committed to the Republican cause and the IRA gunmen who carried out their evil work and I was actively involved in killing as many of them as possible. I doubted strongly that I would ever be able to admit to her that I was a badged member of the SAS, for the IRA always referred to Britain's élite troops as 'death squads'. Understandably, of course, we never saw it that way but we always realised that the SAS would be brought in to carry out dirty work on behalf of the Government.

Throughout the summer of 1987, I spent much of my time in England at the SAS headquarters in Hereford, but whenever I did return to the Province I would find as much time as possible to spend my off-duty hours with Mairead. When in England I led a lonely life, missing Mairead far more than I realised I ever would when we were together. As a result, I found myself drinking too much when off duty and feeling nostalgic and somewhat melancholic, missing her fun and spontaneity.

I wondered whether our affair was simply a case of a love too far, an impossible dream which we would never be able to realise. When apart, we were enemies at war and yet, when together, the strongest of lovers. There was no denying that when we were together in Belfast, we thoroughly enjoyed ourselves.

I also wanted to live with Mairead to see whether the magic we enjoyed during the few hours we spent together would still be as interesting, vital and dynamic after spending weeks and months together. We managed the odd weekend, the occasional night, but most of the time we would only have three or four hours together, during which we both wanted to spend most of the time cuddling, kissing and making love.

Only once did we spend any length of time discussing the possibility of living together, like man and wife, on a permanent basis.

'Would you ever think of coming to England?' I asked as my way of leading the conversation into discussing the possibility of living together.

'I've never thought of it,' she replied, 'and I've never been invited.'

'Do you think it might be a good idea?' I enquired.

'Yes, maybe,' she replied, once again giving me a non-committal answer.

'We could perhaps go over for a couple of weeks, or take a holiday in the sun together.'

'I'd love that,' she said. 'I'd love to go to Spain or Italy with you and spend two weeks in the sun.'

'Me, too,' I replied.

'Really?' she said, surprise in her voice.

'Yes, really,' I said.

'Why have you never mentioned it?' she asked. 'One of the reasons I always thought you had a wife and kids back home was because you never suggested taking a holiday with me.'

'I didn't think you would come,' I replied. 'That's why I never raised the question.'

'You's so silly,' she said. 'Spending two weeks with you in the sun would be absolute heaven for me.'

'Really?' I asked.

'Yes,' she said and began kissing me. 'Then we could do this together all day and all night, and I could buy a bikini so we could do it in the sea as well.'

'You're insatiable,' I said, teasingly.

'It's just that I'm so keen,' she replied. 'Remember, Scott, I've ten years to make up.'

'I know, I know,' I said, and I wondered if those

ten lost years really did play that large a role in her thinking.

It was while we were having a cup of tea later that I suddenly asked, 'Have you ever thought of living with a man?'

'With you?' she asked directly.

'Yes, with me.'

'Of course I have,' she said. 'Are you's silly in the head or something? Sometimes, Scott, I think you's must not have the slightest idea how women think.'

'What do you mean?' I asked, feeling somewhat foolish.

'You should know from the way I am with you ... the very fact that I want to screw you whenever I see you ... the fact that we're still going out together after knowing each other for twelve years and more. I've never wanted another man since the time we first met and I was only a schoolgirl then. I've loved you forever, Scott. You must have been blind not to see that.'

'I was never sure,' I replied honestly. 'I knew that you loved the sex but I wasn't sure whether you wanted me. You always seemed to have so many other things on your mind.'

'Such as?' she replied quickly.

'Such as your university degree, your family, the cause ...'

'You mean the IRA,' she said, interrupting me.

'Yes,' I said. 'Every time we discuss your time inside and the IRA you seem to come alive, to change into someone with a passion as though it interests you far, far more than your love life. So I decided to wait, to see what you would choose to do.'

'I don't do any more of that,' Mairead said.

'What do you mean?'

'Well, they think I'm being watched so I only run a few messages for them.'

'Watched by the Special Branch?' I asked.

'Something like that,' she said.

'And are you?' I asked.

'Sometimes I think I am being followed, at other times I don't think they're taking any notice of me whatsoever. You know, Scott, I never want to go back inside that hell hole again. I couldn't face doing another ten or twenty years inside ... it would kill me. I can think about the cause and discuss it with people and since studying I am far better educated about the politics of the whole ghastly business. But the days of me taking part in anything are gone. They understand.'

'Who's they?' I asked and immediately bit my lip, for I thought that was one question too many.

'Oh, you know,' she said.

'The Provos?'

'Something like that,' she said, and she smiled at what I hoped she believed was my naïveté.

'Remember, Mairead,' I began, 'I don't know anything about your other life. I just know it's so risky and to me, so stupid, because you can get banged up for ten years. Next time it would probably be for 20 years and I think that's a waste of your life. I would love to live with you in England, away from all this, but I don't know whether you could live away from Belfast and the Troubles. Part of me senses that you thrive on it and that I'm your plaything.'

'Don't be so daft,' she countered. 'But you are right

in some respects. If I lived in England I would forever be listening to the radio, watching the TV news, wanting to know how the struggle was going back home. And I don't know whether that would be fair on you. I would never be able to forget my baggage, not after my experiences inside. I will never forget those years.'

'And do you ever want children?' I asked.

Mairead didn't reply but looked me straight in the eye, as though I had asked her a question for which she had no reply.

'What do you's think?' she asked.

'Well, it's natural and you're a very animal sort of person,' I replied.

'Yes, you're right. I would,' she said. As an afterthought, she added, 'Then I could educate them in the way I would want to, telling them about the Troubles. But I don't think I would want to bring them up here. It's an awful existence for kids.'

'And what about a husband?' I teased.

She hit me then, punching my shoulder quite hard. In mock concern at my injury I rubbed it gently as though soothing the bruise. Then I grabbed her and pulled her towards me, laid her on her back and began to kiss her.

'Kiss me all over,' she said. 'Bite me ... you know I love that.'

After it was all over and we were lying close together, Mairead asked, 'Would you really consider settling down with me?'

'Yes, I would,' I said, 'but not here in Ireland. I would want to take you away from the Troubles, to settle in England or maybe overseas somewhere, otherwise I fear you might want to return and that would never work.'

'You's do know me,' she replied. 'And here was I thinking you were stupid. Sorry.'

'That's OK,' I said.

We reached no conclusion and, as I drove her back to the bus station that night, I wondered what Mairead would have said if I had owned up to being one of the SAS men involved in the Loughgall massacre. Thoughts like that, would cross my mind and I feared that, if ever she discovered my real job, she would never speak to me again. We had just been talking about living together, perhaps having children together, but I wondered whether Mairead, too, was telling white lies. Something told me that she was not being entirely honest and I suspected that she was more involved with the Provos than she admitted. So, we were about to say goodbye to each other, perhaps for a week or a month, and yet when we were together we enjoyed a magic affair, exciting, passionate and sexually ecstatic.

But I knew that if we weren't being honest with each other at this stage then there was little chance that a full-time relationship would survive very long. I drove back to the base that night feeling disappointed with our conversation, because we had talked about matters of real importance but had reached no conclusion. I decided to wait, to see how Mairead would react now that we had discussed the possibility of a future together. And, for the first time in my career with the SAS, I began to think what else I could do with my life. Although I loved soldiering and enjoyed the privilege of being an SAS man, I didn't really want to

SCOTT GRAHAM

spend the next ten years on patrol on the Irish border
with occasional trips back to Hereford for R & R and a
few courses.

The following morning, I was told that I was being
posted back to Hereford and I felt that fate had
intervened to make sure that Mairead and I would
never have enough time to make the decision whether
we did want to set up home together. I didn't know
what I would tell her. In some ways, our open
conversation about our future had offered a way
forward for us. Now it seemed that the Army was
about to snap it shut again.

It even seemed to me that the SAS could have been
listening to our conversation and decided that we were
spending too much time together, becoming too
involved and that they had decided the time had come
to separate us, making it difficult, if not impossible, for
the affair to move on to another, more serious level. I
knew that was nonsense but it showed me that I was
becoming somewhat paranoid about the whole damn
relationship. I needed to get a grip of myself.

I would spend three months in England, most of
the time at Hereford but some weeks in London. I was
bored and wanted to return to Northern Ireland and
Mairead. Two remarkable events, however, were about
to shatter my life and end Mairead's extraordinary
secret life as an IRA operative. The first was an
appalling IRA act that repulsed the world; the other, the
start of a chain of events that would lead from a
building site in Belfast to a sunny Sunday afternoon on
the Rock of Gibraltar and cold-blooded killings at the
hands of my mates in the SAS.

12

No single place name in Northern Ireland arouses as much emotion as the word 'Enniskillen'. More than ten years after the name hit TV and newspaper headlines around the world, Enniskillen still conjures up all the horrors of sectarian violence in Northern Ireland.

It was on Sunday, 8 November, 1987, when an IRA bomb exploded without warning at a Remembrance Day parade, killing 11 innocent people and seriously injuring 63 other men, women and children. The ordinary families of Enniskillen were gathered around the town cenotaph to pay homage to the dead of two world wars. Written on the statue were all the names of those local people who had died serving their country.

Without any warning whatsoever, and for no

apparent reason, the IRA triggered a huge bomb that brought tons of rubble down on the 70 people who were standing quietly in prayer around the cenotaph. A television crew captured the agonies of those injured on film, but the pictures were so horrific that the film was never shown on television.

That day's horror shocked so many people and turned so many others away from the Republican cause that its effects took years for Sinn Fein/IRA to live down. Stunned by the worldwide outcry to the Poppy Day bombing, the IRA issued an official statement saying that the leadership 'deeply regretted the catastrophic consequences' of the bombing and claimed there had been a deadly blunder. The IRA statement admitted that one of their Active Service Units had planted the bomb which was targeted at Crown Forces rather than civilians. They claimed the bomb could have been detonated early by army experts trying to block the IRA's remote-controlled attack, and maintained that the bomb blew up without ever being triggered by an IRA radio signal. No one believed the IRA's version of events.

Only days later, when the political storm over the Poppy Day bombing in Enniskillen was still bringing condemnation, an operation began which would have repercussions the following year when my mates in the SAS, working in plain clothes and under cover, would kill three IRA suspects at point-blank range as they strolled together in the sun on the Rock of Gibraltar.

Eric Martin was the managing director of H & J Martin, a major building contractor whose yard and offices were in the Ormeau Road, South Belfast. And his wife was a sister of Lord Lowry, then Northern Ireland's Lord Chief Justice. Technical Intelligence suggested that an Active Service Unit had targeted Eric Martin and planned to murder him.

The reason — his firm carried out building work for the security forces, constructing heavily fortified police stations throughout Northern Ireland, it had fortified barracks for British Army personnel stationed in the Province, and had fortified check-points and construction work for Government offices and buildings.

Builders had always been a main target for the IRA. They would not only strike at the firm's offices and yards, and particularly the bosses, but also anyone who worked for the firms, whether they were carpenters, bricklayers or even secretaries and young apprentices. To the IRA, anyone who worked for a firm that carried out building work for the security forces was fair game, for they were determined to bring a halt to all such construction, making their task of killing and bombing security forces personnel that much easier. Since the Troubles began in the 1970s, more than 100 innocent building workers have been killed by IRA gunmen.

Eric Martin, however, was a prime target for the IRA, for his firm was not only one of the principal employers of workers engaged in construction work for the RUC and the Army but he employed more than 200 skilled and semi-skilled workers at sites around the Province. The IRA believed that if Eric Martin was murdered then his firm would fold, taking 200 skilled men out of the construction industry and making it even more difficult for the security forces and the British Government to find anyone with the courage to continue the heavy building programme necessary to protect the RUC, the Army and government officials and workers. As a result, extraordinary precautions were taken, on the advice of the Special Branch, to protect H & J Martin's workforce, ferrying them in armoured vans around the countryside and even employing helicopters to chopper them to and from out-of-the-way construction sites in South Armagh, the IRA stronghold which for many years was a 'no-go' area to British troops as well as the RUC.

The Tasking and Co-ordination Group, the senior Intelligence co-ordinators from MI5, MI6, the Special Branch, Army Intelligence, the RUC, and the SAS, decided that a high-priority, special 24-hour guard should be kept on Eric Martin, to be undertaken by both the SAS and the HMSU.

It was decided that a four man SAS unit should be tasked to protect Eric Martin and his wife and children at their 1920s mansion home, a detached house surrounded by open fields in Belfast.

The SAS unit were housed in the double garage, a few yards from the main house and they lived there day and night, taking it in turns to stand guard during the hours of darkness. They never went near the main house but ate, cooked, slept and washed in the garage while keeping watch over the Martin household and patrolling the grounds, usually under cover of darkness.

HMSU officers would take Eric Martin to work each and every day and ferry him back home at night. But so concerned were the authorities for his safety, that Martin was driven in a Range Rover with three other Special Branch cars escorting, two in the lead and one behind his vehicle. Before setting out from his home or from work, another Branch car would check the road a few hundred yards ahead and radio back when they believed it was safe for the convoy to proceed. Each morning, bomb disposal experts would check the dirt track and the hedgerows leading to the main road in case any explosives had been laid. And sniffer dogs, trained to smell out explosives, would also be used each day to check fields on either side of the first few hundred yards of his route to work. Nothing was left to chance.

H & J Martin's extensive building yard in Ormeau Road, 200 yards from the North of Ireland Sports Ground, had always been well-guarded and fortified with closed-circuit video cameras and security officers on 24-hour guard duty. But now, Special Branch officers were drafted in to re-check the works, as well as to examine the details of all recent workers taken on by the firm in case one of them was in fact a Republican sympathiser, deliberately planted to spy on Eric Martin. For some years, workers employed by the firm had been routinely checked by the RUC for any past terrorist or Republican connections, but this process would now be intensified.

Whenever Eric Martin needed to attend business meetings away from his offices, the same convoy procedure would be employed and armed Special Branch officers would accompany him as his own personal bodyguards. If he and his wife were invited out for the evening to dinner or a concert, the same intense protection would be brought into action. Even when Eric Martin went hunting, as he loved to do during the winter months, HMSU officers would accompany him to and from the hunt. They would then remain in their cars, driving along the country lanes in an effort to keep their man in view as he cantered and galloped across the fields. Usually, they would need to resort to binoculars when the hunt moved off into deep country, but they would try to keep him safely in their sights throughout his day's sport.

In early December 1987, a few weeks after the security net was thrown around Eric Martin, officers from the HMSU, who had been assigned to watch over him, noticed a young man acting suspiciously, seemingly keeping an eye on the H & J Martin building yard. An E4A officer was assigned to drive up and down the Ormeau Road, taking photographs of the suspect with a covert camera. After four or five attempts, the photographs were good enough for the man to be accurately identified.

Officers methodically sifted through the files of all known IRA sympathisers and former members and came across their man. He was Daniel McCann, aged 30, a butcher from the Lower Falls area of Belfast who had been jailed in 1980 for possession of explosives. In December 1983, however, McCann had been cleared on a charge of possessing firearms. Since that time, however, the Special Branch had learned that McCann had been promoted to become IRA Commander for the district of Clonard in West Belfast. As a result, McCann was high on the list of terrorists to be kept under Special Branch surveillance because the authorities knew that he would be involved in planning, if not carrying out, active service missions.

Nine months earlier, in March 1987, McCann had asked for police protection, complaining that he was a marked man after Loyalist gunmen, one armed with a sawn-off shotgun, burst into his home in Cavendish Street one night when he was out. He had no idea of the identity of the gunmen but was certain that they must have been members of a Loyalist paramilitary unit who had targeted him.

From the moment McCann was identified as the man watching Eric Martin's movements a close surveillance Det unit was detailed to watch his every step. Days later, he would be seen in the lane leading to Eric Martin's home and he was also spotted in the Mary Peters Running Track from where he would have had a clear view of Martin's house. The TCG became convinced that McCann was planning an operation for one of the IRA's Active Service Units. His main task would be to decide the best possible method of attack, whether to use a UCBT, a bomb or the more direct method of using a gunman, perhaps in a car or on a motor-cycle, to shoot Eric Martin at some point during his four-mile journey to and from his works. The TCG knew that McCann would also be responsible for organising the bomb-making equipment deemed necessary and any weapons the Active Service Unit would require. He would also be responsible for organising the best method of escape for the unit after they had completed their deadly mission.

While the Det surveillance team was watching McCann's every movement, they discovered that he occasionally met a young, petite, dark-haired woman whom they could not identify. They saw the two of them walking down the Ormeau Road together not far from H & J Martin's offices. Once again, photographs were obtained of the young woman from the covert camera, and again a detailed search was undertaken for known Provo sympathisers, including not only all those young women who had been arrested, charged and sentenced for IRA activities, but also those young women suspected of being sympathetic to the Republican cause.

The RUC were conscious that the Provos used many young women to carry messages, ferry arms and Semtex, run errands and help the IRA in small, incidental ways without ever becoming hard-line activists. The police had found many instances when young women with babies had been used to ferry a variety of different objects, often in their babies' prams. And many of these young women were never identified or even questioned about their activities. As a result, few ended up identified with their photographs neatly filed away for instant access. First reports from the police archives were negative — they could find no identity for the young woman.

But the Det team were not stood down. They

continued to keep a 24-hour watch on McCann and managed to obtain better quality photographs of the mystery woman. This time, the photo library revealed that the young woman was probably Mairead Farrell, but the fact that her hair had been cut short had so changed her look that they were still not 100 per cent sure that their identification was correct. The RUC, of course, knew her parents' address and this was staked out. It was only 48 hours later that the Det team reported back that the young woman who walked out of Mairead's home was the same woman they had photographed with McCann.

Two days later, Mairead Farrell was once more seen in the Ormeau Road, this time making enquiries about renting a flat which all but overlooked H & J Martin's building yard, a prime spot from which to survey and detail Eric Martin's daily movements, timing them to the second. Anyone watching from that first-floor window would also have been able to check the level of protection the man was being given and work out the best way to attack the man or his vehicle.

As a result, another E4A team was tasked to keep a watch on Mairead's movements. Throughout the week, Mairead Farrell was seen going to Queen's University each morning, where in October 1987, she had enrolled as a first-year arts student in the faculty of economic and social sciences. One of her subjects was political science. She was also traced going shopping for her parents, visiting the centre of Belfast after finishing her studies at Queen's, meeting Danny McCann, not only in the Ormeau Road but also at other rendezvous in pubs and cafés in Belfast city centre. She was also seen taking a train from Belfast main station to Marino station where she would meet a well-built man who was waiting for her in a parked car, the car not parked close to the station but some distance away, as though he did not want people to see that he and Mairead were meeting. Initial reports showed that after the car moved off, the E4A team was unable to follow or say where the couple went or what happened.

The second time the couple met, however, an ID was made of the car and the number was found to belong to a 'Q' car used by members of the SAS billeted at the hangar at Aldergrove. An immediate check showed that the man who borrowed the car on that particular night was Sergeant Scott Graham.

When these facts were reported to the TCG in Belfast the following day, there was surprise and shock. No one in the room had any knowledge that an SAS Sergeant had been detailed to work under cover with Mairead Farrell, whose name, of course, was known to all those present. The SAS representative said he had no knowledge that Graham had been assigned to get close to Farrell. All the other senior officers attending the TCG meeting that day said that they would order an urgent investigation within their own areas of responsibility to see whether Graham was working under cover for one of the agencies other than the SAS.

The TCG agreed that every effort would be made to find out what the hell Graham was doing, secretly meeting a known Provo bomber who had served ten years for The Conway hotel blast. Of course, in Northern Ireland, such situations had arisen before when investigations had been carried out at the same time by two separate agencies which had no idea the other was also involved in the same line of enquiry. To avoid such mistakes had been one of the primary reasons for the three TCGs to be set up, one covering Belfast, the other in the south of the Province and the third covering the north of the country.

An officer who attended the TCG get-togethers explained what happened at the next meeting. 'The SAS representative said that he had checked out the facts and was now certain that Sergeant Graham had taken out that particular vehicle on the night in question and he gave the time the car was signed out to Graham and the time its return was logged. From enquiries, it seemed that Graham had been in charge of the car the entire time. All the other representatives present said that, from their enquiries, there was no question that Sergeant Scott Graham of the SAS had been detailed to be involved in any surveillance work involving Mairead Farrell.

'The meeting decided that nothing whatsoever should be said to Graham at that stage, but that MI5 would be tasked with not only trying to obtain photographs of Graham with Farrell but, more importantly, ascertaining precisely why Graham and Farrell were meeting in secret. The security service was also ordered to keep a 24-hour watch on Mairead Farrell and to prepare a dossier of her life, friends and acquaintances. The RUC were asked to prepare a report on Farrell's time in Armagh jail so they might be better able to judge to what extent she had embraced or turned her back on the Republican cause. The SAS representative was detailed to keep a 24-hour watch on Graham on the condition that he should not be apprised of what was going on.

'One senior RUC man asked, "What the hell can the man be doing?"

'He addressed the question to the meeting in general but, more particularly, to the senior SAS representative.

'"I am at a loss at this stage to tell you what is behind this," the senior SAS officer replied, "but now we know more of the facts, we shall find out as soon as possible and report back."

'At the TCG meeting the following week, MI5 reported that no contact had taken place between Graham and Farrell since their investigations began and their enquiries among the other Security Services, including the RUC Special Branch, revealed that Graham was not working for any of the services in any undercover role.

'The MI5 officer told the meeting, "We have to assume that Graham is either working on his own in some rogue way or that he is simply having a relationship with Farrell. We don't know whether he is aware that Farrell is a member of the Provisional IRA; whether he knows she has served ten years for planting bombs; or whether the couple might simply be enjoying a relationship.

'"And there is another most important point. It may be that Farrell knows that Graham is with the SAS and is waiting for the right moment to have him

288

assassinated by the Provos. We have known IRA girls to act as honey traps many times before. It's one of the oldest tricks in the book. What seems odd in this case, is that Graham and Farrell have obviously known each other for some weeks and most honey traps are sprung within hours."

'The SAS representative confirmed to the meeting that during off-work periods, Graham had spent the entire week either at the hangar or out with friends, visiting pubs.

'He also told the meeting, "It so happens that within a couple of days, Graham is scheduled to return to Hereford because his Squadron is due to take over SP Duty during the next few months. There will be no question of him being in the Province while on SP duty, unless, of course, on some special project, but when that happens, as you all know, it's strictly an "in-out" job. Their feet hardly touch the ground."

'"Are we going to tackle Graham about this one?" the RUC representative asked.

'"We can simply keep an eye on his post and, if necessary, intercept any letters to check their contents," the SAS man volunteered.

'A senior officer asked, "What do we know about this man? Is he likely to be involved with the Provos or do we think he just fancies this girl?"

'The SAS man gave a brief resumé of Scott Graham's military career, pointing out the major highlights, the countries he had visited and the tasks he had been ordered to carry out. He pointed out that his disciplinary record was good, although he had been in trouble on a few occasions but nothing serious. He reported that Graham had never been on orders or brought before the Adjutant or Commanding Officer on any charge. His record noted that he had been in minor skirmishes, usually as a result of excessive drinking. He also had a reputation in the Squadron for being a 'ladies' man'.

'The SAS representative said, "Graham is a popular man with his comrades, he gets on well with his officers and has a reputation as a first-class soldier. His life is the Regiment and he would never do anything to put that at risk. I have no reason to suppose that his relationship with the girl is anything but sexual."

'The MI5 representative asked what was known of Farrell since her release from jail. The Special Branch man reported that she still appeared to be a committed member of the Provisional IRA and had been seen in a number of hard-line republican clubs.

'He went on, "During the days and weeks following her release, she was fêted by the Provos' top people, including Gerry Adams. She was treated as a heroine of the Republican movement in a number of clubs and pubs and one night she was presented with a framed photograph of herself, a tribute to her ten years in Armagh and the leadership qualities she showed during that time. She was also the guest of honour at a commemoration event which was held in the Sloan's Club near Kelly's Corner.

"That particular evening was to commemorate those Provos killed at Loughgall. Parents and relatives of those killed were brought to Belfast in taxis and coaches and the dinner, the drinks and the entertainment were funded by the Provos. On that occasion, Farrell presented mementoes to the families of the dead gunmen. Farrell was chosen to make the presentations because her reputation had grown throughout the movement in West Belfast since her release.

'"The Provos went out of their way to make her famous. She is good-looking, attractive and petite. She is also intelligent. She looks vulnerable though she has a real personality. She won praise and esteem within the movement for her hunger-strikes and her dirty protest in Armagh that went on for some months. Since her release, there have been no reports or sightings of her actively involved with known Provos, but we must assume that she is still a member and a potential activist. We do know that after jail sentences, the Provos tend to keep their celebrated members quiet so as not to draw attention to them, possibly exposing other activists to the security services. They usually meet and socialise in the clubs where they believe they are relatively safe from prying eyes. But, as you all know, we keep the hard-liners under surveillance most of the time."'

I knew I was about to leave Belfast and return to Hereford with the Squadron for three or four months' SP duty. I hoped I would be able to see Mairead before leaving, to explain that, once again, I had been head-hunted to carry out some vital welding work on the Rhine in Germany. But, for some unknown reason, I was called in and told I would be leaving for Hereford within three hours as part of the advance party.

'Shit,' I thought, 'now I won't be able to say goodbye.'

I phoned Mairead and thanked God when I heard her voice on the end of the line.

'What you's phoning for?' she asked in a challenging voice as soon as she realised who was calling.

'I've got bad news,' I replied.

'Shit,' she said, 'what bad news?' and I sensed alarm in her voice.

'I've got to go away,' I said, 'Germany again. I'll be away three months or so.'

She seemed to relax and the tension left her voice. 'You's always going away,' she said. 'Can't you's ever stay in one place for more than a few months?'

'I wish I could stay here', I said, 'but they've released me here and I've got this other job in Germany.'

'Can't you stay here?' she asked, pressing me, 'just for another few months? Can't you skip this job and wait for another?'

'You know I've explained it to you,' I said. 'If you start turning away jobs they forget you. Then you're dead.'

'I understand,' she said, 'but just this once?'

'If I could, Mairead, then I would stay. Listen, I've been thinking. When I finish this job, would you like to go away somewhere ... Spain or Italy?'

'I don't know,' she said, 'I don't know what I'd tell people.'

'You'll think of something.'

'Alright,' she said, 'it would be good to get away.
I've never been anywhere.'

'It's a deal then,' I said. 'We'll take a holiday
together as soon as I get back from Germany.'

'Give me a call when you return,' she said.

'Shall I phone or write?'

'Better not,' she said, 'just think of me instead.
And I'll do the same.'

'OK, I'll say goodbye, then.'

'No, listen a moment,' Mairead said, 'I want to
tell you something. Never forget that I love you. Will
you remember that?'

'Of course I will,' I said, meaning every word.
'Remember, I love you too, far, far more than you
realise.'

'Is that true?' she asked and I could hear the
concern in her voice.

'Yes, absolutely,' I said. 'I always have.'

'I love you when you talk like that,' she said.

'Good, don't forget.'

'Never, never, never will I forget,' she said. 'Bye-
bye.'

'Bye,' I said and I waited until her phone went
'click' before putting down the receiver.

I left Belfast in mid-December to return to
Hereford, wondering when I would see Mairead
again. Of course, I had no idea that I had been spotted
dating her and no one had ever told me that my name
had been bandied about the TCG meetings after I had
been identified as her companion.

Back in Hereford, I threw myself once more into
training with the Squadron but, as usual, being back

at base on SP duty was a boring time, always waiting for some action, hoping an emergency or catastrophe would occur to interrupt the boredom. Every Regiment Squadron took it in turns to undergo SP duty and the only times any of us enjoyed those weeks and months was when something interesting happened and we were called to action.

We all realised that there had to be a Squadron on permanent stand-by because, when any emergency arose, it was the SAS that would be called in to carry out the dirty work. Much of the time, neither the Press nor the general public had any idea that we had been called to sort out some country's internal problem, rescuing someone, kidnapping some undesirable rebel leader, or simply being asked to protect a VIP who had close, friendly relations with Britain. We sometimes had to go simply to guard some highly prized possession in a foreign country or, far more interestingly, take part in a hit on some undesirable elements causing problems to a friendly government.

I spent much of the time wondering about Mairead, wondering what I should do to encourage her to come and live on the mainland. I knew the holiday idea was a good one. I became convinced that if we were away together somewhere overseas, lying on a beach in some far away country, it would then be possible to broach the whole subject, tell her the truth, own up to being a member of the SAS and try to persuade her to come and live with me in England. I knew that if I had raised the matter in Belfast, or anywhere in Ireland, she would have gone berserk and I would have had to make a quick exit. I always knew that wouldn't work because I would then be forced to tell my CO everything that had happened and that would put me in deep shit.

My plan to 'come clean' while on holiday, with just the two of us, became increasingly attractive and I would lie awake at night planning what I would say to her, and when. I thought I would tell her one night after a good dinner and some booze and after a really good session in bed. I felt that after an initial burst of anger, Mairead would calm down and realise that if we made a go of it, living together away from the Troubles in Ireland, she would realise that there was another life outside the Provos and the Republican movement. I didn't know, of course, how she would react, but I had this blind faith that it would all work out OK. I might have been naïve, knowing that love is blind, but I felt in my heart that Mairead did love me, and hopefully more than she loved the Provos. But I was never 100 per cent certain.

The Det and the HMSU kept a close watch on Danny McCann and Mairead but they were more concerned about making sure that Eric Martin was well protected day and night. They were taking no chances. TCG knew that if the Provos could get to Eric Martin and take him out then no builder in Northern Ireland would be safe. Eric Martin was the big one, the most important builder in the Province and already the authorities had enormous problems persuading smaller builders to work on government projects. If he, too, was killed, then the problem of finding good, qualified, trustworthy builders to carry out all the necessary work would have been all but impossible.

Two weeks before Christmas 1987, however, Danny McCann disappeared from Belfast and Mairead Farrell was not seen anywhere near H & J Martin's works nor the Martin mansion. Checks were made at every known haunt but McCann seemed to have disappeared into thin air. Mairead continued to live at her parents' home, and continued her daily trek to her studies at Queen's University in Belfast but she was not seen again in the vicinity of H & J Martin.

For some weeks, however, the extraordinary level of protection was continued because the IRA were well known for checking out a victim, taking detailed notes of their every day movements, drawing up a plan of action and then moving away from the target, leaving him or her alone for some weeks before returning to their target and taking them out swiftly and without compassion. With Eric Martin, no one was taking any chances.

In January, it was decided to scale down the level of Eric Martin's protection but he would not be left completely alone, vulnerable to attack. The SAS team who lived in his garage at home was taken away, but for some months his daily ride to work and back was always undertaken with police protection.

In November 1987, Spanish police became suspicious of a young woman after noting that the unknown woman with an Irish passport travelled each and every Tuesday from Spain into Gibraltar. She was

followed and seen to spend some of her time on the
Rock in the area around Government House and the
Governor's official residence, taking photographs and
acting as though she was a normal tourist. After
spending a couple of hours or so walking around the
town, she would return to Spain. Photographs were
secretly taken of the woman and sent to London.
These photographs were passed on to Belfast and the
woman was identified by the RUC Special Branch as
a member of the Provisional IRA. But it was not
Mairead Farrell.

On 15 November, McCann and Sean Savage,
travelling under the names of Reilly and Cohen, were
spotted by undercover police at Madrid airport
arriving from Malaga. After telephone calls with
British Intelligence in London, the Spanish police
realised they had two high-profile IRA gunmen to
contend with. But they had no idea what they were
doing on the Spanish mainland. They concluded that
the two gunmen might be intending to murder British
ex-patriots living in Spain. As a result the police
began the mammoth task of checking through the
names of 89,000 British people then living in Spain to
see whether there were any obvious targets among
them.

The police were searching for former high-profile
judges, politicians, police, army personnel or anyone
who had been connected with law and order in
Northern Ireland, people who might be seen as
natural targets for the IRA. Some names were
discovered and checks were made on their
whereabouts but there had been no sign of McCann

or Savage, or the IRA woman sympathiser, anywhere near their homes. They were at a loss as to why the two men should be in Spain.

In January 1988, TCG in Belfast heard that Danny McCann had been sighted once again in Spain, this time accompanied by the young woman who continued to visit Gibraltar on a weekly basis. They knew the woman was not Mairead Farrell, for she was still attending studies each day at Queen's University.

It was in February that TCG received the vital missing piece of the jigsaw. An agent working for the Force Research Unit, an intelligence-gathering organisation staffed mainly by Army personnel, which handled agents throughout the Province, discovered from inside the IRA's Belfast Brigade that a spectacular bombing was being planned at the weekly changing of the guard ceremony in Gibraltar. Checks showed that the Royal Anglican Regiment, then serving in Gibraltar, had recently completed a two-year tour of duty in Londonderry.

The IRA had carried out a series of attacks against British targets on the Continent during the previous ten years. In August 1978, the IRA carried out bombing attacks on eight British Army bases in West Germany on a single night. In March 1979, the British Ambassador to The Hague, Sir Richard Sykes, was assassinated. His Dutch footman also died in the attack. On the same day, a Belgian businessman was shot dead after he was mistaken for the British envoy to NATO. Four British Army bandsmen and eight Belgian civilians were injured in an attack in Brussels in August 1979 and in June of the same year, the NATO Supreme Commander in Europe, General Alexander Haig, was caught in a landmine explosion in Belgium which local police believed was intended for a senior British Army officer. Early in 1980, a British Army lieutenant was killed at the garrison in Belefield, West Germany, with the same gun that was used to murder Sir Richard Sykes. In 1987, the IRA set off a massive car bomb outside a British military barracks in West Germany which injured 33 people.

At one of the weekly meetings of the Central Intelligence Committee held in February 1988, all the information concerning the Provos' recent interest in Gibraltar and the intelligence from Belfast was discussed in detail. This highly secret committee comprised the Chief Officers of Britain's secret services, MI5 and MI6, the Special Branch, Army, Navy and Air Force Intelligence, as well as the Northern Ireland Special Branch, and met at 10 Downing Street. The meeting was chaired by Prime Minister Margaret Thatcher, who, ever since the IRA's bombing of Brighton's Grand Hotel during the Tory Party Conference in October 1984, had taken a very personal interest in what she called 'the Irish Question'.

Britain had been unable to monitor, arrest or, if necessary, kill any members of the IRA Active Service Units operating in continental Europe because international law had to be respected. But Gibraltar was a different matter. Once a Crown Colony, under the Constitution of Gibraltar, its defence, internal security and foreign affairs are controlled by the

British Government-appointed Governor, then Sir Peter Terry. His authority was above that of the local legislature, the House of Assembly, which had only limited powers. With the Governor's permission, British forces could operate freely on the Rock.

The Downing Street meeting agreed that the IRA Active Service Unit should be kept under the closest possible surveillance, their every move monitored, but that no attempt should be made to curtail their preparations or arrest any members of the unit. And the SAS were ordered to have a team from their Special Projects squadron on permanent stand-by.

13

I HAD NO IDEA, OF COURSE, that my SAS commanders
knew of my involvement with Mairead Farrell, and
yet I did find it a little odd, disconcerting even, that
on my return to Hereford I found myself somehow
sidelined. It wasn't that I was ignored by the officers,
and never for one moment did I believe my
Commanders were acting suspiciously towards me,
but I sensed that I was not the most important SAS
soldier around.

Patrols would be sent off on various missions
during January and February while I stayed behind at
Stirling Lines, the SAS headquarters, keeping fit,
undergoing endurance marches and taking part in
rigorous exercises in the bitter winter weather on
Brecon Beacons. I would also find myself detailed to
train cadre, specialist units, which were always being

brought into headquarters for specific training of one
sort or another.

Everyone back at base, of course, hears rumours
of what is going on in the Regiment and I began to
hear stories of squads being sent to Spain on
reconnaisance missions. I also heard that the missions
related to an IRA Active Service Unit which was
apparently planning a bombing campaign. We knew
that the IRA had often had a crack at British forces
overseas, particularly those attached to BAOR, but we
could not see why they might be targeting Spain.
When I discussed the matter with mates, however, no
one put forward the theory that the ASU were in
Spain en route to Gibraltar.

We knew that Britain had one infantry battalion
permanently stationed on the Rock because of its
importance as a NATO base. But we didn't realise at
that time that with all the support men and women,
the entire garrison totalled nearly 2,000 — 750 from
the Army, 430 from the RAF and 720 Royal Navy
personnel. There was also a local defence force, the
Gibraltar Regiment, a volunteer reserve force and a
Royal Navy Reserve Unit. There were also 200 local
police on the Rock, the Royal Gibraltar Constabulary.
All these units kept an eye on a population of just
29,000 men, women and children all living in an area
two miles square.

On Friday 4 March 1988, I was called in to the
Adjutant's office and told that I must report to RAF
Brize Norton at 0700hrs the following morning,
where I would report to the RAF flight controller

dressed in civvies together with my passport, ID card and an overnight bag.

'What for?' I asked.

'Can't tell you,' he said, 'I don't know myself. We've just received the orders.'

'Do I take any weapon with me?' I asked.

'No,' he replied. 'I asked if you needed side-arms or anything, and was told that it was simply an ID task.'

'Do you know where I'm going?' I asked again, thoroughly perplexed at what was happening.

'I really haven't the faintest idea,' he said.

'Do you know for how long?'

'Not a clue ... but if it's only an ID it probably won't be for long,' he suggested.

'Is anyone else coming with me?' I asked.

'No,' he replied, 'you're on your own on this one.'

'And you really haven't any idea what this is all about?' I asked one last time.

'Seriously, Scott, I don't know,' he said. 'Only that it's an ID and they need you. They asked for you by name and number. That's all I know.'

'Thanks,' I said, 'I'll be seeing you, then,' and walked out, totally perplexed at what on earth this job was all about. Not for one moment did I think this had anything whatsoever to do with Mairead.

All that night, I couldn't sleep wondering what the hell was the reason why some unknown, unnamed officer would want me on my own at such short notice. It was obvious that I was going somewhere because I had to take my passport.

I thought it would probably be related to Northern Ireland and wondered whom they wanted me to ID.

At 0400 hrs, I was awake, and after shaving and taking a shower, I was dressed in jeans, a shirt and a leather jacket before driving to Brize Norton, arriving well before 0700hrs. I had a couple of cups of coffee and a bacon sandwich while I waited for the Flight Controller to come on duty.

As I introduced myself to him, he said, 'Ah yes, you're one of the men going to Gibraltar this morning.'

'Gibraltar?' I queried, a distinct note of disbelief in my voice.

'That's right,' he said, 'that's what I've got down here. You're due to fly at 0800hrs. All right?'

'All right by me,' I replied. 'How many of us are travelling?'

'About a dozen,' he said.

'Only 12?' I queried again in the same tone.

He was getting exasperated with the conversation. 'Listen, mate,' he said, 'I'm just the Flight Controller. I've got my orders. I've got 12 names down here on this manifesto and you're one of them. That's all I know. Stick around here and you'll soon find out. OK?'

'Thanks,' I said, as he walked off still examining the clipboard in his hand.

'Hi.'

I looked round to see my old mate Peter O'Kane walking towards me, dressed in civvies and holding a small overnight bag.

'What are you doing here?' I asked.

'Same as you,' he said.

'What do you mean?'

'Going to Gibraltar, of course.'

'How do you know I'm going to Gib?' I asked.

'Because that's why I'm here. Come and have a cup of coffee and I'll explain it to you.'

'Will I understand it?' I said sarcastically, fed up with all the cloak and dagger antics of the last 24 hours.

'Of course you will,' he said, 'there's nothing to it. It's just a weekend away in the sun.'

When we finally sat down, I hardly let him have a sip of coffee before jumping in. 'Well, for God's sake, put me out of my misery. What the fuck's going on?'

'It's Mairead Farrell,' he said, saying the words slowly and distinctly and looking at me intently to gauge my reaction.

'Mairead Farrell?' I asked, with a strong tinge of disbelief in my voice, because I knew that I had never in my life mentioned Mairead's name to him.

'Aye,' he said, 'Mairead Farrell.'

'What about her?' I queried, wondering if I sounded somewhat nervous because suddenly everything was falling into place. I tried to remain calm and matter-of-fact but my mind was racing. If Peter O'Kane of the HMSU knew about my relationship with Mairead, then the information must be almost public knowledge, with every spook in Northern Ireland aware that I had been having an affair with Mairead.

'Listen,' he said, 'I volunteered for this job

because I know you. I persuaded them that it would be better coming from me than from a stranger.'

'What?' I asked. 'What's coming to me?'

'Listen Scott,' he said, 'we've been mates for some years now and you've always helped me out of tight corners, given me advice, and we've had a ball together on occasions.'

'True,' I replied.

'TCG know all about your relationship with Mairead Farrell.'

'What?' I exploded, throwing caution to the wind and putting my faith in Peter. 'How the fuck do you know that?'

'I was briefed a couple of days ago by HMSU Intelligence. They have photographs of you with Mairead. They showed me the pictures. They don't know why you've been involved with her or for how long but it sure worried the shit out of them.'

'Fuck,' I said quietly. 'What else do they know?'

'Nothing, as far as I know. They asked every security outfit to find out if you were working under cover and everyone reported a negative. So they put two and two together and believed you've just been having an affair, a relationship, whatever.'

He looked at me again, straight in the eyes, to see how I reacted to the news.

'Is there anything else they should know?' he asked, speaking in a very serious voice.

'What do you mean?' I asked.

'You know,' he said, 'you must know that she is in the IRA; that she did The Conway bombing job back in the 1970s and that she did ten years inside for that.'

'Yes,' I said, 'I know all that.'

'Anything else I should know?' he asked, as though tempting me to tell all.

'No,' I replied, 'nothing.'

'She didn't compromise you, or anything?' he asked. 'Didn't put the hard word on you?'

'No, nothing like that.'

'But she must have known you were SAS?' he asked.

'Never,' I said and then I looked at him in some alarm. My mouth went dry — the penny had finally dropped.

'Jesus Christ,' I said. 'You don't think that I've been giving her information or anything do you?'

'I don't know,' he said.

'Listen,' I began, speaking somewhat desperately, knowing that I must keep my cool to make sure Pete believed me. 'She never knew I was SAS. She thinks I'm a welder, working in the shipyards. She has no idea I'm even Army, let alone Regiment.'

'But you know she's IRA?' he asked.

'Yes,' I knew. 'I've known for ages.'

'What do you mean, you've known for ages?'

'I tipped off the police before The Conway bombing.'

'You what?' he exploded. 'You knew about that?'

'Mairead told me about the planned bombing a few nights before the bomb was planted. I didn't know the exact time or date but I knew it was on. I told a mate in the RUC. You can check it out if you want. I told him a couple of days or so before the bomb was planted.'

'So what the fuck went wrong?' he asked.

'That's exactly what I asked at the time,' I said.

'Well, that's good for you,' Pete said. 'If needs be, you can give the officer's name and rank and everything?'

'Yes, sure I can,' I said. 'He'll back my story.'

'Thank fuck for that,' he said, 'that will get you off the hook.'

'Off the hook?' I queried.

'Yes,' he repeated, sounding adamant, 'off the hook. Back in Ireland, they ran a fine tooth comb over your record. They had to … they couldn't take anything for granted. But because of your record, no one could believe that you were in bed with the IRA, giving them information.'

'Thank God for that,' I said, sounding relieved. 'You never doubted me, did you?'

'No, never,' he replied, 'though I thought you were a fucking idiot to go laying some IRA tart. If that isn't asking for trouble, then God knows what is. You must have realised that you would be caught some day.'

'I know, I know,' I said and I realised how dreadful my affair with Mairead must have looked to everyone. We didn't speak for some minutes.

'What's going to happen now?' I queried.

'About you?' he asked. 'Fuck knows, but it can't exactly have done your chances of promotion much good.'

'I can see that,' I replied. 'Do you think it's curtains?'

'As I see it, you've got one chance and this is it.'

'What is?' I asked.

'This job we're on. This is top priority. It's come from Number 10.'

'Shit,' I said, 'from Number 10. You had better tell me. I know zero.'

'You're required in Gibraltar to identify Mairead Farrell. Apparently, she is there as part of an IRA Active Service Unit. There are three of them and they are planning a spectacular. They intend to explode a car bomb during the Changing of the Guard ceremony next Tuesday. They've got the Semtex packed into a car and the authorities are ready to go but there's been a problem. That's where you come in.'

'What's that?' I interjected.

'The authorities, the Governor or the Police Chief or whoever want a positive identification of the three IRA people. They have positive IDs of the two men but not of Mairead Farrell. Intelligence is certain that the girl is Mairead but the Gib authorities want to be 100 per cent certain. When that info was passed back to TCG, your name came up and I was called in ... they knew we were mates.'

'So they want me to fly with you to Gib to ID Mairead. Then what?'

'They'll arrest her and the other two and they'll all be taken back to Belfast.'

'I understand,' I said, speaking slowly as I struggled to grasp everything I had been told in the last few minutes. 'I understand.'

We would talk later on the RAF aircraft as we made the three-hour journey to Gibraltar. There were about a dozen on the plane but I don't think any of the other passengers were Army. I sat towards the back with Pete, some way from the others.

I had a great deal of thinking to do. Now I understood that my vibes about the way I had been treated back at Hereford had been correct. Suspicion, that was the word that leapt to my mind. Now, they weren't certain of my allegiance, my total loyalty. Fuck, I thought, that's all I need. If you lose your mates' trust in the SAS, then it's curtains, you might as well fuck off immediately because no one would ever trust you again.

I began to realise what a bloody idiot I had been to continue the affair with Mairead. Now I could see that no one else in Northern Ireland would believe that our relationship was simply a mutual attraction between two people, especially the Army.

I began to wonder whether it might be possible to use the whole situation to my advantage. If Mairead really was part of another bombing mission, and this was proved in court, then they would put her away for life and throw away the key. That was for sure. But if I was only going to ID her and the police arrested her, she would probably be sent back to Belfast under escort. Maybe there was no evidence of a car bomb, maybe it was just the presence of the three of them together in Gibraltar that had alarmed the authorities. But that didn't ring true. I was kidding myself.

I raised the question with Pete. Now I had nothing to lose and decided to put my trust in him and lay my cards on the table.

'Could we have a private conversation, just between the two of us?' I asked. 'Or does everything I say have to go back to TCG?'

'Of course we can,' he said immediately, 'what's on your mind?'

'I've got a confession to make,' I said. 'I know this sounds ridiculous, implausible, stupid even, but it's the truth. I love this girl. She's magic. I've never met another woman like her. And when we're together it's just fantastic and she feels the same, I'm sure.'

'You've got it bad then?' he asked.

'Yep,' I replied. 'I've tried to walk away from this relationship countless times, but I can't. I just want to be with her. I want to settle down with her. I've never felt like this before, but that's how I feel towards her.'

'But she doesn't even know you're Army, let alone Regiment,' he said. 'She could never stomach settling down with a British Army soldier. Talk about sleeping with the enemy! You're nuts. If you ever told her the truth, she would go mad.'

'That is a problem,' I agreed.

'Forget it, then,' he said, 'forget whatever you're thinking. It would never work.'

But I wasn't finished yet. 'If they simply pick up this trio and find no car bomb, what would happen then?' I asked.

'I would expect the authorities to take them back to Belfast and find something to hold them on and then charge them with some offence or other,' he replied.

'But that could be difficult if they can't pin

anything definitive on them?' I suggested.

'Yes,' he said, 'that's true. But Scott, you know the business ... they can always charge them with some offence.'

'They would release them?' I asked.

'They could,' he replied, 'but it's bloody unlikely. Once they've three IRA suspects, members of an ASU under lock and key, they'll never let them go free. But why do you ask? What are you getting at?'

'Listen,' I said. 'If they pick them up and find no car bomb, no guns, nothing, the three have done nothing wrong.'

'So?'

'So ... it might be possible for me to see Mairead after she's picked up and put a suggestion to her.'

'I doubt if they would let you get within a mile of her,' he replied.

'But if I approached a senior officer and asked to speak to her, tell him that I wanted to return to London with her rather than Belfast, don't you think he would allow me to speak to her?'

'It depends,' Pete replied, 'but I suppose it's a possibility though I doubt if it would work, with the authorities or with Mairead. You wouldn't exactly be her favourite person, now would you?'

'True,' I said, 'but then I could tell her the truth and let her make the decision. You see, Pete, I know her, know her really well. And I believe if we were together somewhere out of Ireland, with all its pressures, then she would welcome my suggestion. I know it sounds corny, but I think she loves me, too. I'm sure of it. If only we could be together, away from

Belfast, then we would get on brilliantly together. And from what you're saying, I don't have much future in the Regiment.'

I knew in my heart that my idea was reckless and probably stupid but I had nothing else to cling to, no hope of a future together with Mairead and no future with the Regiment. I didn't care that I might sound naïve and ridiculous, sentimental and besotted. It was the way I felt. But there was nothing else I could do but wait until we arrived at Gibraltar and see what happened. I knew all would depend on whether the girl was indeed Mairead and whether a car bomb was found. If there was a bomb then I knew I would just have to walk away from Gibraltar and forget all about Mairead. But if no car bomb and no guns were found, maybe I stood a chance.

When we touched down at Gibraltar, there was a fair wind cutting across the tarmac and we were met after we passed through Passport Control.

'There's a car to take the two of you to an apartment,' said the army officer who greeted us. 'You will be asked to stay there and you will then be contacted when necessary. As you can understand, this is a most sensitive situation and we must ask you to stay in the apartment at all times. Downstairs there is a restaurant of sorts where you can have some food. Just sign the bill. I needn't tell you that you are both on active duty and therefore no drinking.'

We both nodded. He was curt and to the point but we understood he was just doing his job.

'Could I just ask ...' I began.

'I'm afraid I don't know anything else,' he

313

interrupted. 'You will be contacted later in the apartment. There is a telephone there. OK?'

We walked out of the airport building to the waiting car and were driven to the Queensway apartment block arriving shortly after lunch. The RAF had done us proud on the flight over so we weren't in the least hungry. The first-floor apartment was obviously a holiday let, an ordinary, rather dowdy two-bed flat with just the bare essentials. I took a shower and lay down for a kip.

I found it all but impossible to sleep, thinking over what had happened and what might happen. Whenever I thought of my present predicament I would become angry, annoyed with myself for being so stupid as to think I could carry on a relationship with a known Provo bomber and get away with it. I cursed myself for being so weak-willed, unable to walk away from Mairead and yet knowing all along that the risks I was taking were unbelievably high. How I thought that no Northern Ireland security service would check on Mairead after her years in jail I don't know. I chastised myself for being both blind and fucking stupid.

And yet, and yet ...

I could see that there was a possible window of opportunity. If, in fact, Mairead and her Provo mates were only on a recce, then there would be no proof that they were about to detonate a bomb. And without any proof there was nothing the authorities could do. Without any evidence they could not arrest or charge them but would have to let them go. I wondered if that would give me the opportunity which had been playing on my mind for months, if not years, to persuade her to quit Belfast and come to live with me in England. And her Provo friends back home need never know that I had been SAS because it was obvious to me, that whatever the outcome of this trip to Gib, I had to be realistic, get the hell out of the Regiment, and find a new career.

I thought long and hard that afternoon. I had enjoyed, indeed loved, the life of an SAS soldier but I was now over 30 and I knew there was no point in hanging on with the Regiment if my name had been dragged through the mud. I knew I had done nothing wrong but I also knew that the CO would never again put any trust in a Sergeant who had the stupidity and lack of forethought to get involved with a Provo bomber.

I must have dozed off for an hour or more for Pete walked in after sleeping for a few hours and told me it was nearly 6.00pm and he was feeling peckish.

'What do you fancy?' I asked.

'Don't mind,' he said. 'We could go downstairs for a bite in the restaurant, but I don't think we should both leave the apartment at the same time. They might need us. Do you fancy a take-away?'

'Indian or Chinese?' I asked.

'Chinese,' Pete said. 'What about you?'

'Yeah,' I replied, 'suits me. Will you go or shall I?'

'You stay here,' he said, 'I'll go and find something. Shall I grab some beers while I'm at it?'

'Great, get a six pack, will you?'

'Sure,' he said. 'Lager OK? I'll probably be half-an-hour. If anything happens, leave me a note with a phone number.'

'Right,' I said, and Pete walked out.

I put on the television and waited. I was glad we were in Gibraltar because they had a BBC channel, so it felt I was back home in Blighty even though I was 2,000 miles away. We ate the mountain of food that Pete brought back and sat around drinking the lager and watching TV, waiting for the phone to ring. Occasionally I went over to the phone to check for was a ringing tone. I couldn't understand why no one had contacted us.

At 11.00pm we decided to call it a day. There was nothing decent to watch on the box and so we turned in. We figured that if nothing had happened by that time of night, nothing would. We would have to wait and see.

We were both up, shaved and showered by 8.00am, not wanting to be caught napping by some urgent phonecall from headquarters demanding our presence somewhere or other. We were both on duty and realised that such slack behaviour would never be accepted, especially if there really was the danger of a major bomb explosion.

Pete took a phonecall at about 9.00am, apparently just to check we would be ready at a moment's notice to ID the suspect. No names were mentioned on the phone. The officer at the other end of the line told Pete that when the time came, a police car would be sent to the apartment to pick me up and I would be taken to a spot from where I would be able to identify the suspect without the person seeing me. He stressed that it was important that the suspect had no idea of my presence. After ascertaining the identity of the suspect, I would immediately use the radio in the police car to pass a message through the police network to the Operations Room at HQ. There I would ask to speak to the Duty Officer. I was to give my name but not my Regiment. All I had to report was whether the ID of the suspect was positive or negative. Nothing else was required. After passing that message to headquarters, I would then be returned to the apartment to await further orders.

'Seems straightforward enough,' I said after Pete had relayed the conversation to me.

'Yeah,' he replied, 'but you'd better not let her see you.'

'I get the point,' I replied, knowing that Pete was warning me against any idea I might have had about contacting Mairead or warning her off the scene. 'Don't worry, even I wouldn't be that stupid.'

He smiled.

'Do you know who's going to make the arrests?' I asked, wondering if Pete knew more of the operation than he had, in fact, told me.

'Scotty,' he said, 'I promise you I know nothing more than you do. I was called in and told I was flying to Brize Norton and to meet you. They told me of the accusations and the circumstances and said that my job was to accompany you to Gibraltar. I've told you everything I know and, having spoken to you, I now know more about the situation than they do. They just have to have a positive ID and you're the best person to make that. There's nothing more to it.'

'Do you know anything about the bomb or the target?' I asked.

'Only what I've told you. They believe there's an ASU about to plant a bomb outside Government House where they hold the Changing of the Guard. And one of the three-man team is meant to be Mairead Farrell. I don't even know the names of the other two.'

'OK, I understand ... it's just that all this waiting around is getting on my nerves. I feel I should be doing something but we've been kicking our heels in this place for nearly 24 hours and nothing's happened. It's just frustration. I'm always like this before an operation but this time there's no risk in it for me. I've just got to ID someone.'

'There's nothing to it,' Pete said, trying to reassure me and calm my nerves. 'You'll just go along, check out the girl and tell them whether it's a positive or a negative. Look, Scott, it might not even be her. Have you thought of that?'

'Of course I've thought of that,' I told him, with some exasperation in my voice, 'but don't pull the wool, Pete. They've got me here because they're pretty certain it's Mairead. I'm not that dumb.'

'You're probably right,' he said, not wanting to start an argument.

'What happens if she sees me or recognises me?' I asked. 'What happens if she comes over to me and talks to me. What do I do? What do I say?'

Pete turned on me, raising his voice, 'You make fucking sure that she never sees you. You heard the orders and make sure you fucking obey them. We don't want any heroics, Scott. You're in enough shit with the Regiment already. If you fuck up this operation they'll have your guts for garters. Forget it ... no heroics, no fancy stuff. Just do what you've been ordered to do. OK?'

I looked at him, knowing he was simply giving me sound, sensible advice. 'I know,' I said, 'I know.'

I found myself pacing around the apartment, going over to the balcony, looking around the place, not knowing what the hell to do while I waited for the go-ahead. At about noon, the phone rang again. Pete answered.

He listened and simply said, 'I understand,' a couple of times before replacing the receiver.

'Yes,' I said, a note of anticipation in my voice.

'Cool it,' he said, 'just a friendly call to say we're not forgotten. They're waiting for the ASU to turn up. No point in us doing anything until they've been sighted.'

An hour later, the phone rang again. Once again, Pete took the call.

'They've been sighted,' he said. 'Two of them, one a woman, have been seen crossing the border from Spain on foot. They've told us to stand by. A police car will be here shortly.'

'Shit,' I replied, for in my heart I knew that Mairead would be the woman. I don't know how I knew, but I was certain it would be her.

'Good luck,' Pete said as we heard a car drive up below the apartment. We presumed the vehicle below was the Q car.

'I'll need it,' I said, taking a deep breath and

walking down the stairs, knowing that I was about to betray Mairead once again.

As I sat in the front of the car, I thought how awful it was that I was being taken on a journey to betray the woman I loved. I had already been responsible for her serving ten years in jail and now there was a good chance that she would once again be arrested. Even if there was no car bomb, even if none of the ASU had any weapons on them, I felt certain that the Gibraltar authorities, with help from Belfast, would concoct some trumped-up charge on which to arrest and hold them and drag them into court to face more years inside. I had no idea of the names of the other two, but I did know that if Mairead was convicted of another IRA-type offence, she would be facing 20 years inside. The thought left an empty feeling in my stomach.

The driver told me that he had been instructed to take me to the area near Government House to a place called Ince's Hall, where it was believed the three suspects would meet. I had no idea, of course, where we were driving. I had never been to the Rock in my life and it all seemed strange. Although it was Sunday in early March, there seemed to be a lot of visitors around the place, walking about. It wasn't a hot day but the weather was warm and many of those walking around, whom I presumed were tourists, were dressed in shirt sleeves, the women in summer dresses and sweaters.

And the traffic kept slowing to a crawl.

'How long will it take us to get to Ince's Hall?' I kept asking the driver, frustrated at our slow progress.

'Can't say,' he would reply, 'it all depends on the traffic. This place is so small, the traffic is worse here than in the centre of London. I hardly ever get into top gear.'

As we drove along, he pointed out various landmarks to me, including the Governor's Residence, Government House, an old people's home and, finally, Ince's Hall.

'Keep your eyes peeled,' the driver advised as we approached Ince's Hall, 'the suspects should be somewhere around here.'

But I could see no young woman who looked remotely like Mairead. I wondered if she had bought a wig as a disguise or bleached her dark hair or something and so I checked out all the short, good-looking young women I could see walking around. I also looked at all the young couples wandering around the area because I thought Mairead and one of the suspects might be acting as a young married couple, sightseeing. There was no one who looked remotely like Mairead. There were some dark-haired young women around, but they were obviously Spanish and were more thick-set than Mairead.

After 30 minutes of driving slowly along in the queues of traffic, I thought I should radio in to say we had been unable to see anyone who looked remotely like Mairead.

I picked up the radio and, taking instructions from the driver, radioed through and asked to be put through to the Operations Room. There, I asked to speak to the Duty Officer and gave my name.

'Yes,' he replied, 'Duty Officer speaking.'

'We have seen no one who looks remotely like the suspect. We are in the area around Government House, driving along the harbour, but have seen no one. Have you any further information so that I can ID the suspect?'

'Wait one,' he said.

Two minutes later, the Duty Officer came back on the blower. 'Keep driving around, will you? It is likely that all three suspects might be together, so you will be looking for two men and the suspect. Exact whereabouts not known.'

'Roger,' I answered and put down the radio mike.

'Just keep driving around,' I said to the driver. 'I suppose they will let us know when they have a precise location for us.'

'Anywhere in particular?' he asked.

'Don't ask me,' I said, 'but let's keep driving up and down the harbour, but not so that we will become too conspicuous. I should imagine some of these people on the streets are your plain-clothes men, aren't they?'

'I haven't seen anyone I recognise,' he replied, 'but I should imagine we've flooded the place.'

We seemed to be getting nowhere fast. I scanned every possible area in the hope of seeing Mairead or someone who might resemble her, but I saw no one. I checked my watch. It was now just after 3.30pm and we drove away from the centre towards the Spanish border.

'You might care to know that we are now driving along Winston Churchill Avenue,' the driver said.

On the right was a Shell petrol station and, behind that, a large housing estate. We drove through the Shell station and began making our way back towards the Governor's Residence once again. Still we saw no one who looked remotely like Mairead and I wondered if I had been sent on some wild goose chase.

We drove slowly with the flow of Sunday afternoon traffic along the harbour, past the Governor's Residence and to the dry docks some distance past the wharf.

'Shall we turn and go back again?' asked the driver.

'Well, there's fuck all down here,' I said. 'Better drive back again and take another look.'

I kept telling myself to stay calm and cool. I had been involved in scores of similar situations with the SAS, waiting for someone to turn up, waiting for something to happen, needing the patience of a saint to stay calm as the minutes became hours and the hours became days. Watching and waiting yet having to stay alert, never permitting myself to become complacent, fed up or impatient in such circumstances. But this time it was so very different. This time I kept thinking that I had seen Mairead, but when I looked closely, the woman I had spotted looked nothing like her at all and I would smile to myself that my eyes were playing tricks on me.

As we headed back, I checked my watch again. It was 3.55pm.

'Time for tea,' I thought to myself and remembered the times Mairead had clambered out of bed in the morning, happy to boil the kettle and bring a hot, steaming cuppa back to bed in the cottage we had used back in Ireland when she was still a young girl.

As we drove through the town centre once more, we were heading towards the Spanish border and Gibraltar airport again, when I saw a young woman walking on the right side of a young man. They were also walking towards the border, approaching the Shell service station, so I could not see her face. I looked intently at her back, suddenly convinced by her walk that the woman was Mairead. She was wearing a dress and carrying a shoulder bag. They looked like any young couple out for a Sunday stroll.

'Is that her?' said the driver.

'Wait 'til we pass her and I'll make sure,' I said as we crawled along in the traffic.

As we drew level with Mairead, travelling at about five miles an hour, I immediately recognised her. There was no mistaking her. I picked up the mike again and a voice answered.

'Headquarters.'

For a split-second, I froze, not wanting to betray her, but the voice cut in again.

'Headquarters. Can I help you?'

Instinct, training, took over. 'Ops room, Duty Officer,' I said, as I looked back towards Mairead and her companion.

'Duty Officer,' said the voice.

'Graham here. Positive ID of suspect ... positive ID.'

As I spoke those words, I was looking straight at

Mairead and our eyes met. She was looking towards me, not more than ten yards away from me, and her mouth opened as she stared towards me. Suddenly, her attention and mine was startled by the sound of a police siren behind our car. I spun round to see the police car, taking my eyes off Mairead. As I turned, my attention was drawn to two men behind her. The two men were moving towards her as though for the kill and, instinctively, I knew they were SAS.

Then I saw a gun appear in the hand of one of them as he took three brisk steps forward towards Mairead who was still looking around her, oblivious to the man with the gun.

'No!' I yelled at the top of my voice. 'No!'

The police driver looked at me, stunned, stopped the car and began to say something.

Then I heard the shots.

They sounded like bursts of machine-gun fire and I saw another man close in on Mairead and the man. All this happened in a split-second and I only had eyes for Mairead. I saw her throw her hands in the air and the young man did the same, but as they threw their hands upwards they both fell forward, then crumpled to the ground. The firing continued. Two men were only a matter of six feet or so from Mairead and the man. I must have heard ten or a dozen shots.

'Are you all right, Sir?' asked my police driver and I just nodded in reply. I didn't move a muscle, didn't make another sound, nor did I attempt to get out of the car. I was rooted to the spot, unable to move, devastated by what I had seen.

All of a sudden, I was brought back to life as I heard more shots fired, but some distance away. This time, there must have been a dozen shots or more. I looked through the back window of the car from where the shots seemed to be coming, but I saw nothing. I saw three police officers clamber out of the car behind and run across the road towards Mairead and the man lying on the ground and, as we drove slowly away from the scene, I saw five or six plain-clothes men approach Mairead and the young man. Their guns had been put away. To me, that could only mean one thing — the men knew Mairead and the young man were dead. I had witnessed such scenes hundreds of times in training and I knew without a doubt that the men responsible for the shooting were SAS. They had to be.

The driver said nothing and continued to inch along as the cars once more began moving away from the scene, as though not wanting to be involved in anything so gruesome as a shooting. I looked back at the scene and saw men bending over their victims. Then the men got to their feet again, and took out black army berets which they put on their heads.

'Fucking SAS,' I said to myself under my breath. The black army berets confirmed my suspicions. I knew that no other unit, except the SAS, would have been brought into carry out such a cold-blooded killing. I looked to see if I recognised the men, but though their faces seemed vaguely familiar I had no idea of their names or in which Squadron they operated. In that instant, I was more concerned about their guns than who they were.

As we drove away, I could see the area swarming with police and officials. Cars arrived as if from nowhere and I saw people getting in and out of them and driving away. I would learn later that the Provo accompanying Mairead was the ASU leader, Danny McCann, and the other young Provo who had been gunned down 150 yards away was Sean Savage.

'Back to the apartment?' the driver asked, startling me somewhat as I tried to focus on what had just happened.

'Yeah, yeah,' I gasped, hardly aware of what I was saying.

I slumped back in my seat, one moment my mind racing at the horror of what had occurred, the next moment my mind a blank as I tried to block out the awful sight of seeing my beloved Mairead shot dead in front of me.

Pete must have been looking out for me when I arrived back at the apartment block for he ran out as we drove up.

'Well?' he asked, eager to discover what had happened. 'How did it go?'

'She's dead,' I said. 'They shot her right in front of me, and the other lad.'

'What!' he exclaimed, hardly able to comprehend what I was saying. 'They shot her? When? How? Where? Tell me!'

'Later,' I said. 'Let's get inside.'

'Do you need me any more?' the driver asked.

'Er, no, no thanks,' I said. 'We'll call.'

'Thanks,' he said. 'I'll head back, then. Goodbye.'

When we were sitting inside the flat, I told Pete

everything that had happened, everything that I could remember. He let me complete the whole story before he asked any questions, but as I spoke he would occasionally interrupt with the odd 'shit' or 'fuck'. He looked concerned.

When I had finished, I looked at him, my face blank.

'So that's it,' I said. 'It's over, finished. She's gone ... dead ... killed ... she's gone for ever. And I've got my mates in the SAS to thank for that.'

'You can't blame the Regiment for that,' Pete said. 'You know they were only following orders.'

'Aye,' I replied, 'you're right. But now I know that I'll be leaving the Regiment, I feel drained of all emotion, as though I was never a part of the SAS.'

'Let me make you a cup of tea,' Pete said, trying to sound friendly.

But he had no time even to put on the kettle before the phone rang. Pete took the call.

Seconds later, he turned to me. 'That was the Duty Officer informing us that a car will come to pick us up shortly to take us to the airfield. We'll be back at Brize Norton before midnight. We'd better pack.'

The rest of that day was a blur. I did pack, go to the airfield and clamber aboard the RAF plane for Brize. I hardly remember the journey. I had two beers but refused any food. Pete sat next to me but just left me with my thoughts. I liked him for that. I didn't want to talk to him or to anybody, I just wanted to be left alone, to think of Mairead and what might have been.

14

'WELL, SERGEANT GRAHAM,' the Adjutant said in a perfectly pleasant voice. 'I see that you're due to terminate your service later this year unless, of course, you sign on for another term.'

'That is correct, Sir,' I replied.

'Do you intend to apply for an extension, serve another five years or whatever?'

'In the circumstances, Sir, I think it would be best if I terminated my service later this year when I will have completed my 12 years.'

'I think that would be a very good idea,' he said. 'Shall we take that as definite?'

'Yes please, Sir,' I replied.

'There is one point,' he said as I was about to salute and leave the room. 'As a result of everything that has happened, I think it might be more suitable if you were taken out of mainstream Regiment duties and became more involved in training. We need good men with long service to help with training the next generation of SAS soldiers. What do you say to that?'

I was in no position to argue. When I marched in to see the Adjutant that day, I feared that I was for the high-jump and wondered if I might even be RTU'd for my association with Mairead. I was thankful for any mercy the SAS might show me.

'That would be fine, Sir,' I lied, 'I would enjoy the challenge.'

'Good,' he replied, 'I felt sure we could sort everything out. I'll organise it.'

'Thank you, Sir,' I said.

I heaved a sigh of relief as I left the room, thankful that I had not only been able to stay with the Regiment until my time was completed, but also that I hadn't had the ignominy of being RTU'd and then perhaps kicked out of the Army by the Paras, the regiment I would have had to rejoin for my remaining months in the Army.

In the blanket Press coverage of Mairead's death, which covered the return of her body to Belfast and the dramatic scenes at the graveside, I had noticed that a man called Seamus Finnucane was named as her boyfriend. Seamus Finnucane and his brother Patrick were members of a well-known republican family. Patrick, a lawyer who had become famous for his dedication to helping Republicans in trouble with the law, was later murdered, shot dead by a Protestant Loyalist hit-squad. I smiled as I recalled the conversation I had had with Mairead only a few months earlier when she had explained how the IRA 'arranged' for high-profile Provo women to have 'relationships' with suitable Republican men. And I looked at photographs of Seamus Finnucane and wondered whether Mairead would have been attracted to the man. But I would never know.

In the days following my return from Gibraltar, I had been having second thoughts about what had happened on the Rock. Though I had been flown over to Gib to ID Mairead, I had barely been given the opportunity to carry out the task they had assigned me. I had also been reading the British newspapers, watching the television news and listening to the radio. And I had videoed the TV programme *Death on the Rock* and watched it many times. It seemed that those killings on the Rock had caused a maelstrom of debate which the Government was having problems burying. Even Margaret Thatcher's intervention during House of Commons Question Time failed to dampen the furore which enveloped the Government. But I noted that Thatcher stuck to her guns, refusing to permit an official inquiry into the shootings. That decision, more than any of the media hullabaloo, convinced me that the Government had a secret they were determined to keep under wraps.

I collected all the statements made at the time by the Prime Minister, by Foreign Secretary Sir Geoffrey Howe and the Ministry of Defence. I noted that there had been no explosives in the rented IRA car found at the scene and no detonators; I noted that none of the three shot dead had been armed; and I noted that no 'trigger' or 'device', suggesting that they were about to detonate a bomb, was found on the bodies of any of those killed. I also noted that some days after the shootings, 60 Labour MPs sponsored a motion in the House of Commons denouncing the Gibraltar shootings by SAS troops as an 'act of terrorism' and 'tantamount to capital punishment without trial'.

I was still determined to get to the bottom of what really happened that day. To me, it seemed extraordinary that the three had been shot dead at point-blank range by members of the SAS and yet no one, no civilians, soldiers or police, was at any risk whatsoever at the time they were shot dead. I had to find out what really happened and why. I decided to talk to my SAS mates who had been part of 'Operation Flavius', the official name given to the Gibraltar mission. And one of them on the Rock that fateful day was a very good pal of mine with whom I had shared some good times and some rough ones over five years. More importantly, I also knew I could trust him implicitly.

I was amazed at what I learned.

Twenty-seven shots had been fired by the SAS when they killed Mairead, Danny McCann and the third member of the group, Sean Savage. It seemed obvious that Danny McCann was the leader of the ASU, a one-time Commander of the IRA Belfast Brigade. Sean Savage, 23, the youngest of the trio from Downfine Gardens, Belfast, was little known to the security forces. In 1982, along with four other men, he had been charged with IRA membership and with causing an explosion but the charges were later dropped by the Crown. At the time of their deaths, however, not one of the trio was wanted in connection with any specific offences.

Photographs of the three dead showed that Sean Savage had been shot 16 times and sustained 27 wounds, covering almost his entire body, in what the Crown pathologist described as a 'frenzied attack'. Entry holes sustained by Savage included five in the head, five in the back, five in the front and one to the hand. Mairead's wounds showed she had been shot three times in the back from a distance of less than three feet. She had also been shot at close range in the face. McCann had two wounds in the chest, two wounds on his back and three wounds to the head. It seemed obvious to me from my SAS training that such an attack from such a close range could only mean that the SAS soldiers were under orders to kill all three.

According to documents found on the bodies, Mairead was travelling under the name of Catherine Alison Harper, now Mrs Smith; McCann under the name Robert Reilly; and Sean Savage had documentation naming him as Brendan Coyne. In Savage's pocket was also a driving licence, and birth and baptism certificates all in the name of Brendan Coyne. He also had £1,700 in a money belt around his body.

In McCann's clothing was found more money and a hotel reservation form from Spain. Mairead had a wrist watch with the inscription 'Good luck from your comrades at Maghaberry, September '86', the prison

Mairead had been moved to immediately prior to her release in 1986. There was an unopened packet of cigarettes and, in her black shoulder bag, an Aer Lingus boarding card for a flight to Brussels in the name of Johnston, some make-up and some sun cream. She had also been wearing a simple pair of gold earrings.

At the inquest into the deaths of the three, held in Gibraltar, senior MI5 officers, along with seven SAS soldiers and other security service officers, were called to give evidence, explaining why the SAS men felt obliged to open fire. The coroner's court had to decide whether the killings were justified or unlawful.

The man who masterminded the entire SAS operation was named only as 'Mr O' and he was responsible for briefing not only the Governor and the Gibraltar Police Chief, but also the local Special Branch, police officers and all military personnel involved. He told how he believed that a three-member Active Service Unit, as the IRA called it, would be despatched to the Rock to carry out a car bombing designed to kill as many soldiers as possible. It would probably be detonated by remote control and brought across the Spanish border in a vehicle in which it would remain hidden.

He stated under oath that the three ASU members had not been under surveillance but were believed to be in the area around Malaga in southern Spain. He said that a car had been discovered in Brussels in January 1988 containing 110lb of Semtex, four detonators and equipment for a radio-detonation system, though that car bomb had been defused.

However, Mr O said that the Intelligence services believed that the ASU planned to drive a car bomb into Gibraltar some time before the Changing of the Guard parade, scheduled for 11.00am on Tuesday, 8 March. They believed that a blocking car might be put in place beforehand, but discounted this because that would have entailed two vehicles and two trips across the border, which was always guarded.

Mr O claimed that subsequent events confirmed his initial suspicions in all but three aspects. The IRA did plan a massive car bomb, the target was Gibraltar and the target area was correct. But he admitted that intelligence was incorrect in assuming the three to be armed, in assuming the car parked in Gibraltar was the car containing the bomb, and thirdly in assuming that the car later found in Marbella, containing a massive bomb, was to be triggered by a timing device and not a radio device.

The Commissioner of Police for Gibraltar, Mr Joseph Canepa, told how he had been briefed by Mr O, as a result of which he came to the conclusion that his armed police would not be able to cope with the situation and that he therefore accepted that he would need military assistance. He issued instructions that an operational order be prepared to handle the situation, which stated that every effort should be made to protect life, to foil any attempt to take life, to make arrests and to take custody of prisoners.

Mr Canepa also read to the Coroner's Court orders handed to the Gibraltar Special Branch and their armed officers, listing the instructions for use of firearms, including giving a warning and ordering a suspect to stop. The order stated that someone could only fire without warning in circumstances where delay would cause danger to themselves or to others.

On the morning of Sunday, 6 March, Mr Canepa said that he received information that two members of the ASU, a man and a woman, had crossed into Gibraltar. He then went to the central Operations Room and was informed by British security chiefs that the two had met a third person, whom they believed to be the third member of the ASU, near Ince's Hall where he had parked a white Renault car. It was known that the band of the Anglican Regiment would muster near Ince's Hall at 11.00am on the morning of Tuesday, 8 March.

He told how, when it became known that the three ASU members, whom he had been assured had been positively identified as McCann, Savage and Farrell, walked away from the Renault car, the British security chiefs had reached a conclusion that the car must have contained a bomb. A British bomb expert was detailed to check out the car to see whether it contained a bomb and he advised the British security chiefs that the car was a suspect bomb.

For some time, Mr Canepa was questioned as to why no effort was made by the police to seal off the area around the suspect car bomb when hundreds of people were walking about in the immediate vicinity. Many would have been killed or injured if the car bomb had exploded. The area was never sealed off and no attempt was made to defuse the bomb. Mr Canepa said no one had suggested the idea of sealing off the area and making it safe for the public.

At about 3.00pm, Mr Canepa said a decision was nearly taken to apprehend the three suspects, but no one suggested arresting them and nothing was done.

Mr Canepa told the court how he was informed 30 minutes later that the three suspects had turned round and were seen heading for the border and he formed the view that they should be arrested on suspicion of conspiracy to murder. He feared there was a possibility that they could make their escape and carry out their mission successfully. At that stage, he signed a form requesting the British military to intercept and apprehend the three persons.

After signing the form and handing it over to the British security chiefs, he saw a senior officer go over to the radio and issue some instructions. He heard nothing else until shortly after 4.00pm when a report came in that the three had been shot dead.

He told the Coroner, 'I was shocked by what had happened. I was expecting arrests.'

He said that one minute after the shootings the senior British officer signed a document referring control back to him.

Mr Canepa told the Coroner that the entire operation that day had been run from the joint operations room in which all members of the advisory group, the tactical command, the surveillance unit and the seven SAS soldiers — all from Britain — controlled all the events.

The SAS soldiers, who gave evidence without having to disclose their names or rank, all said that the military part of the plan was to assist the Gibraltar police in arresting the Provisional IRA bombing unit.

When the shooting began, the soldier who fired the first shot, codenamed 'Soldier A', said he could not remember whether he had issued a warning to Mairead and McCann to stop. He said that he intended to shout 'Stop, police,' but he was not sure whether he actually spoke the words before he began shooting. Other witnesses were called, including some of the SAS men who had taken part in the killings. Some claimed warnings were given to the IRA team, while most witnesses said that no warnings whatsoever were given.

All the SAS soldiers giving evidence said that the three Provos all made 'threatening movements'. The two IRA men apparently appeared to be going for guns concealed in their jackets, while Mairead was alleged to have made a movement towards her handbag, which led the soldiers to believe she was trying to detonate a bomb with a device concealed in the shoulder bag.

However, all the SAS men told the court that no weapons were found on the bodies and no device for detonating a bomb was found in Mairead's handbag.

Earlier, Police Commissioner Mr Canepa had told the inquest jury that when the Renault car was found to contain no bomb, the British security chiefs suggested that the Spanish authorities should be informed that a bomb might be hidden in a car parked somewhere in the nearby frontier town of La Linea. A Ford car key had apparently been found in Mairead's handbag. Consequently, a red Ford Fiesta was found in La Linea with documents and also an anorak, a mackintosh, a money belt with £2,400 in cash, some tape, some pieces of black wire and some cable which was similar to that found later with the bomb. There was also a pair of gloves. Two days later, another car, a white Ford Fiesta, was discovered in an underground car park in Marbella. This vehicle had been rented in one of Mairead's false names — Catherine Smith. It contained 64 kilos of Semtex from Czechoslovakia, ammunition from Yugoslavia, four detonators from Canada, light bulbs from Poland, batteries and small timers from Spain which had been used by ETA in the past. For some years, Special Branch officers in Belfast had been liaising closely with Spanish anti-terrorist police responsible for keeping close surveillance on ETA, the Basque terrorist movement seeking separation from Spain. It was known the Sinn Fein/IRA had links with the Basque separatist organisation and its political wing, Herri Batasuna, and that the two military wings frequently collaborated. Each year, representatives of ETA's political wing, which used to field candidates in regional elections, would travel to Ireland to attend Sinn Fein's *ard fheis* held in Dublin. Sinn Fein representatives would also travel to Spain to attend Herri Batasuna conferences.

The explosive from the car was in five packages and, although not primed, the detonators were connected to the explosive mass. The timers were set for 10 hours, 45 minutes and 11 hours and 16 minutes.

But my mates in the SAS, plus a member of 14th Intelligence Unit based in Belfast, told a totally different story to that put forward by the British Intelligence witnesses at the Gibraltar inquest.

They informed me that after intelligence was received in Belfast that a Provo ASU planned a spectacular in Gibraltar, 14th Intelligence Unit, whose highly-trained men and women operated in plain clothes, was alerted to take over surveillance. At first, they only knew that McCann was involved in planning the bombing and whenever he left Britain, he was followed 24 hours a day. Later, when Sean Savage joined the team, he, too, was kept under constant surveillance. At first, there had been another woman, not Mairead, who had helped to plan and recce the bombing area, but she had dropped out of the ASU some time in January.

The operation was so politically sensitive that all details were restricted to only a few people and all documentation was marked 'Top Secret'. Control of Operation Flavius was based in Hereford, but progress reports were made available to the Central Intelligence Committee which Margaret Thatcher chaired in London. All decisions were taken at those CIC meetings and passed on to Hereford for action.

Two months before it became almost certain that the bombing was planned for 8 March, four members of D Section of 14th Intelligence were sent to take over Intelligence operations in Gibraltar, and those who had been manning the Gibraltar Intelligence and Security section were moved to other jobs.

When the Provo unit, including Mairead, left Dublin for France and Spain towards the end of February, they were kept under constant surveillance by 14th Intelligence. Members of the SAS were also drafted in to work with the Intelligence officers, but